Progressive

FINGERPICKING GUITAR

by

Gary Turner and Brenton White

The exercises in this book have been recorded onto a CD

CD TRACK LISTING

Track	Content
1	Tuning
2	Lesson 1 Ex 1
3	Lesson 2 Ex 2-3
4	Lesson 3 Ex 4-5
5	Lesson 4 Ex 6
6	Lesson 5 Ex 7-8
7	Lesson 6 Ex 9 - Pattern Seven A
8	Lesson 7 Ex 11-12
9	Lesson 8 Ex 13-14
10	Lesson 9 Ex 15
11	Lesson 10 Ex 16-17
12	Lesson 11 Ex 18
13	Lesson 12 Ex 19
14	Lesson 13 Ex 20
15	Lesson 14 Ex 21
16	Lesson 15 Ex 22-23
17	Lesson 16 Ex 24-25
18	Lesson 17 Ex 26
19	Lesson 18 Ex 27
20	Lesson 19 Ex 28
21	Lesson 20 Ex 29-30
22	Songs - Aura Lee- Scarborough Fair
23	Progression 1-10
24	Greensleeves
25	Amazing Grace (Arpeggio)
26	Turnaround
27	12 Bar Blues
28	Melody with Clawhammer Accompaniment
29	Supplementary Pieces - Group 1
30	Supplementary Pieces - Group 2

Acknowledgments
Cover Photograph: Phil Martin
Photographs: Phil Martin

I.S.B.N. 0 947183 13 2
Order Code:
CD Pack CP-18313

For information on the *Progressive* series contact;
L.T.P. Publishing Pty Ltd
email: info@learntoplaymusic.com
or visit our website;
www.learntoplaymusic.com

CONTENTS

INTRODUCTION

Progressive Fingerpicking Guitar will provide you with an essential guide into the most common fingerpicking patterns used by modern folk and acoustic guitarists. A lesson by lesson structure has been used to give a clear and carefully-graded method of study.
No previous musical background is assumed, however it is advisable to have a basic knowledge of open chords before commencing the text.* This will enable you to concentrate fully upon the right hand fingerpicking techniques.
Although only open chord progressions are used in this book, the fingerpicking patterns are universal in that they may also be applied to other chord progressions involving bar or "jazz" flavoured chords.

You should combine the study of this book with constant experimentation and listening to other players.

* See Progressive Rhythm Guitar by Gary Turner and Brenton White.

APPROACH TO PRACTICE

It is important to have a correct approach to practice. The points below outline a method by which you will achieve maximum benefit from your practice sessions.

1. Practice as often as possible, having several short practice sessions (e.g. 15-20 minutes) rather than one long session.
2. Become thoroughly familiar with the chords and chord changes of each progression before commencing any fingerpicking (e.g. strum through each progression and make full use of slide and pivot fingers if applicable).
3. Practice each fingerpicking pattern on one chord before playing it with the given chord progression.
4. Apply each fingerpicking pattern to as many different chord progressions as possible (e.g. use more than just the one or two example progressions given for each pattern). In particular, apply the fingerpicking patterns to songs that you know.
5. Divide your practice time evenly between the study of new material and the revision of past work.

TUNING YOUR GUITAR TO THE CD

Before you commence each lesson or practice session you will need to tune your guitar. If your guitar is out of tune everything you play will sound incorrect even though you are holding the correct notes. On the accompanying CD the **first track** contains tuning notes for all six strings.

1.

ACOUSTIC GUITARS

The two types of guitar most commonly used in fingerpicking are the nylon string acoustic (classical) and the steel string acoustic.

Classical Guitar (Nylon Strings) / Steel String Acoustic

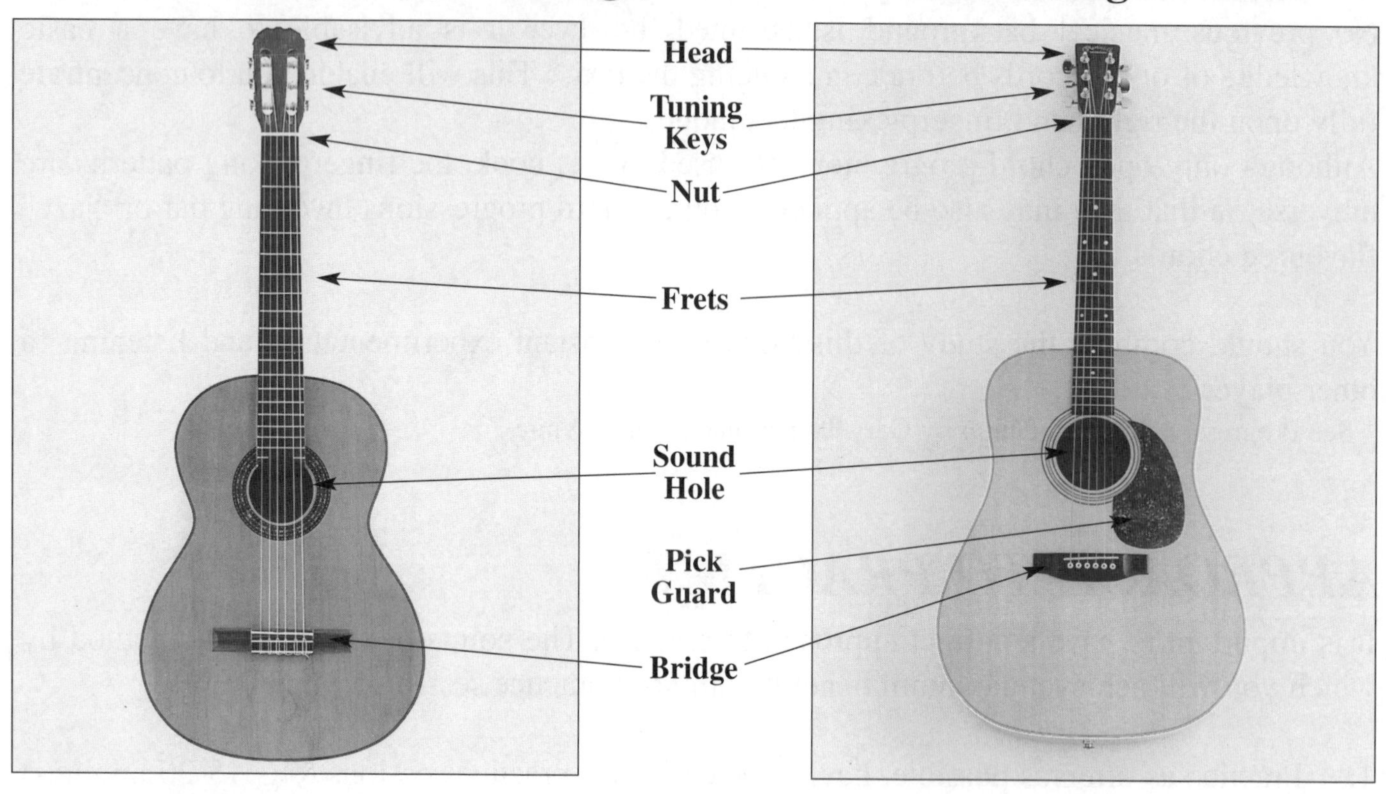

SEATING

Before you commence playing, a comfortable seating position is required. Most modern guitarists prefer to sit with their right leg raised, as shown in the photos below. The guitar should be held close to the body in an upright position with the neck of the guitar pointing slightly upwards. The main aim is for comfort and easy access to the strings.

Practice fingerpicking guitar styles by sitting with your right leg crossed or by using a foot stand.

RIGHT HAND FINGER NAMES

The right hand fingers are named using the following fingering symbols.

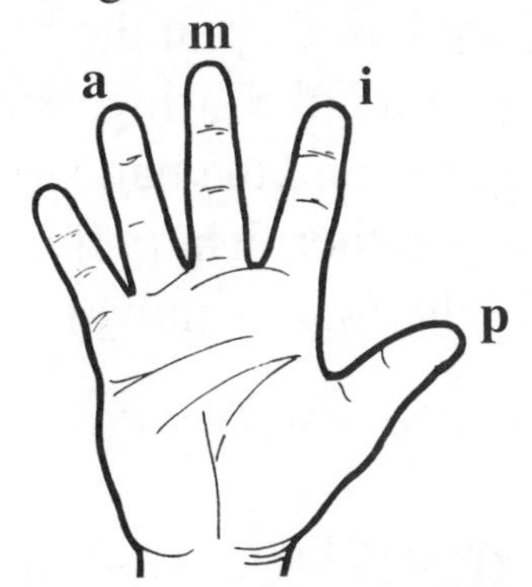

p = primary
i = index
m = middle
a = annular (ring finger)

The little finger is not used in fingerpicking.

THE POSITION OF THE RIGHT HAND

In fingerpicking the right hand adopts the classical position as illustrated in the photos below:

FRONT VIEW

SIDE VIEW

1. Forearm rests on top part of guitar.
2. Hand is at right angles to the strings.
3. Thumb is parallel with the strings and clear of other fingers.

The photos below illustrate some common faults to be aware of:

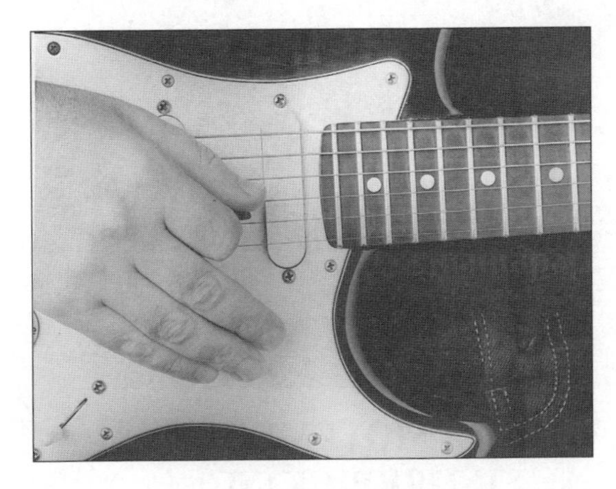

INCORRECT

1. Forearm position too low (created by elbow resting on guitar body).
2. Hand not at right angles to strings.
3. Thumb playing behind the index finger.
4. Hand position too low and too close to strings (created by holding the hand in a strumming position).
5. Hand should not be supported by placing any fingers on the guitar body.

THE FREESTROKE

Most of the fingerpicking patterns presented in this book are based upon the **freestroke** style. Freestroke is a method of playing where the finger, after picking the string, does not come to rest on any other string. The sound is produced by the fingertip and the nail striking the string simultaneously. The fingertip should move across the string, rather than pull out from it. This movement will enable the hand to remain steady (i.e. only the fingers move).

FREESTROKE MOVEMENT

First finger joint should be flexible, and move with the stroke.

Finger moves across the string in an arc - it does not pull away.

A different technique is used for picking with the thumb. Firstly, the thumb, unlike the fingers, does not bend when making its stroke. It is kept rigid at all times. Secondly, the thumb picks with a downward motion, and strikes the string with its left hand side.

THUMB MOVEMENT IN FINGERPICKING

Thumb strikes string with left hand side, and moves through in an arc.

THUMB POSITION AGAINST STRING

THE REST STROKE

The rest stroke involves fingerpicking a string and then coming to rest on the next string. It is extremely useful in accenting (playing louder) a given note.

The diagram below illustrates the movement of the finger in executing the rest stroke.

RIGHT HAND FINGERNAILS

For fingerpicking it is common practice (and most desirable) to grow your right hand fingernails. This will give you a greater control over the volume and tone of the notes you play.

The desired length of fingernails varies from player to player, however, as a general guide, the nail should be at least 1/16" (one millimetre) clear of the fingertip (most people prefer the thumb nail to be slightly longer).

Fingernails should be shaped so that they have a rounded edge, e.g.:

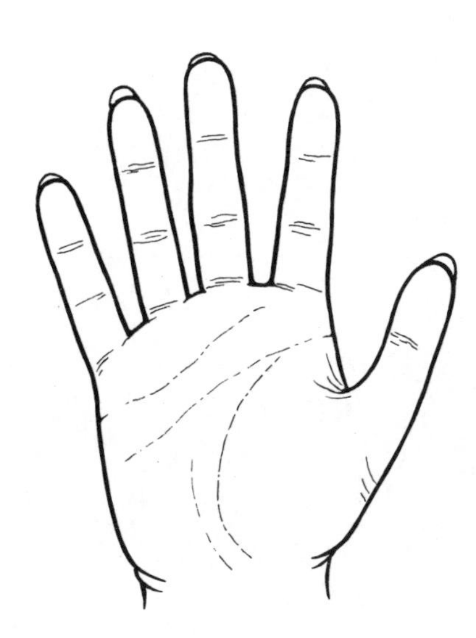

Fingernails should be filed and shaped regularly, working from the underside of the nail.

SECTION I

In this section the concept of pattern picking is introduced. This is the easiest method of fingerpicking and it involves the right hand playing a set pattern throughout different chord changes (i.e. a chord progression). Each pattern is numbered for easy reference and together they form a basic fingerpicking repertoire.

A supplementary list of songs is provided at the end of this section for additional use of the fingerpicking patterns introduced.

Appendices 1 and 2, covering the topics of tuning and notation, should be read before the commencement of this section.

LESSON ONE

FINGERPICKING PATTERN ONE

Fingerpicking pattern **one** involves the use of the thumb (**p**), index finger (**i**), and middle finger (**m**). They will be played in the following order:

p i m i   p i m i   etc.

The thumb will play a bass note, and the index and middle fingers will play the second and first strings respectively.

Hold a C chord and play fingerpicking pattern **one**:

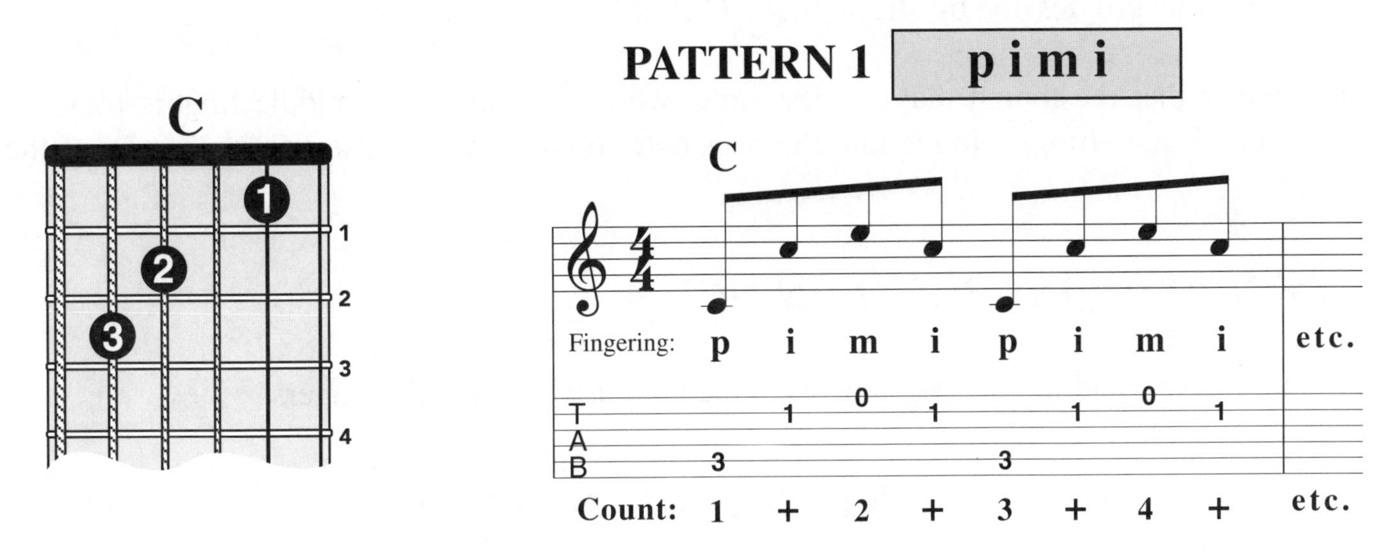

This pattern (and all future patterns) can be applied to any chord. Become thoroughly familiar with it.

TURNAROUND IN C

The following turnaround progression uses the chords, C, Am, Dm and G7.

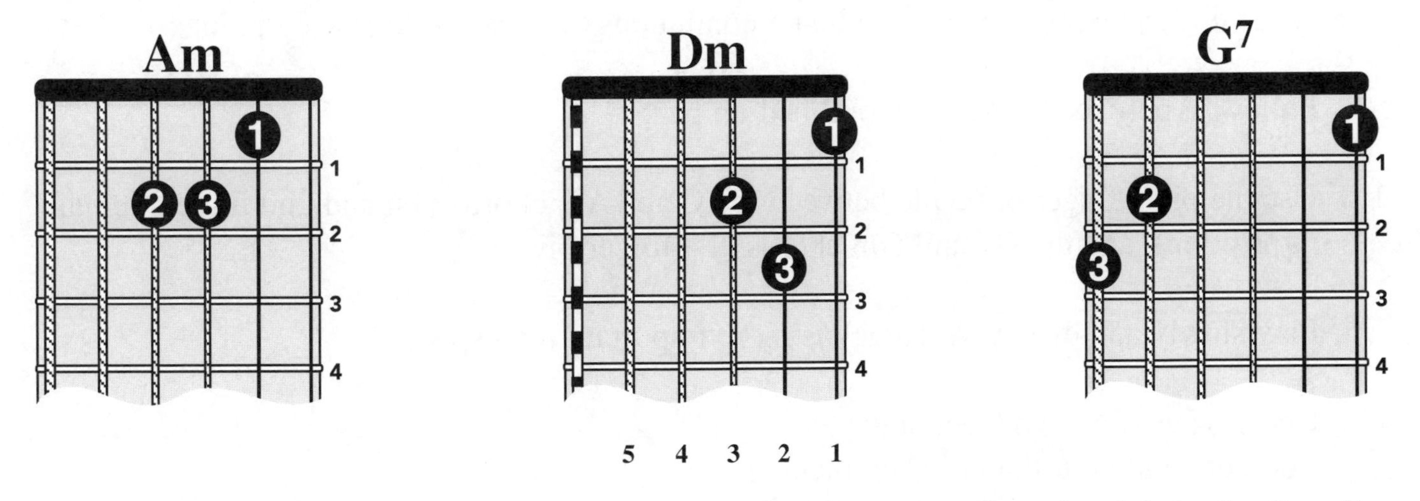

A dotted line indicates that a string is not to be played. In the Dm chord only the first five strings are played.

Exercise 1

PATTERN ONE

p i m i

Any progression with a repeat sign should be ended by a single strum of the opening chord, e.g. finish this progression by strumming a C chord.

Remember that the thumb plays a bass note, while the index and middle fingers play the second and first strings. Notice that the bass note in each case is also the root note* of the chord.

FINGERPICKING PATTERN ONE-A

An alternative fingering for the same example is to use the **m** and **a** fingers:

PATTERN 1-A **p m a m**

This fingering is important for the development of the **a** finger, which will be used in some future examples.

TROUBLESHOOTING

Does your fingerpicking sound smooth and continuous? Check the following points:

1. Follow 'Approach to Practice' outlined on page 5.

2. Use the pivot finger principle between the C and Am chords (1st and 2nd fingers remain in position), and the G7 and Dm chords (1st finger pivot).

3. Play slowly and evenly. Accuracy is more important than speed.

4. Check your right hand technique:
   - do not bend your thumb when picking
   - maintain the correct right hand position (see photo, page 7).

* The root note is the letter note of each chord, e.g. Am - root note A, G7 - root note G.

LESSON TWO

PROGRESSION

The following progression uses the chords A, Asus (**sus** is an abbreviation for suspended) and E. The Asus chord is formed by adding the little finger to an A chord, as shown in the chord diagram below. The open circle indicates that the third finger note is held but not played.

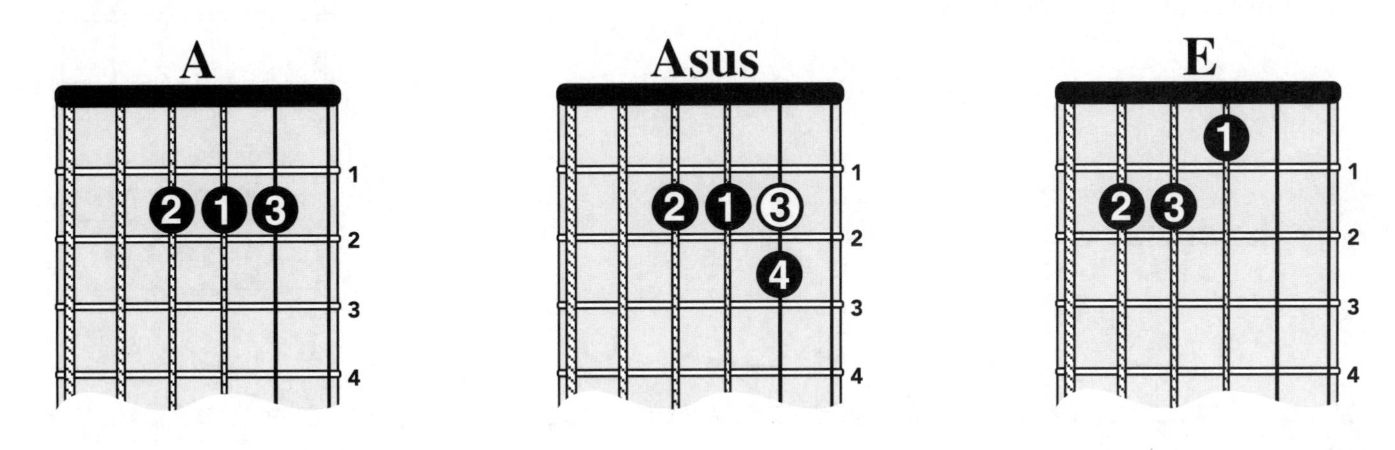

In the following example **pattern 1 (p i m i)** is used, with the **i** and **m** fingers playing the third and second strings respectively. For smooth chord changing, use the slide technique from A to E (first finger slides along the third string).

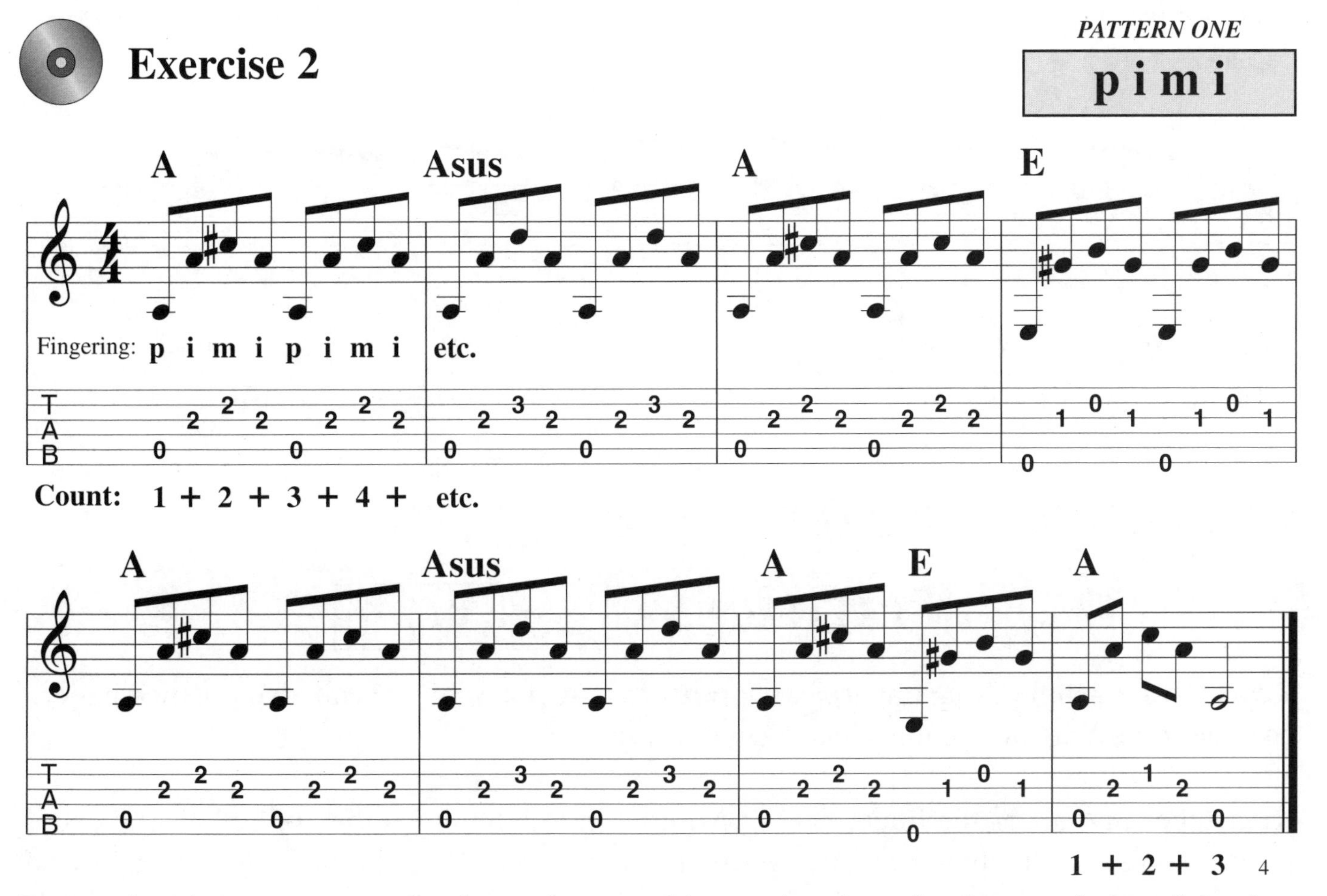

Remember that once a note has been sharpened it remains sharp for the remainder of that bar (e.g. bar one contains two C♯ notes).

FINGERPICKING PATTERN TWO

Fingerpicking **pattern 2** is a variation of pattern one, reversing the order of the **i** and **m** fingers, i.e.

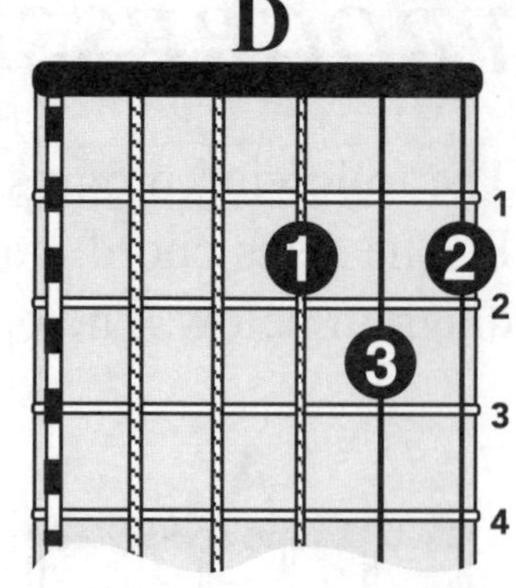

PATTERN 2 | **p m i m** |

Try this new pattern with the following chord progression, where a new chord, D major, is introduced.

Exercise 3

PATTERN TWO

p m i m

Count: 1 + 2 + 3 + 4 + **etc.**

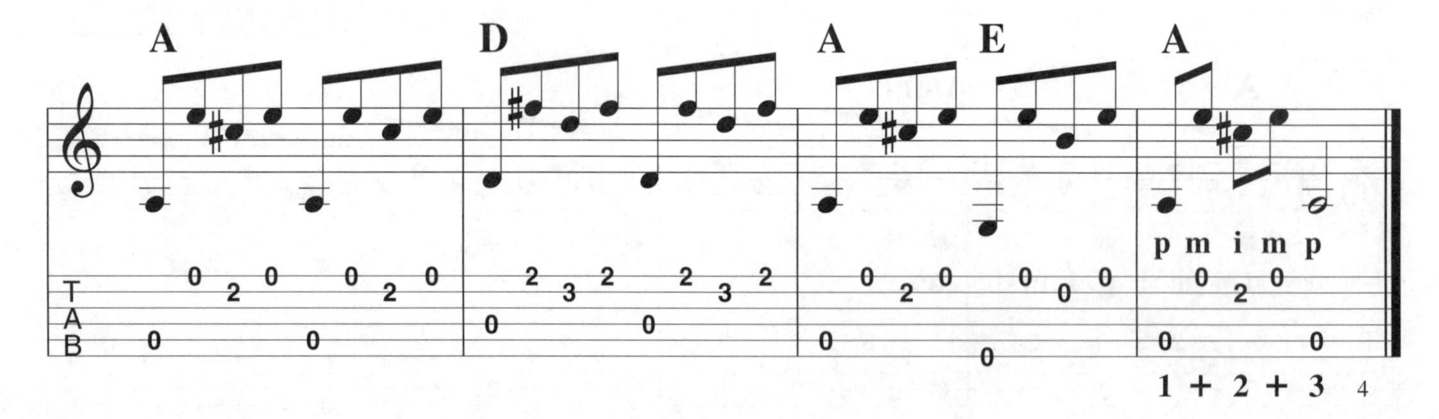

FINGERPICKING PATTERN TWO-A

PATTERN 2-A | **p a m a** |

Repeat this example using fingerpicking **pattern 2-A p a m a**. You can also practice pattern **two** and **two-A** using the third and second strings.

Remember that all of the fingerpicking patterns in this book can be applied to any chord progression, so you should practice **patterns 2** and **2-A** using the progression in Lesson One. You should also practice these patterns against any of the songs at the end of this section.

LESSON THREE

FINGERPICKING PATTERN THREE

Fingerpicking **pattern 3** involves the use of the thumb and three fingers, as such:

PATTERN 3 **p i m a**

Play the following progression using the chords Am, Dm and E7.

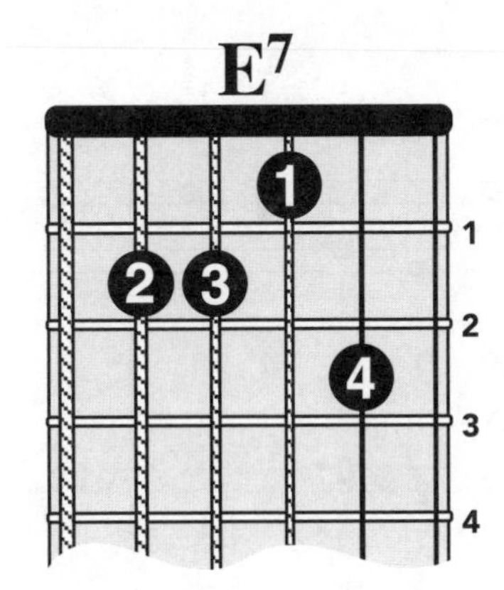

To play this chord, first hold an E shape and then add the 4th finger.

Exercise 4

PATTERN THREE
p i m a

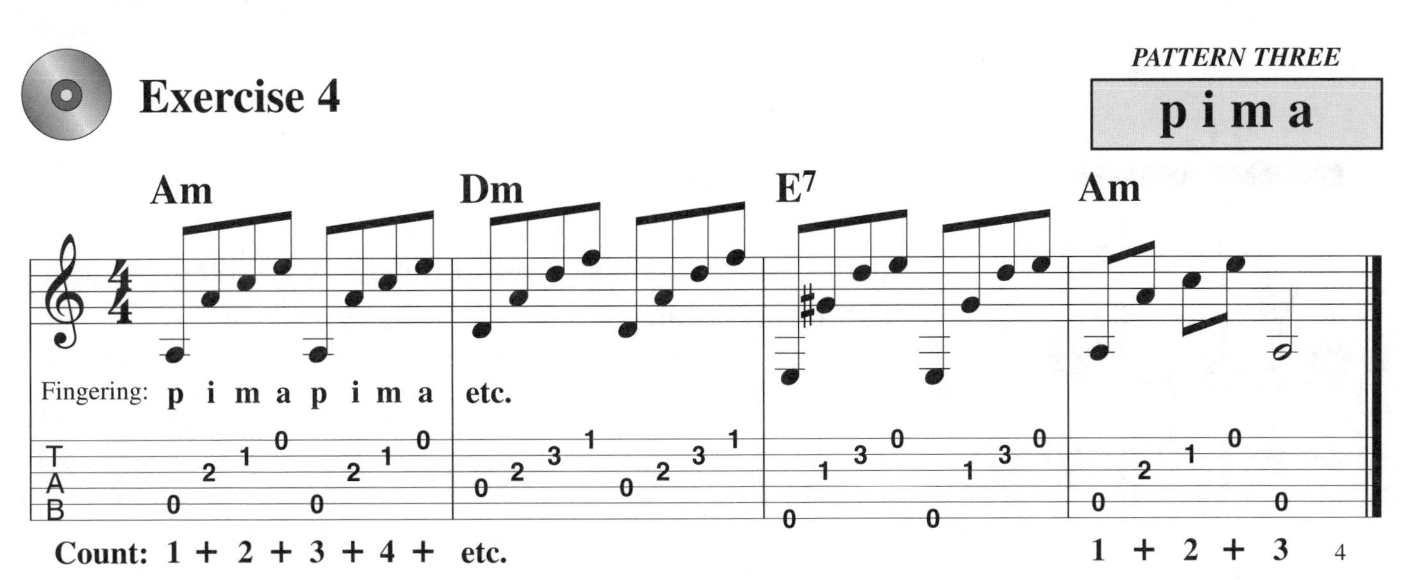

Now play the same progression with fingerpicking **pattern 3-A**: **p a m i**.

Exercise 5

PATTERN THREE-A
p a m i

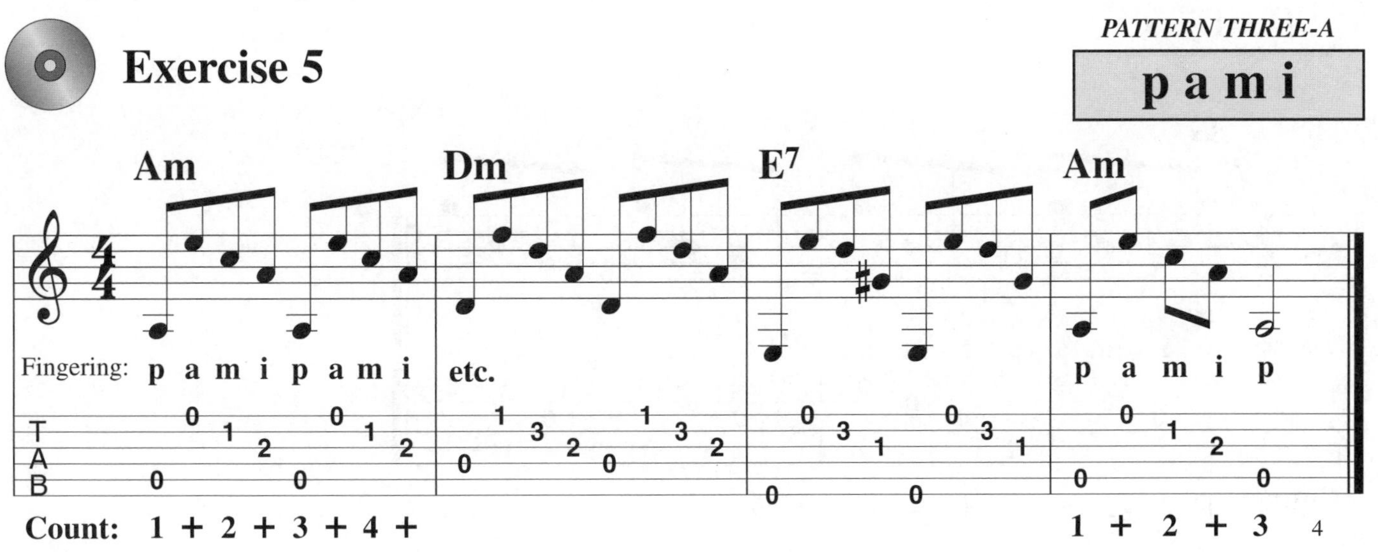

LESSON FOUR

ALTERNATING BASS

So far your fingerpicking has involved playing only the root note of each chord for the bass. To create a more interesting sound, the bass note may be varied. For example:

PATTERN ONE

PATTERN THREE

pima

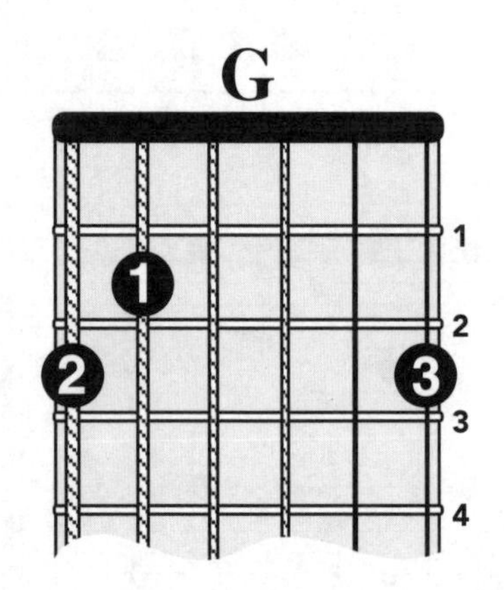

In this next example, three different bass notes are used, holding a G chord.

PATTERN THREE

pima

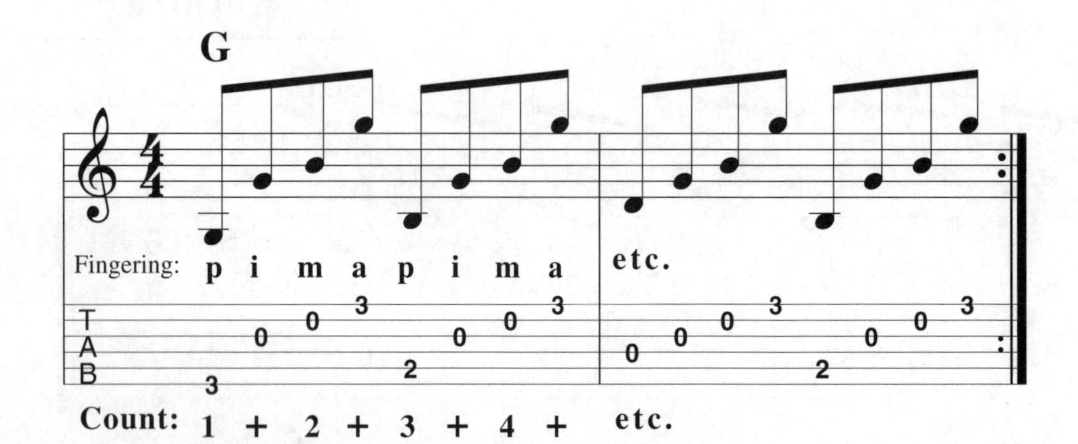

Try the following progression, using alternate bass:

Exercise 6

PATTERN THREE

p i m a

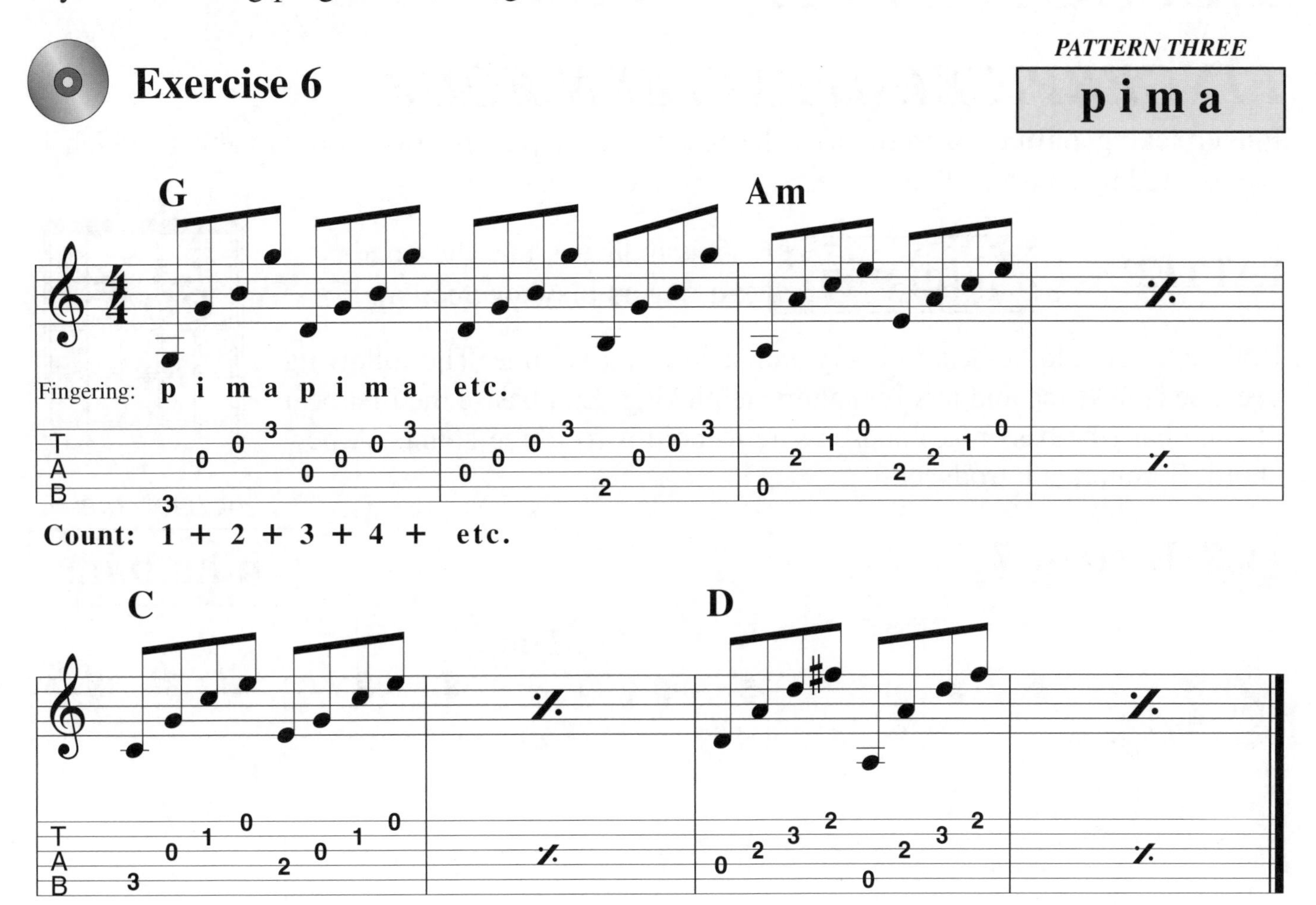

⁒ = Repeat sign; indicating an exact repeat of the previous bar.
In an alternating bass line there are two main rules governing the choice of notes:

1. They should be chosen from notes on the 4th, 5th and 6th strings (the bass strings).
2. They should only be selected from notes that are found in the chord.

You should also take into consideration the overall sound, since some of the combinations will sound better than others.

LESSON FIVE

FINGERPICKING PATTERN FOUR

Fingerpicking **pattern 4** introduces the technique of playing two notes together, which is represented by a curved line: ⌒

PATTERN 4 **p im p im** ← This indicates that the **i** and **m** fingers play together.

Em

Both notes should be heard clearly and have equal volume. The following exercise is in $\frac{3}{4}$ time and involves alternate picking. Emphasise the first beat of each bar (the bass note) and be sure to hold it for three counts. A new chord, E minor, is introduced.

PATTERN FOUR

p im p im

Exercise 7

FINGERPICKING PATTERN FIVE

A new fingerpicking pattern can be created by playing the above example in **arpeggio** style. An arpeggio is the playing of the notes of a chord separately rather than together.

Exercise 8

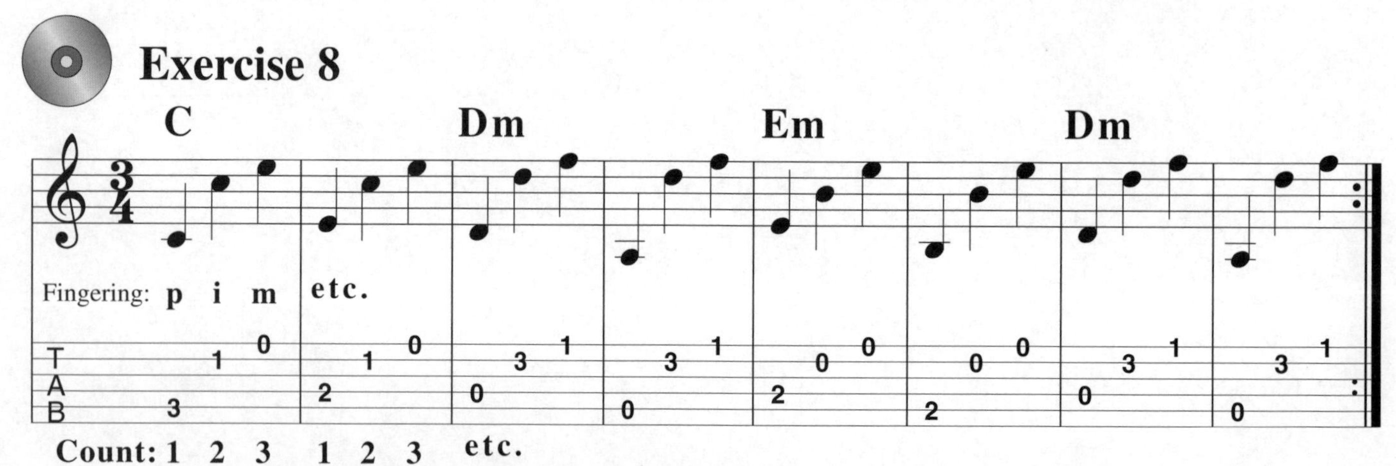

LESSON SIX

FINGERPICKING PATTERN SIX

Fingerpicking **pattern 6** involves the playing of three notes together, as such:

PATTERN 6 | **p ima p ima** | ← Play **i** , **m** and **a** together.

Try the following example, which introduces the chords A7, D7 and G7.

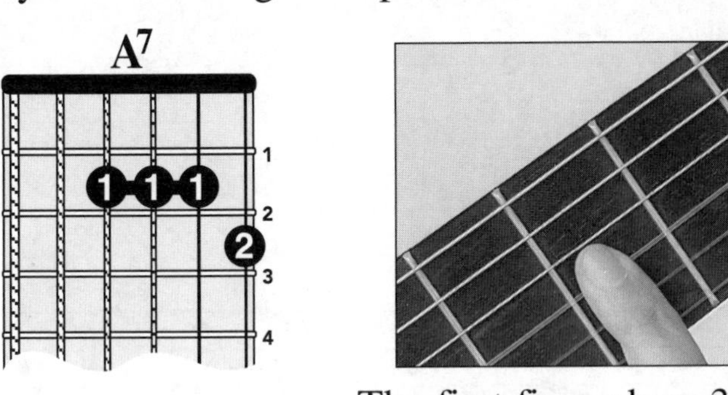

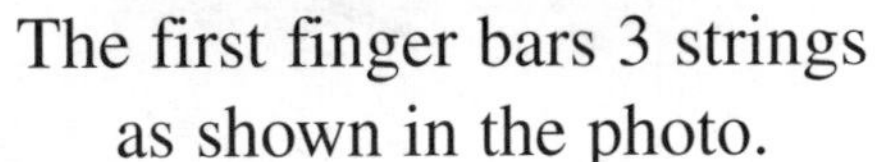
The first finger bars 3 strings as shown in the photo.

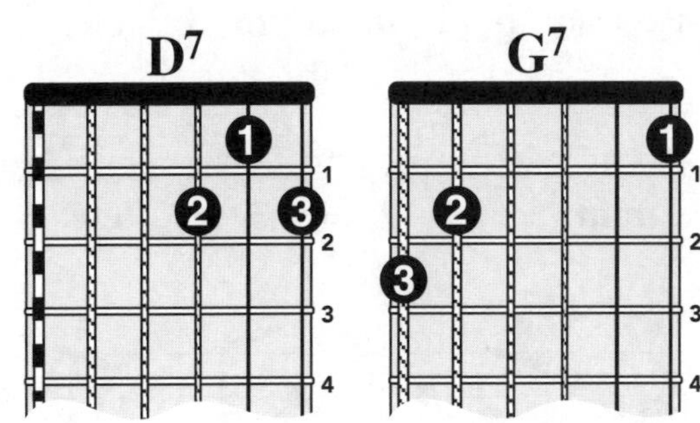

Exercise 9

PATTERN SIX

p ima p ima

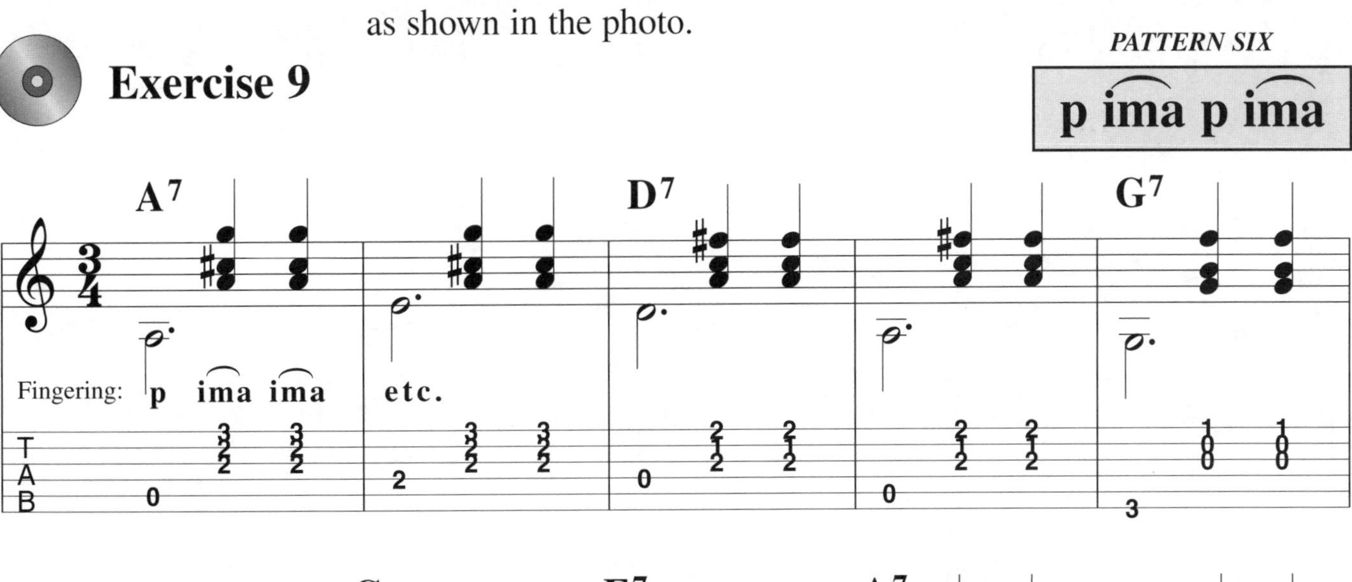

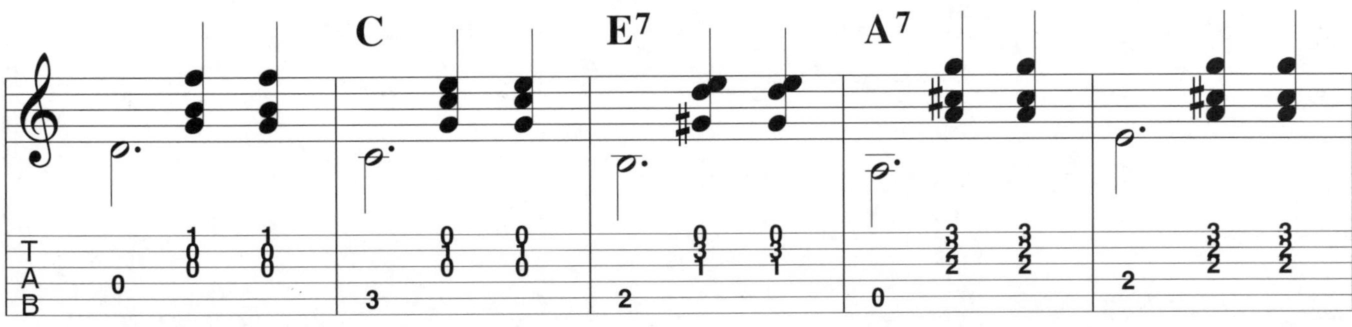

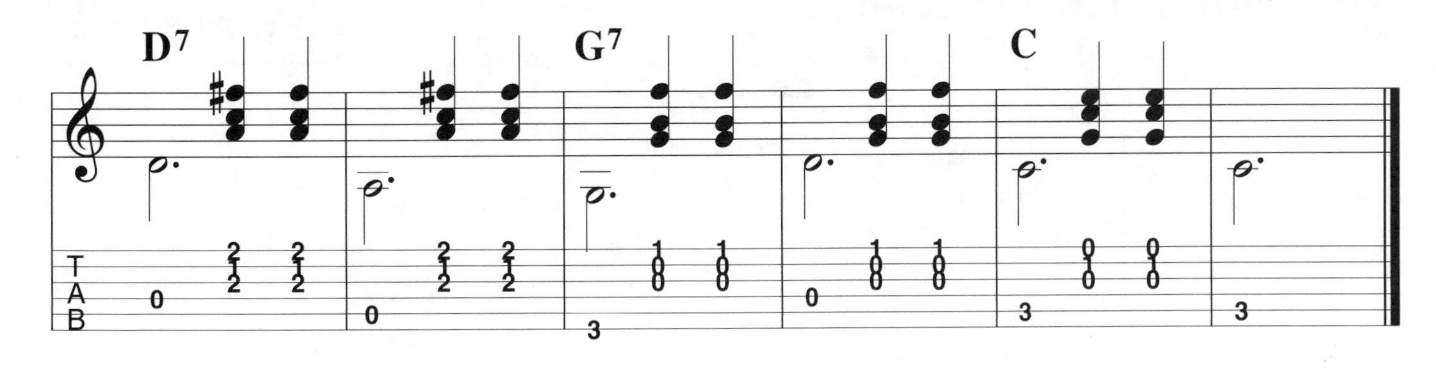

FINGERPICKING PATTERN SEVEN

Pattern 6 can be played in arpeggio style, which gives the following new patterns:

LESSON SEVEN

FINGERPICKING PATTERN EIGHT

The following new pattern is played in $\frac{4}{4}$ time and involves a bass note on the 1st and 4th beats.

PATTERN EIGHT

pimamipi

Exercise 11

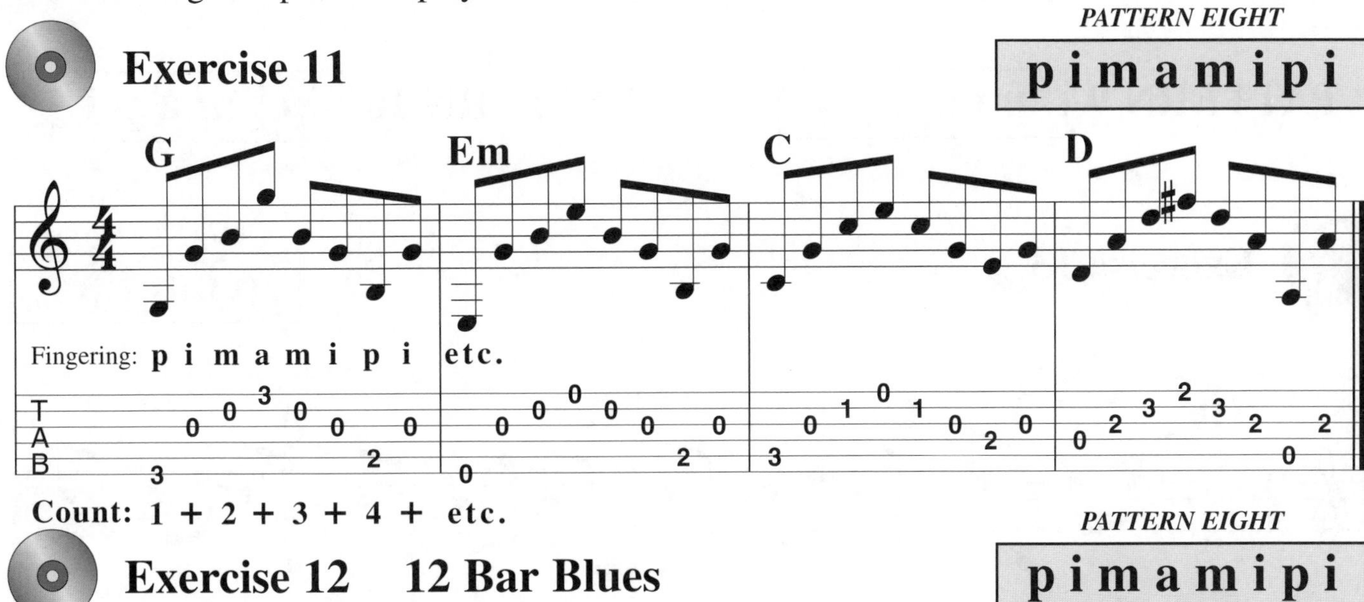

PATTERN EIGHT

pimamipi

Exercise 12 12 Bar Blues

12 Bar Blues is a set pattern of chords which repeats every 12 bars. Many songs are based upon the 12 Bar Blues progression, an example of which is outlined below. Use **pattern 8**.

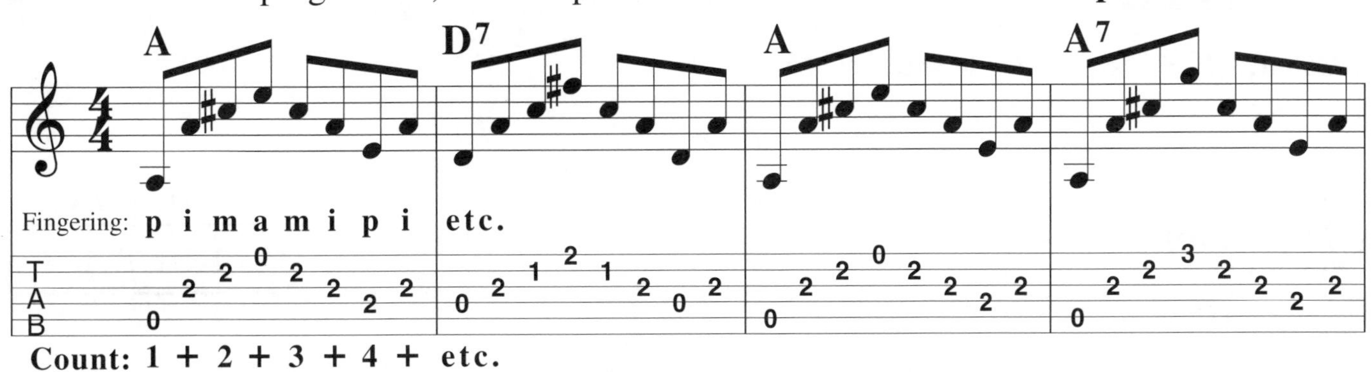

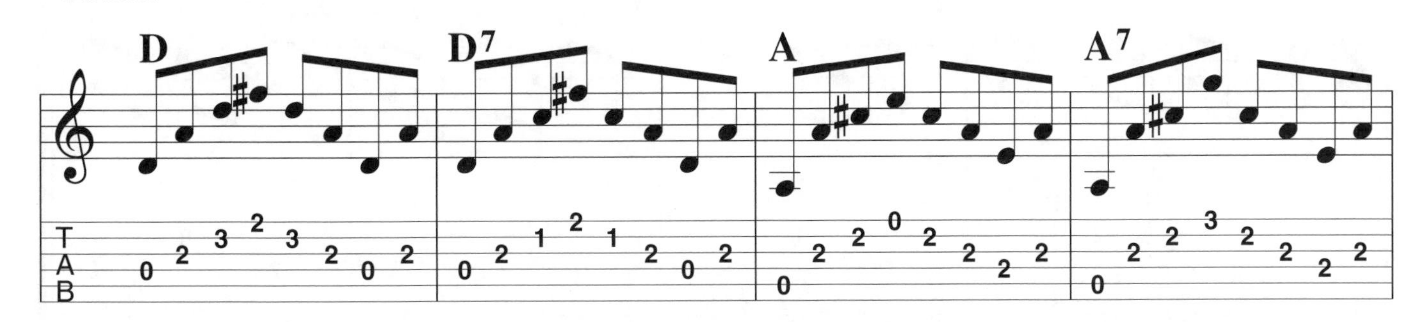

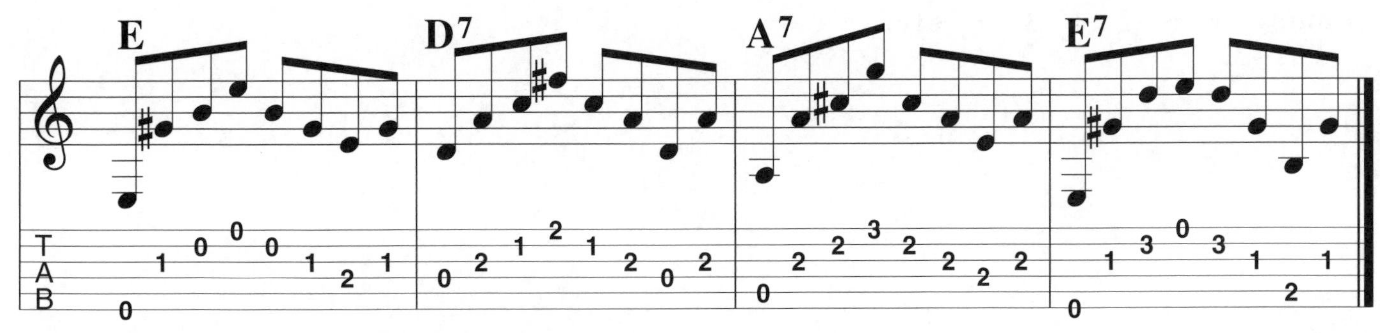

In bar 11 use the A7 chord shape introduced in Lesson Six. However, in bars 4 and 8, it is easier to play the A7 by adding the little finger to the A chord shape:

A7
(alternate fingering)

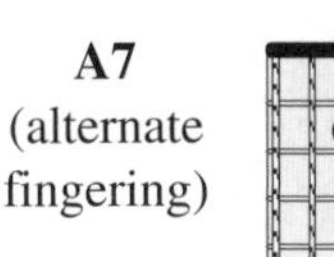

LESSON EIGHT

In Lesson Five and Six patterns in $\frac{3}{4}$ time were introduced with the bass notes being played on the first beat only. The following patterns use bass notes on the first and third beats.

PATTERN 9 **p i m i p i** **PATTERN 10** **p i m a p i**

Exercise 13

PATTERN NINE

p i m i p i

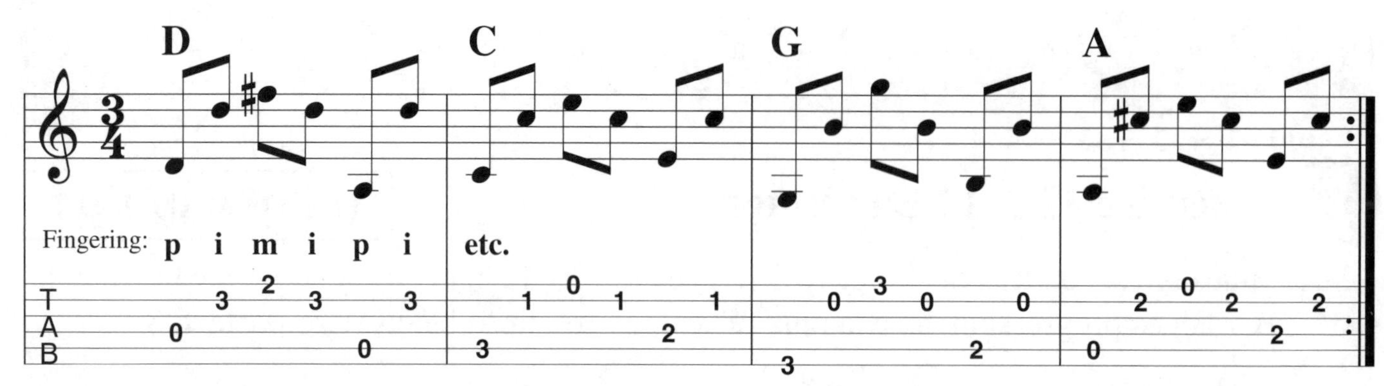

Exercise 14

PATTERN TEN

p i m a p i

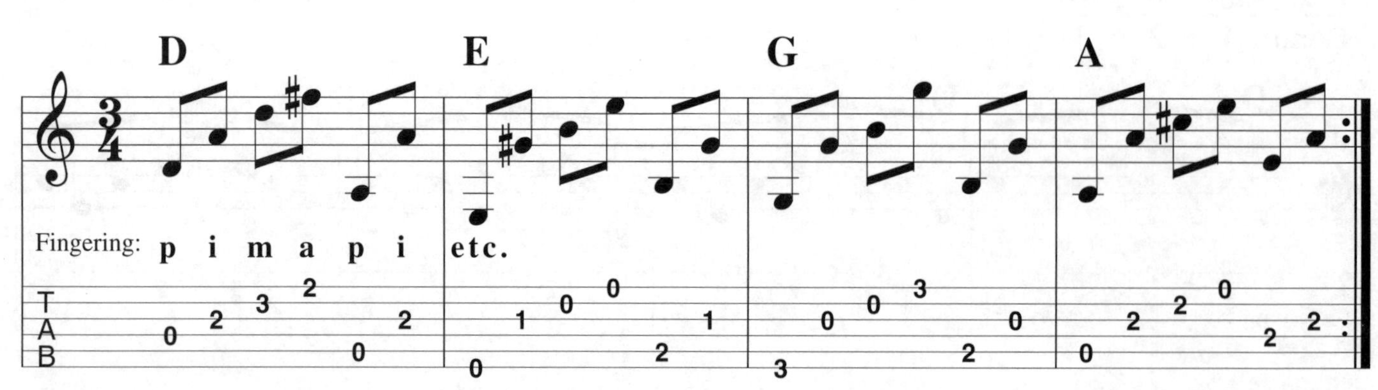

LESSON NINE

BASS NOTE RUNS

A bass note run is a series of single notes played on the bass strings. They are used to connect two chords, adding interest to a given progression.

In the following example each bass note run begins on the 4th beat of the bar (indicated by the brackets). The run is played by the thumb, giving the pattern:

PATTERN 11 **p i m a m i p p**

Bass note runs introduce the technique of playing notes that are **outside** the chord, e.g. the F♯ note in the first bar is not a part of the G chord. This is in contrast to all previous exercises, which have involved only the playing of notes within a chord (i.e. holding a chord shape).

You should experiment with your own bass note run, using the above progression and others that you have studied.

LESSON TEN

FINGERPICKING PATTERN TWELVE

Fingerpicking **pattern 12** introduces the thumb playing a bass note on every beat:

In all previous examples only the 4th, 5th and 6th strings have been used as bass notes. However, in this example, the 3rd and 4th strings are being used.

Use **pattern 12** on the following examples, which introduces three new chords:

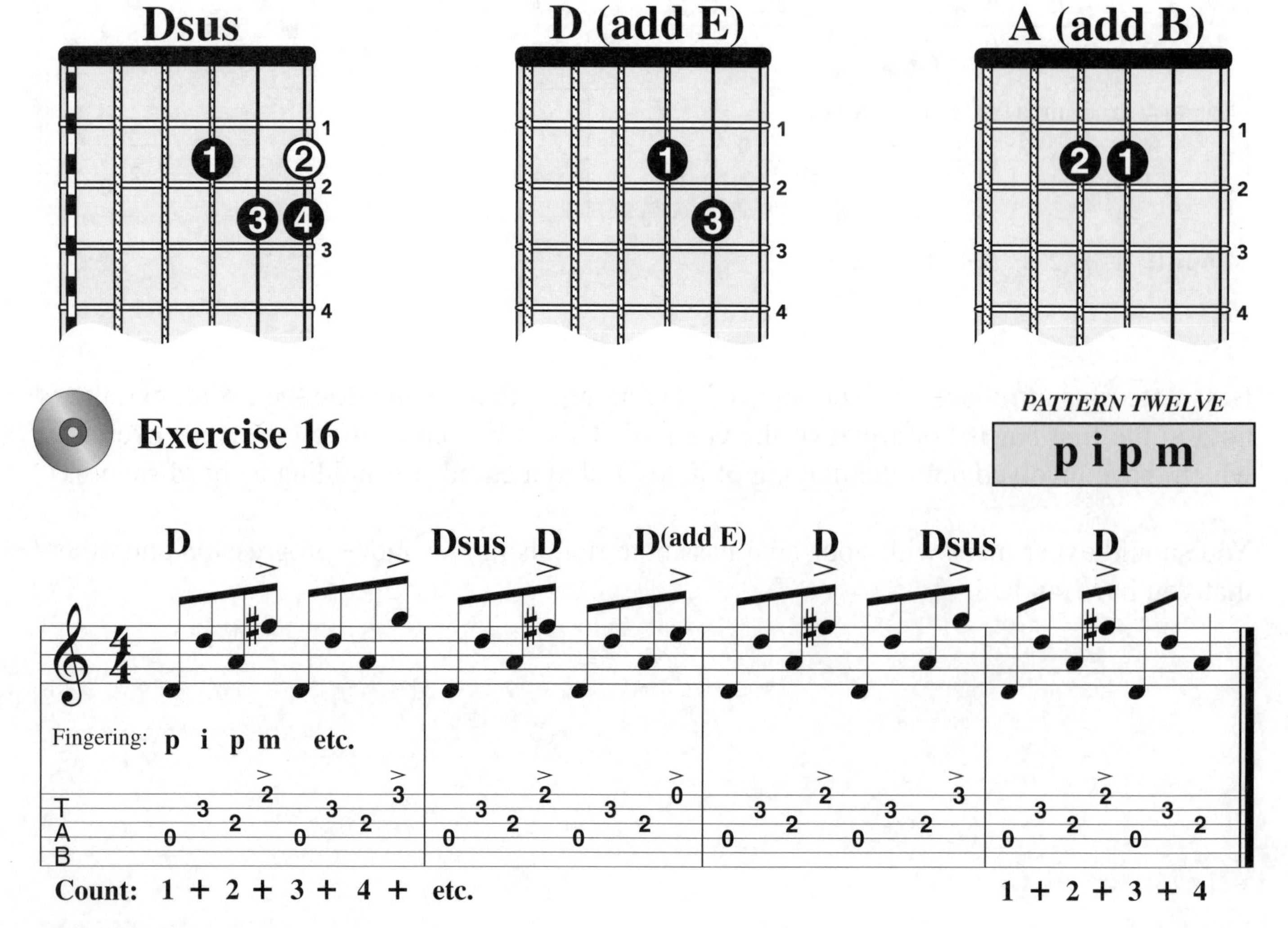

> This is an accent sign - play louder.

* This is a D chord shape with an E note added. It is also another form of the Asus chord.
Likewise, A (add B) is an A chord shape with the B note added and is another form of the Esus chord.

This example is similar to the previous one, except based around the A chord. The bass notes are played on the 4th and 5th strings.

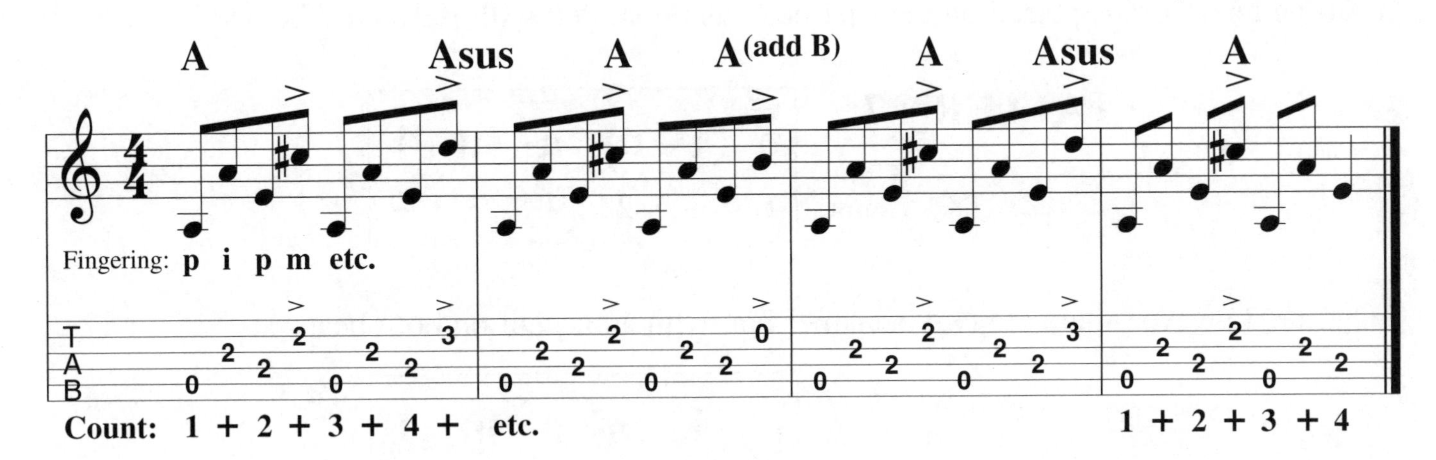

Combine the two examples and pay special attention to smooth changes between all chords.

LESSON ELEVEN

FINGERPICKING PATTERN SEVEN IN $\frac{6}{8}$ TIME

In $\frac{3}{4}$ time an accent is placed on the first beat, as illustrated with **pattern 7** below:

PATTERN 7

	> p	i	m	a	m	i
Count:	1	+	2	+	3	+

In $\frac{6}{8}$ time, however, there are two beats per bar, with an accent on both beats:*

	> p	i	m	> a	m	i
Count:	1	2	3	4	5	6

In the following example the thumb is playing the root note for each chord and the **i**, **m** and **a** fingers play the 3rd, 2nd and 1st strings respectively. Be sure to accent the two beats, as indicated, to create a $\frac{6}{8}$ **feel**.

An F chord is also introduced, illustrated below.

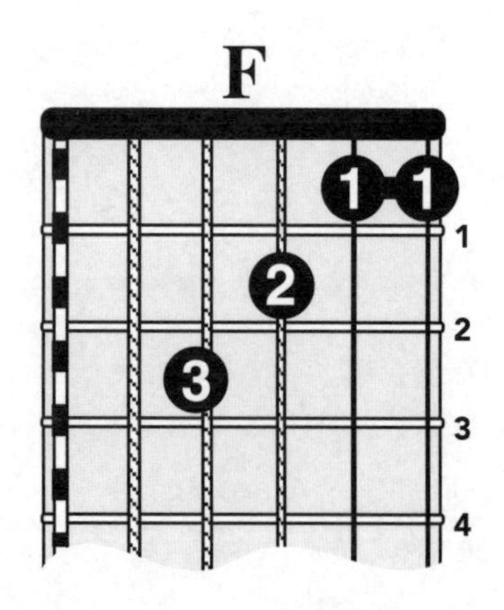

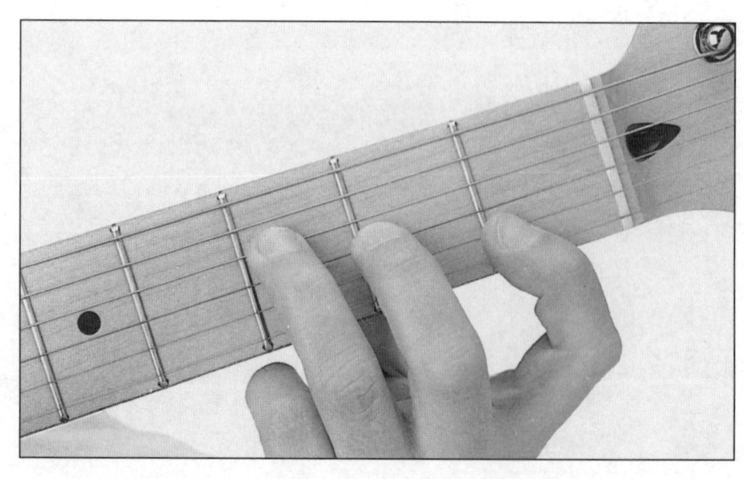

The first finger bars across two strings, as shown in the photo.

* See page 119 for an explanation of $\frac{6}{8}$ time.

Exercise 18

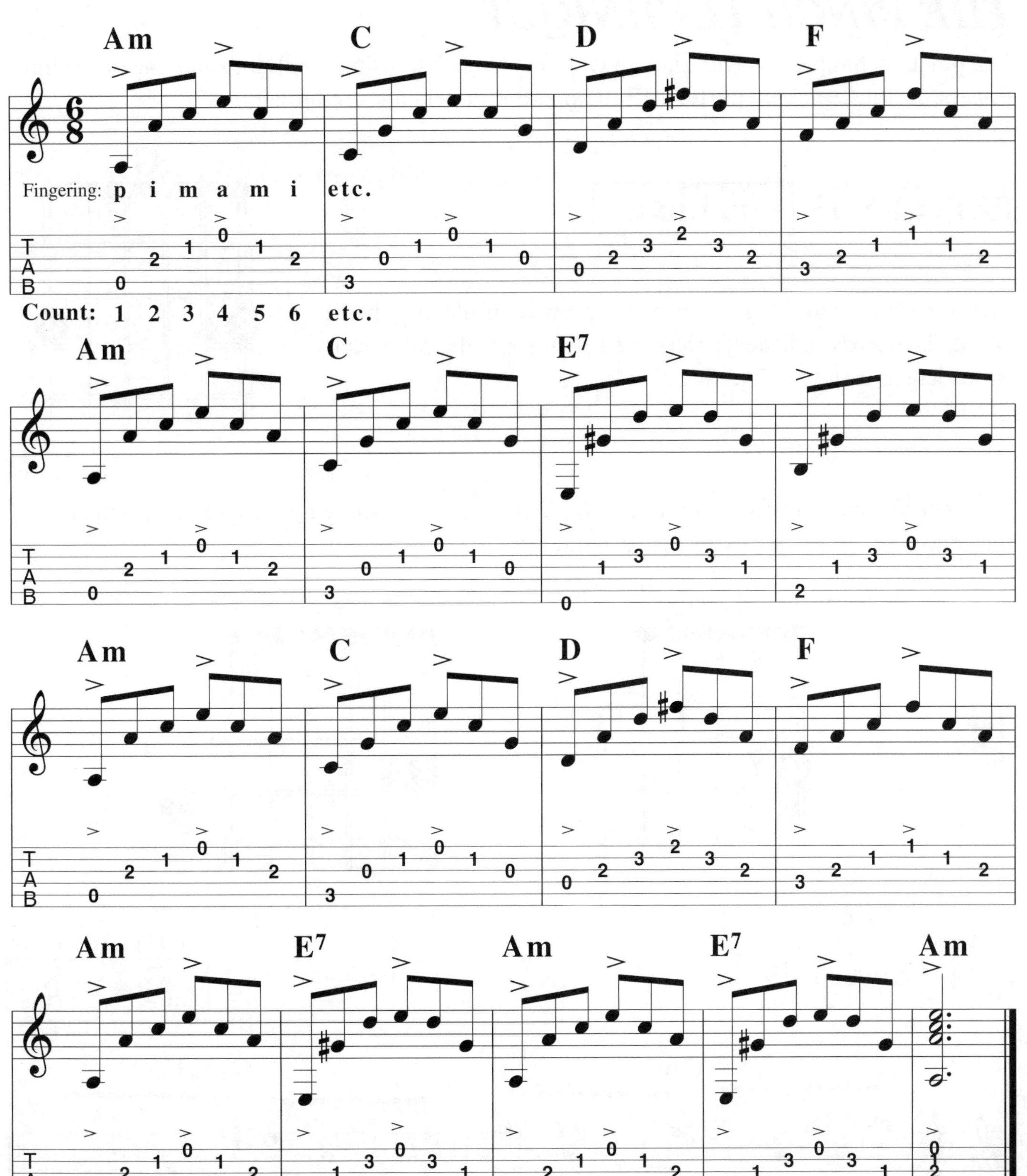

In the last bar, the thumb and fingers play together and the chord is held for the full bar.

To achieve the accent with the **a** finger, a rest stroke (see page 9) can be used. The use of the rest stroke will be quite difficult at first, but it is very useful for accenting a note.

LESSON TWELVE

THE PINCH TECHNIQUE

The pinch technique involves playing two notes together, using the thumb and one of the three fingers. In fingerpicking **pattern 13** the **p** and **a** fingers are used together.

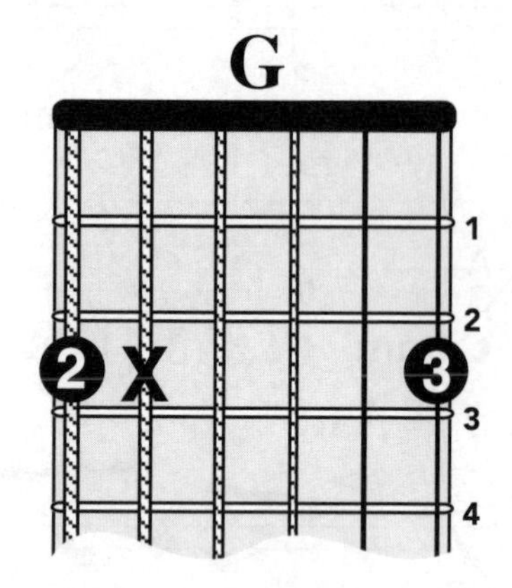

PATTERN 13 pa i m a

The following example introduces a new way of playing the G chord. The cross indicates a deadened string, i.e. the 5th string is deadened, using the 2nd finger.

This chord shape is used for ease of playing in the following progression, which also introduces two new chords, G major 7 and G6.

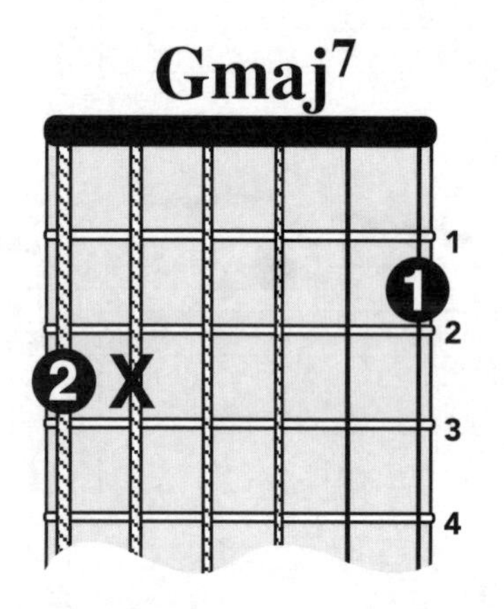

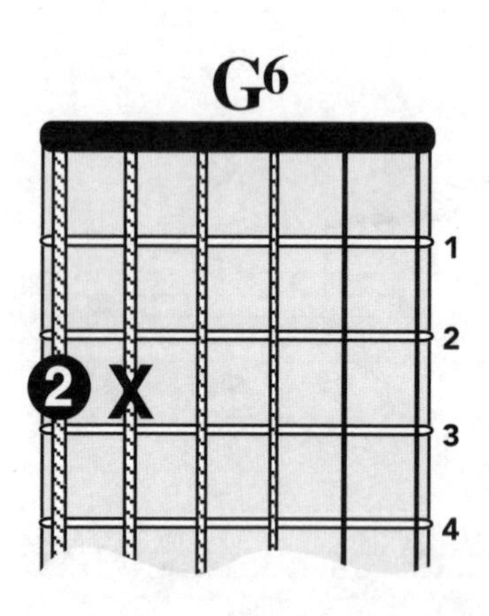

Exercise 19 .

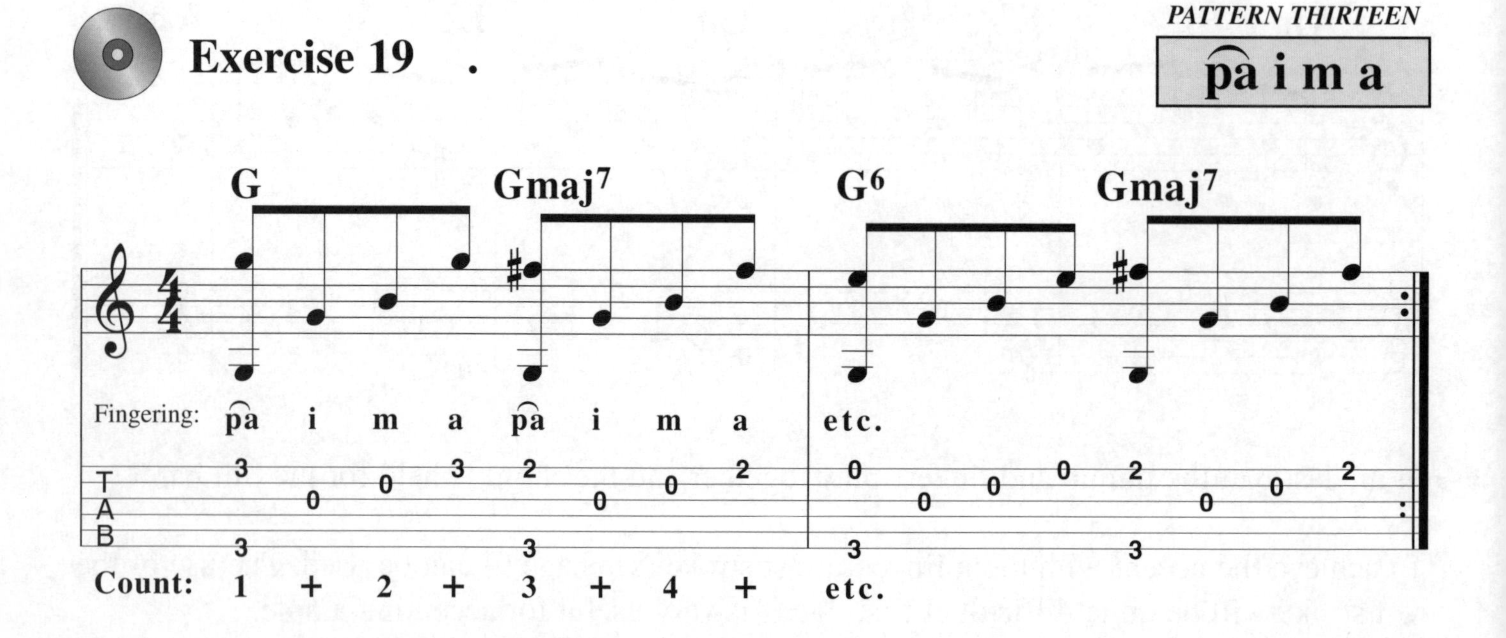

LESSON THIRTEEN

TRIPLETS

Eighth note triplets are three evenly-spaced notes played in one beat, e.g.

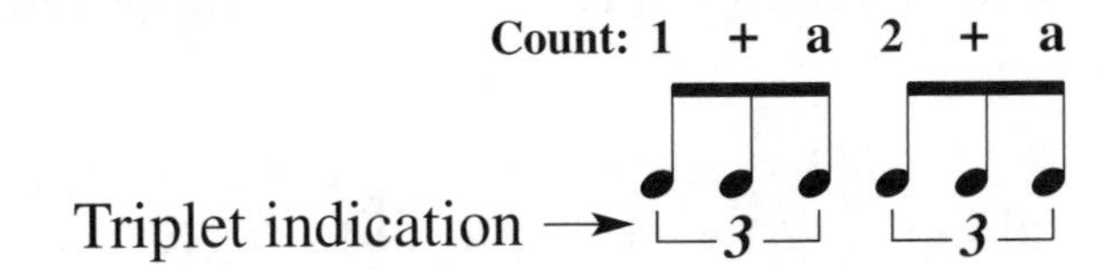

An ideal pattern for playing triplets is pattern 5, introduced in Lesson Five.

Try the following progression:

Exercise 20

PATTERN FIVE

p i m

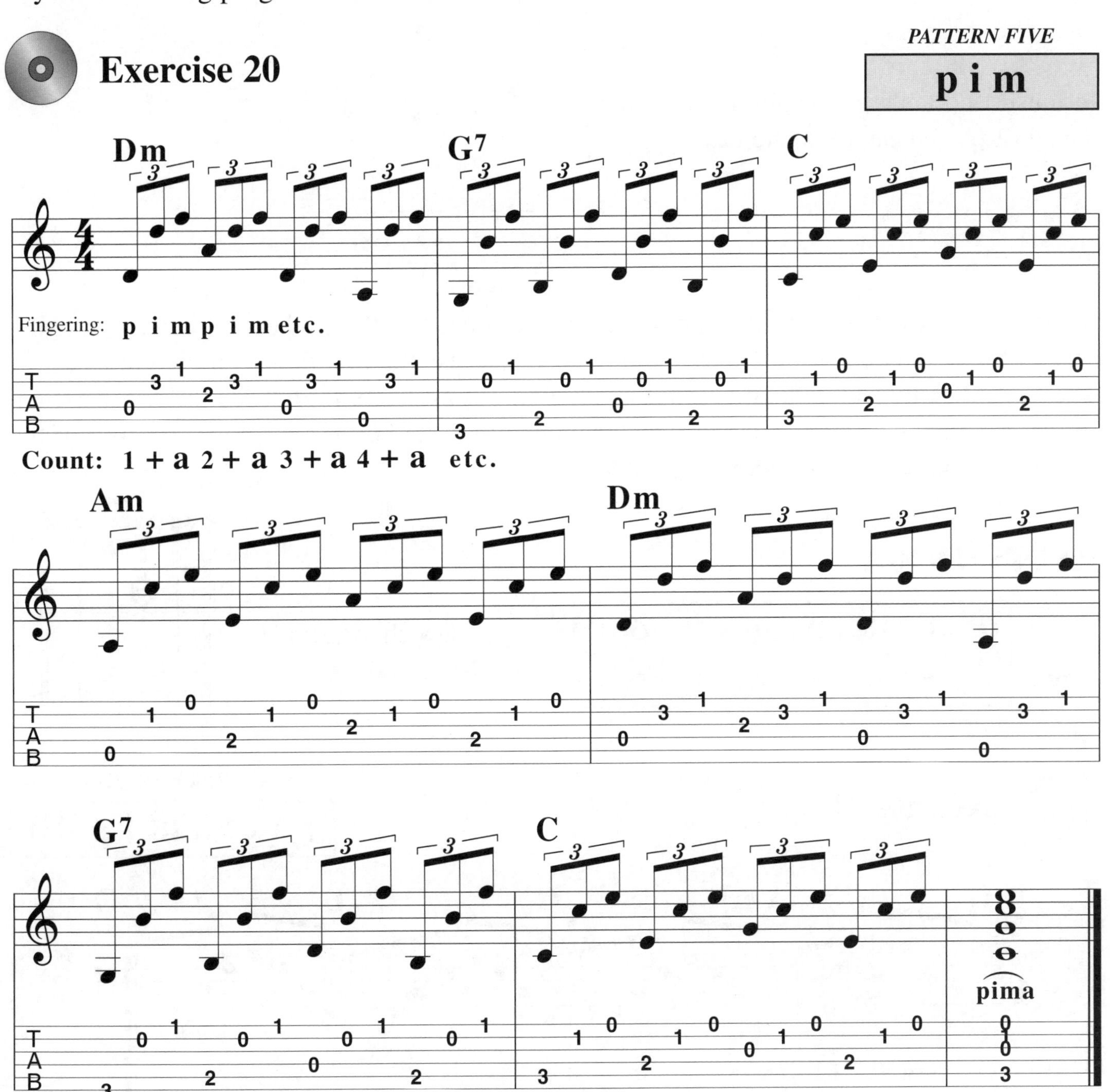

Other examples of triplets can be found in the Supplementary Pieces, beginning on page 95. Try **the Etude** on page 104.

LESSON FOURTEEN

THE HAMMER-ON

A **hammer-on** refers to the technique of sounding a note without actually picking the string with a right hand finger. Instead, the note's sound is produced by striking the string with one of the left hand fingers.

As an example, hold the Am chord and keeping the first and third fingers in position, lift the second finger off the 4th string. Play the open 4th string (use **p**), then bring the second finger down firmly and quickly to its position on the second fret, without picking the string again. This left hand movement should produce an E note quite clearly.

In music and tablature notation, what you have just played can be written as:

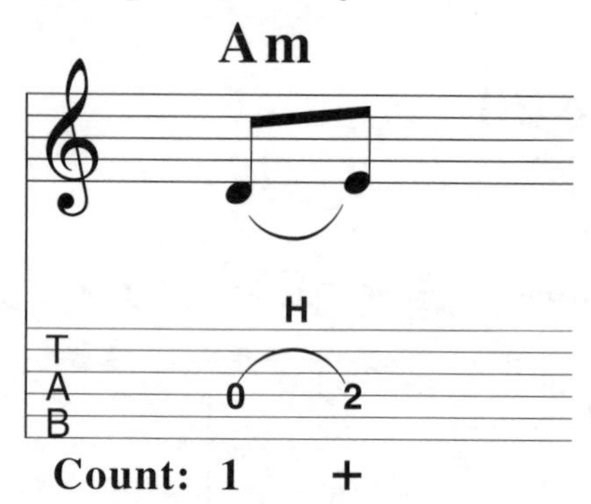

In the following example the hammer-on technique is used on the 4th beat of each bar. Use the second finger to hammer-on in the first three bars and use the first finger for the 4th bar. The fingerpicking pattern being used is a variation of **pattern 8**, introduced in Lesson Seven. In this pattern, however, the hammer-on technique (indicated by **H**) is used on the **and** of the 4th beat, in place of the **i** finger.

PATTERN 8-A

	p	i	m	a	m	i	p	(H)
Count:	1	+	2	+	3	+	4	+

A new chord, Am7 is also introduced.

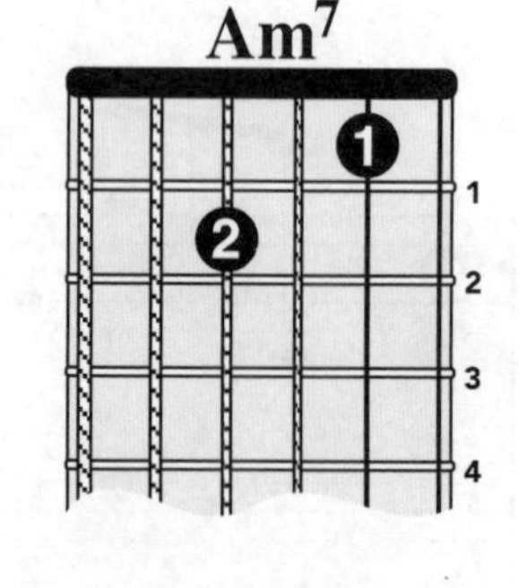

Exercise 21

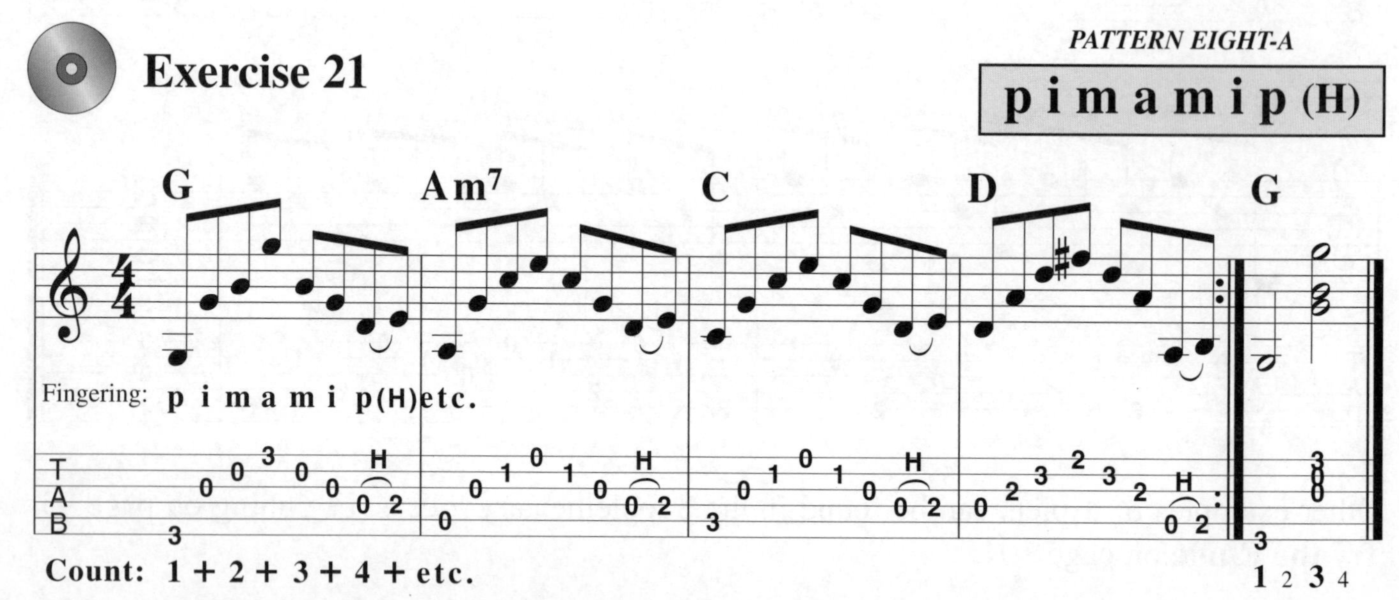

LESSON FIFTEEN

THE FLICK-OFF

The flick-off technique can be described as a reversal of the hammer-on. the note's sound is produced by the left hand finger flicking the open string as it lifts off a fretted note, e.g.: hold C chord and play the second string (C note). Now lift the first finger off the string, flicking it as you do so. This left hand movement should create the sound of a B note quite clearly. In music and tablature notation what you have just played can be written as:

Try the following example, using a flick-off on the first beat and introducing the C major 7 chord.

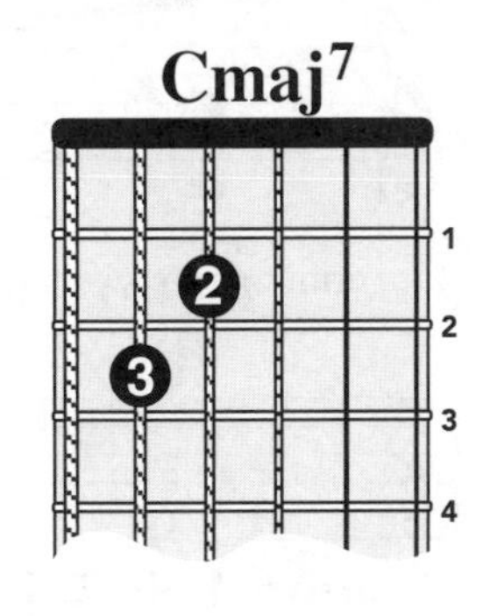

The fingerpicking pattern being used is as such:

PATTERN 14

	pm (F)		i	p	a	m	i	p
Count:	1	+	2	+	3	+	4	+

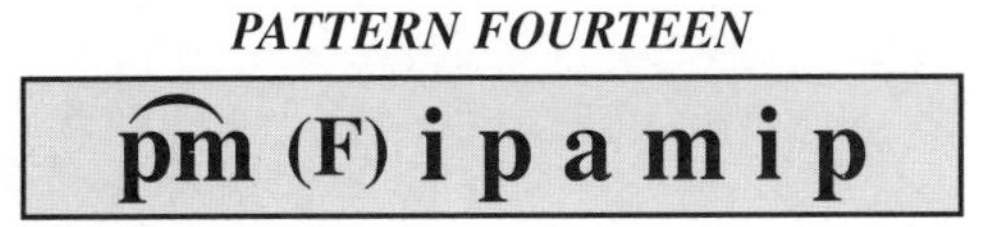

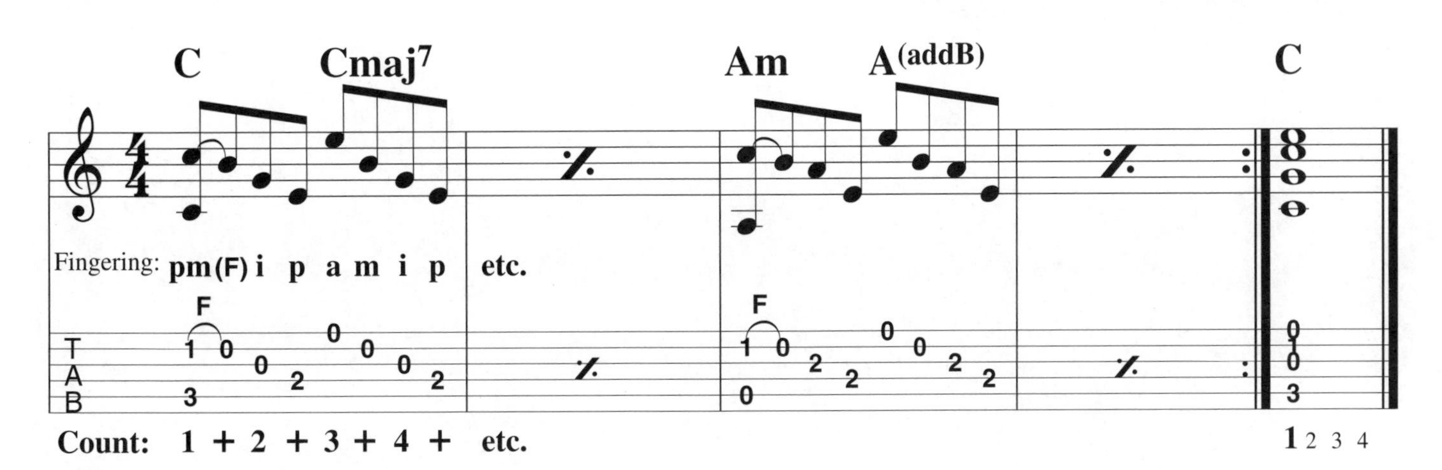

Although **pattern 14** specifically applies to this example, the principles involved (i.e. the combination of pinch and flick-off techniques) can be applied to other chord progressions and songs.

COMBINING HAMMER-ON AND FLICK-OFF TECHNIQUES

The following pattern uses a combination of the hammer-on and flick-off techniques.

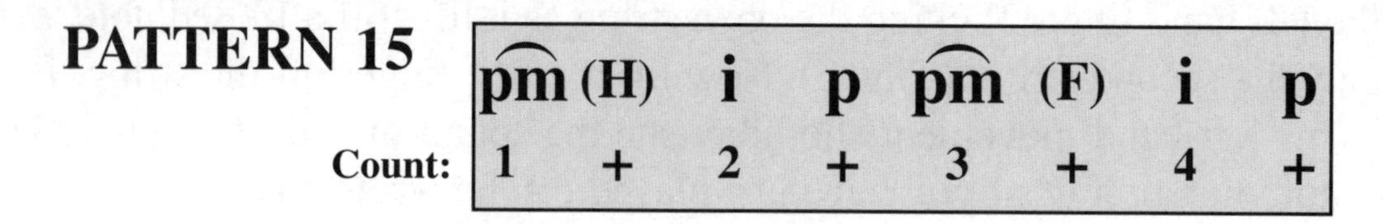

This pattern is applied to the following chord progression:

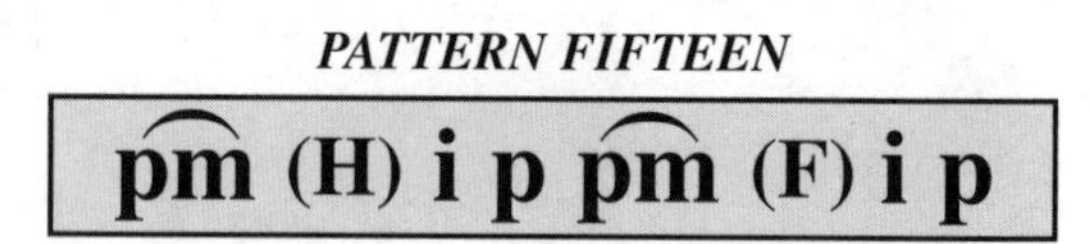

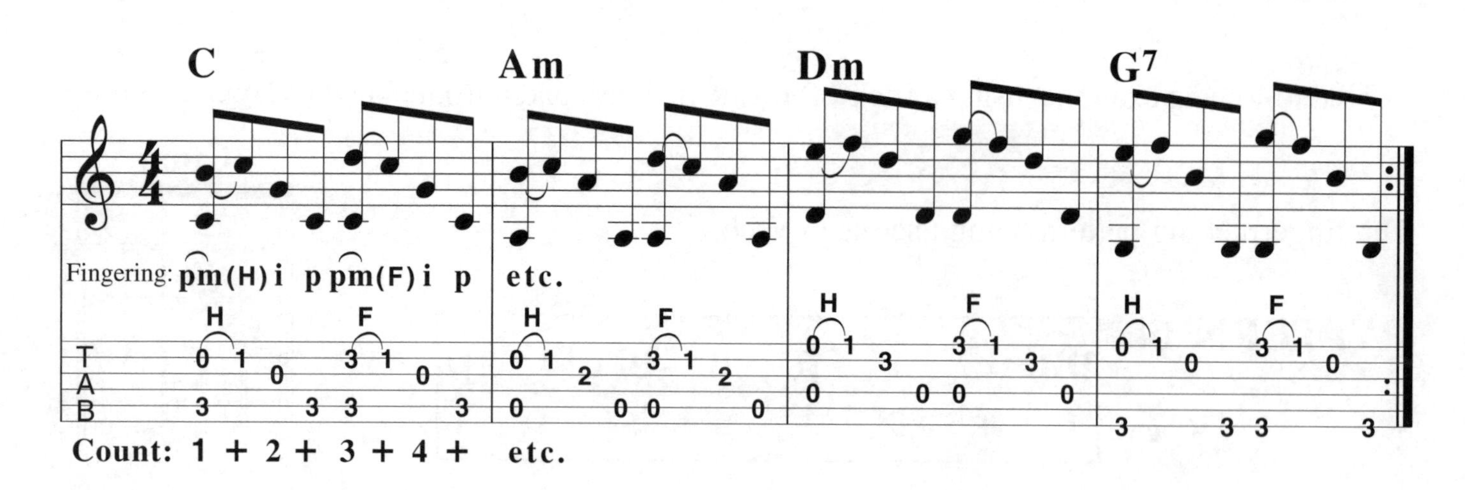

LESSON SIXTEEN

CLAWHAMMER

One of the most popular styles of fingerpicking is called **clawhammer** which involves the following pattern:

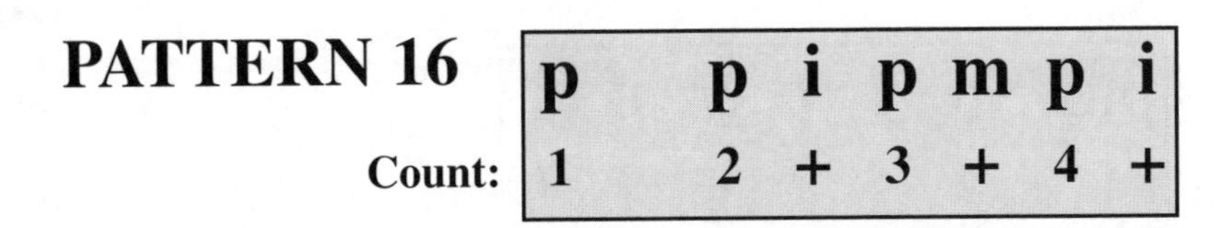

Try the following **clawhammer** example, using the C and Am chords.

Exercise 24

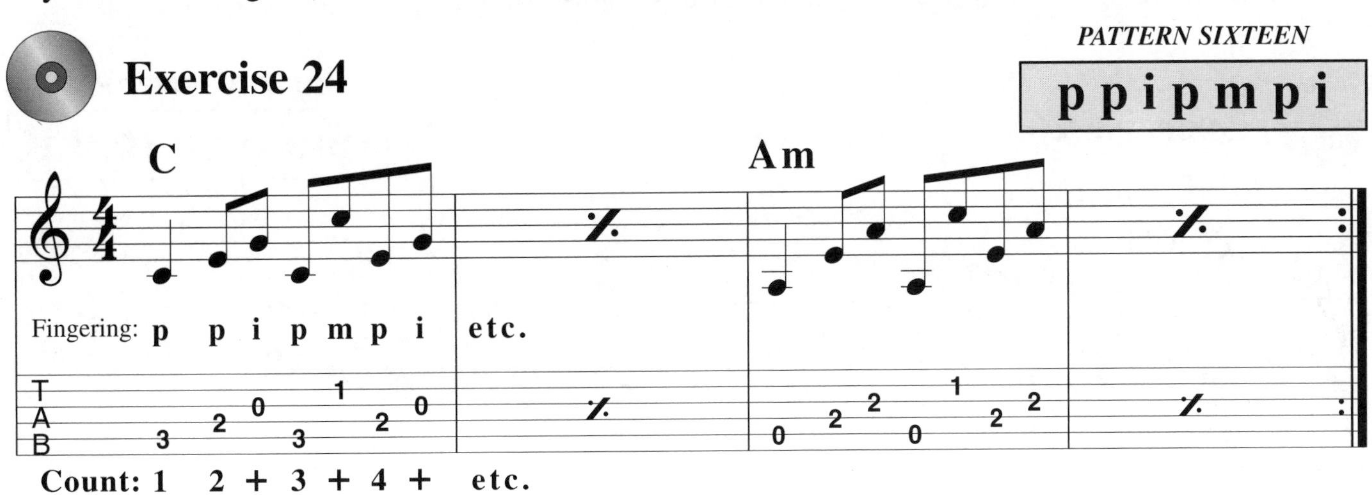

A bass note run and the pinch technique can be added to this example.

Exercise 25

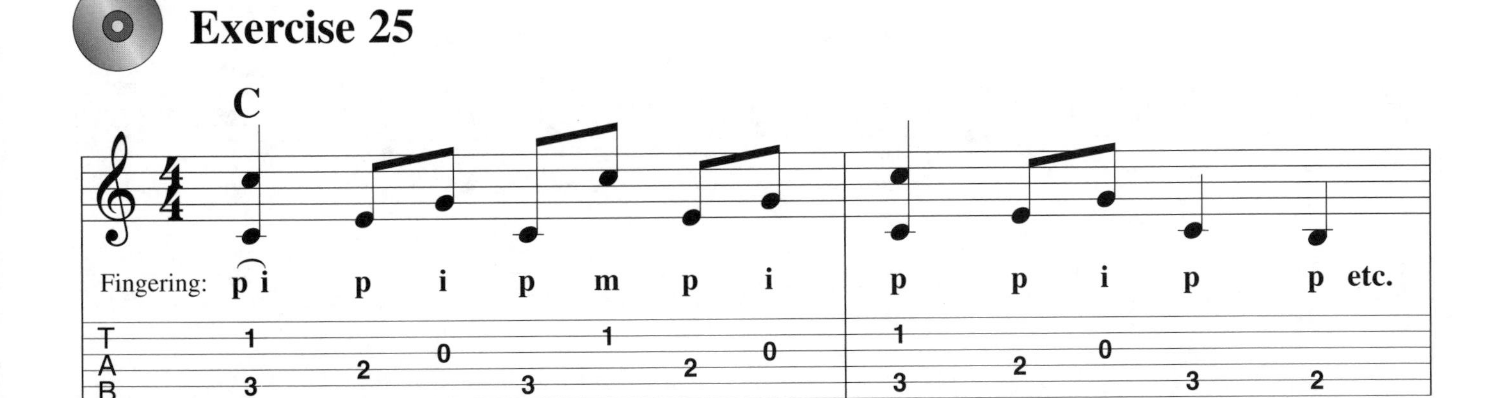

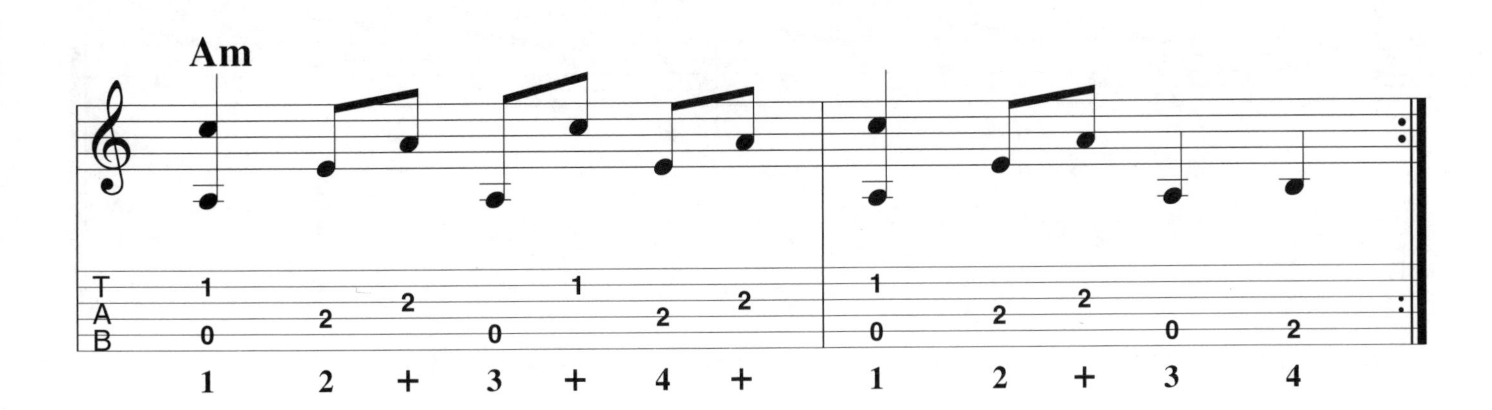

LESSON SEVENTEEN

CLAWHAMMER - THE PINCH TECHNIQUE

The pinch technique (Lesson Twelve) is commonly used in conjunction with clawhammer, giving the following pattern:

C (add D)

PATTERN 17

pm	p	i	p	m	p	i
Count: 1	2	+	3	+	4	+

The following example introduces a new chord: C (add D).

Exercise 26

PATTERN SEVENTEEN

pm p i p m p i

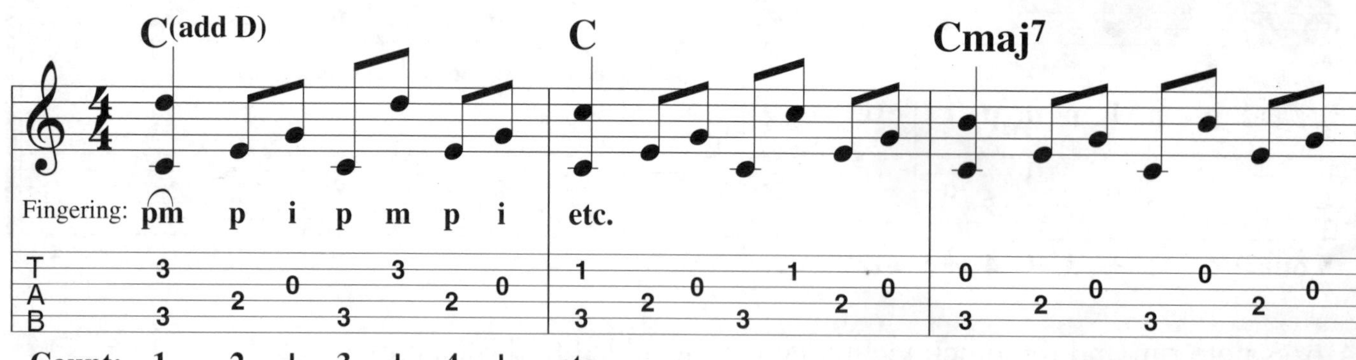

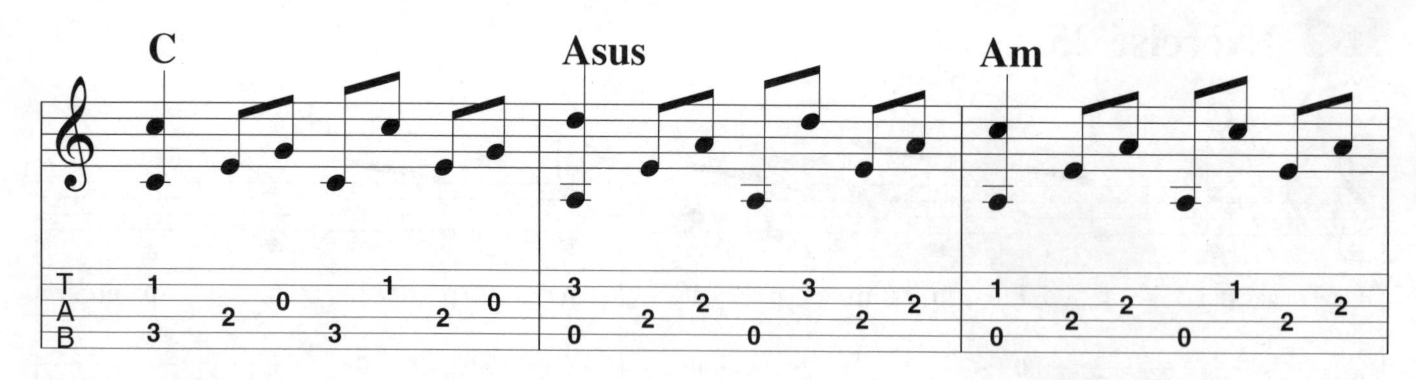

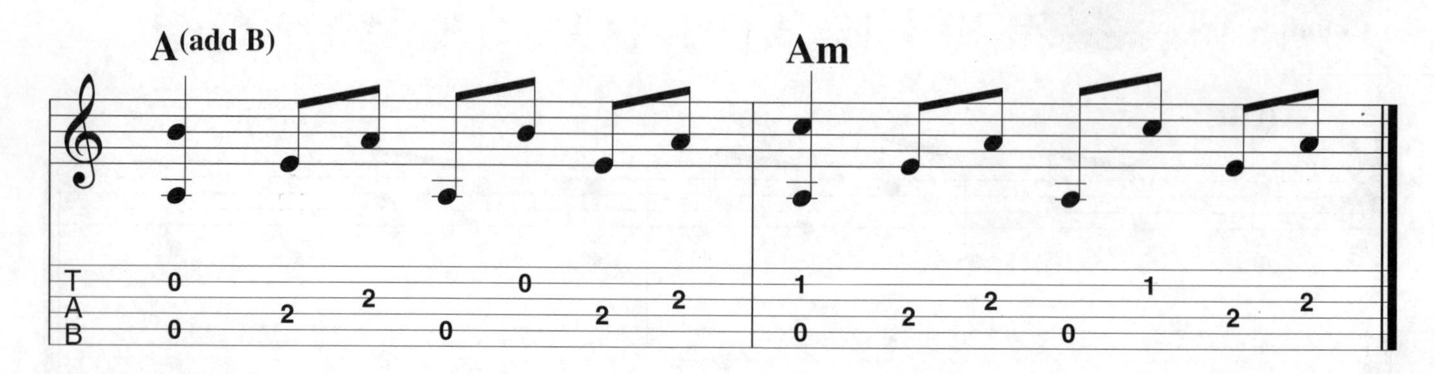

This progression is based around the C (bars 1 and 2) and Am (bar 3 and 4) chords.

LESSON EIGHTEEN

6-STRING CLAWHAMMER

In the last two lessons the clawhammer examples have involved the use of only four strings. The following clawhammer pattern uses all six stings:

PATTERN 18

	pm	p	i	p	a	p	i
String:	52	4	3	6	1	4	3
Count:	1	2	+	3	+	4	+

This pattern can only be used on chords that involve the playing of all six strings. e.g G, E, Am, G7 etc. For five or four string chord shapes (e.g. open D, open F) the standard clawhammer pattern, as outlined in Lessons Sixteen and Seventeen is used.

Try the six string clawhammer using the E chord with the following fingering:

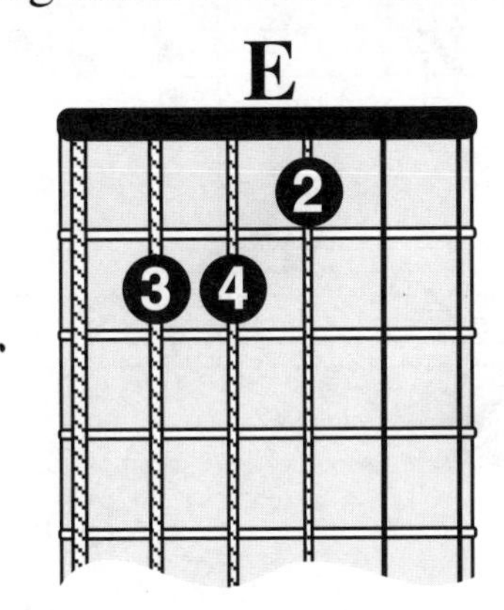

The following example uses the six string clawhammer and introduces the chords A6 (add B), E major 7 and A (add B).

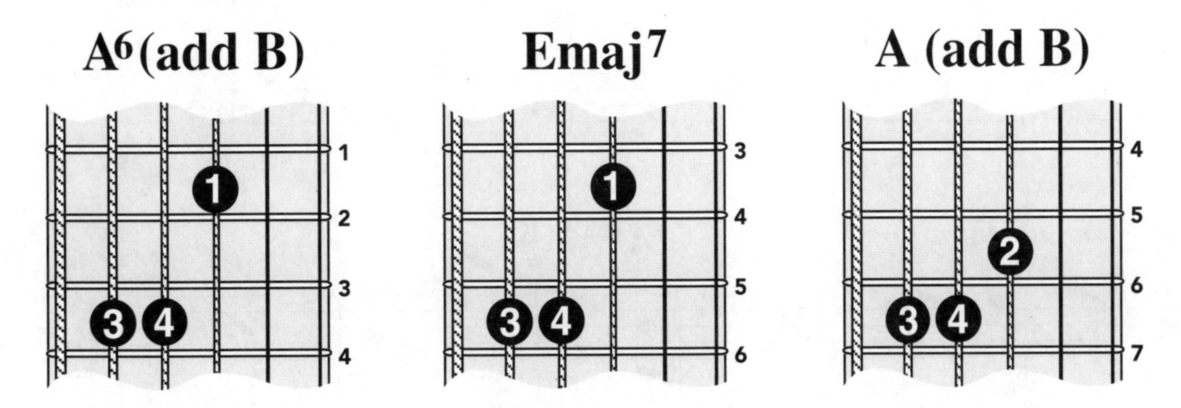

* An alternative fingering for the 6 string clawhammer is as such:

pm	p	i	p	m	p	i
52	4	3	6	1	4	3

This fingering omits the use of the **a** finger.

Although music and tablature notation has been given, it is possible to play this example by simply applying **pattern 18** to each chord.

Exercise 27

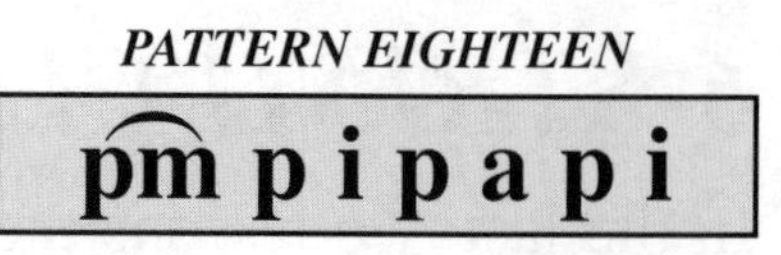

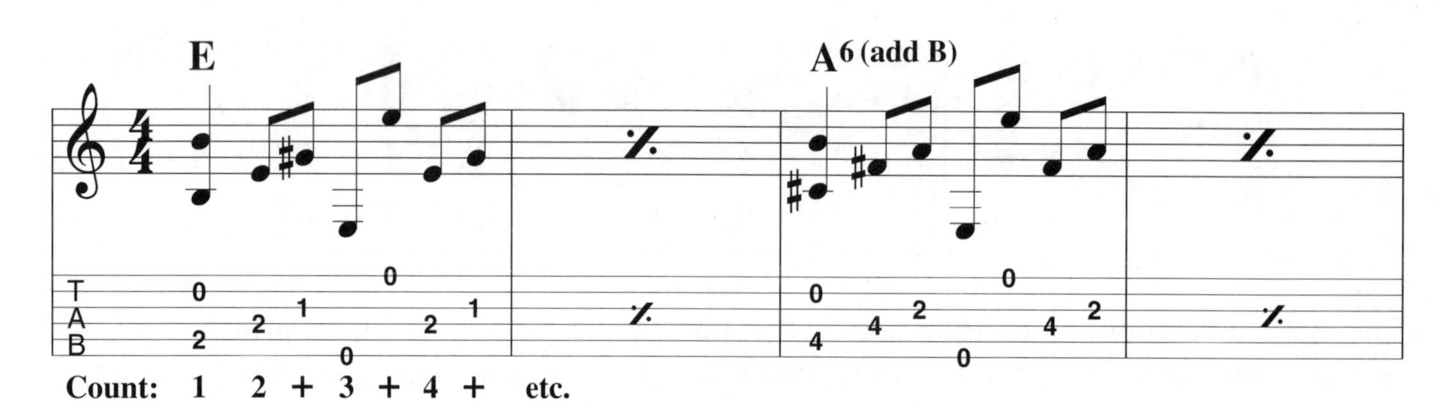

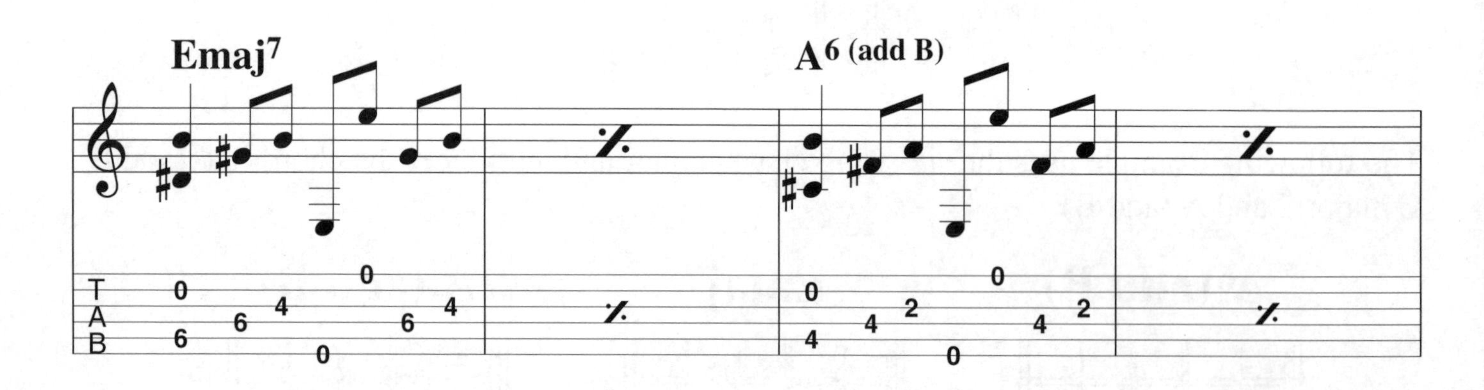

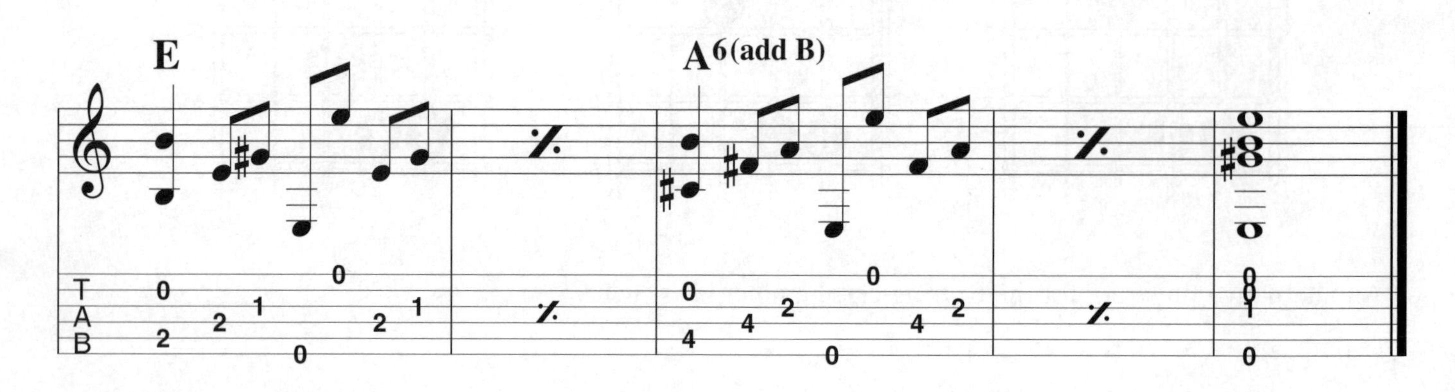

LESSON NINETEEN

CLAWHAMMER IN $\frac{3}{4}$ TIME

Although claw hammer is more commonly used in $\frac{6}{8}$ time, it can also be played in $\frac{3}{4}$ time, using the following pattern:

PATTERN 19

	pm	p	i	p	a
Count:	1	2	+	3	+

The following chord progression introduces a G diminished chord (written G°) and an alternative shape for the G chord.

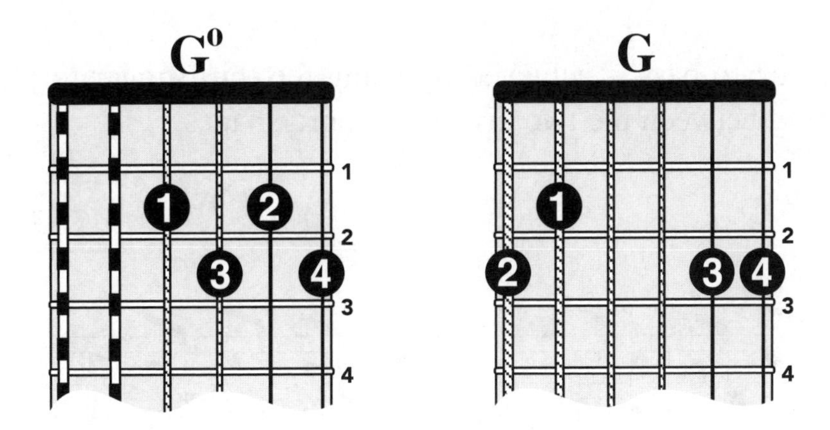

Exercise 28

PATTERN NINETEEN

pm p i p a

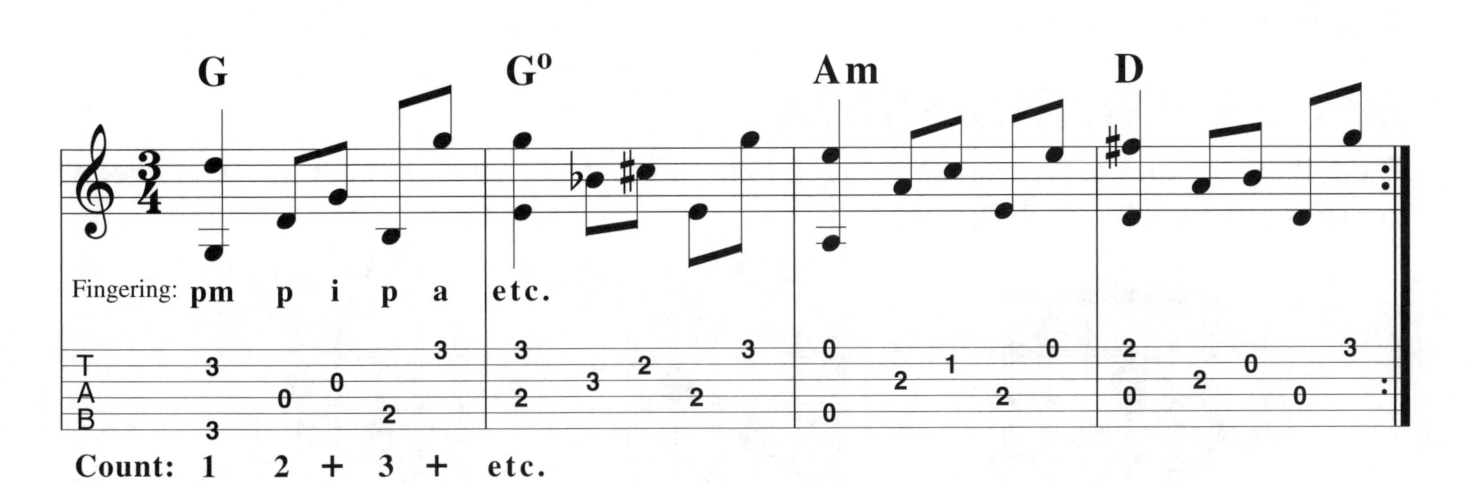

Use the 4th finger pivot between the G and G° chords.

LESSON TWENTY

STACCATO BASS

Staccato means to play short and detached. In fingerpicking, this is achieved by releasing pressure on a fretted note immediately after it is played. In music and TAB notation **staccato** is indicated by a dot placed above or below the note.

The following example introduces the C7 chord, using two different shapes:

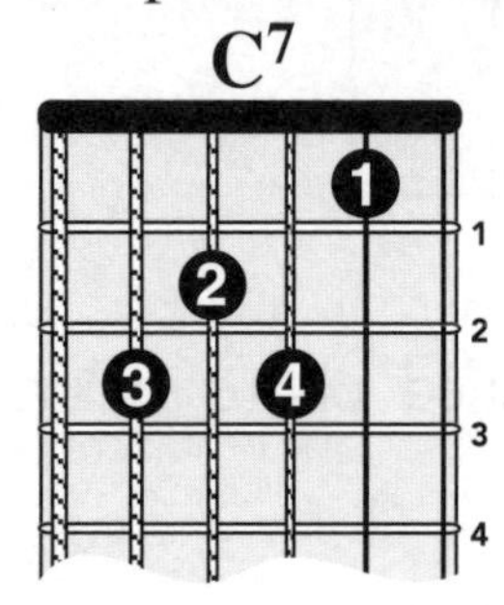

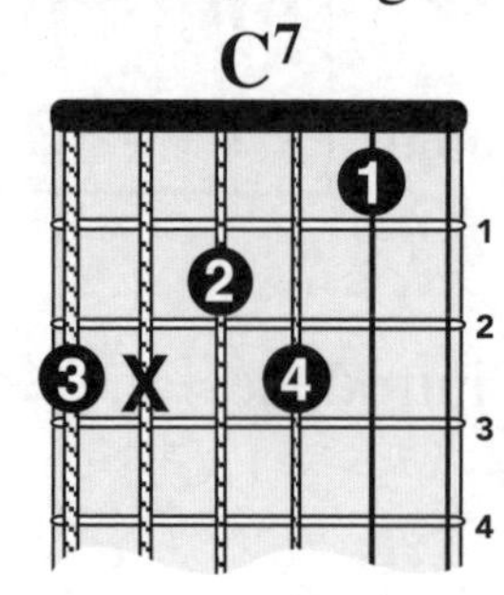

The third finger deadens the fifth string.

In this example a staccato bass is achieved by using the third finger to play the 5th and 6th strings (i.e. alternating between the two given C7 chord shapes).

BLUES PROGRESSION

The following blues progression uses the C7 chord shape played at the first fret (C7), the 6th fret (F7) and the 8th fret (G7).

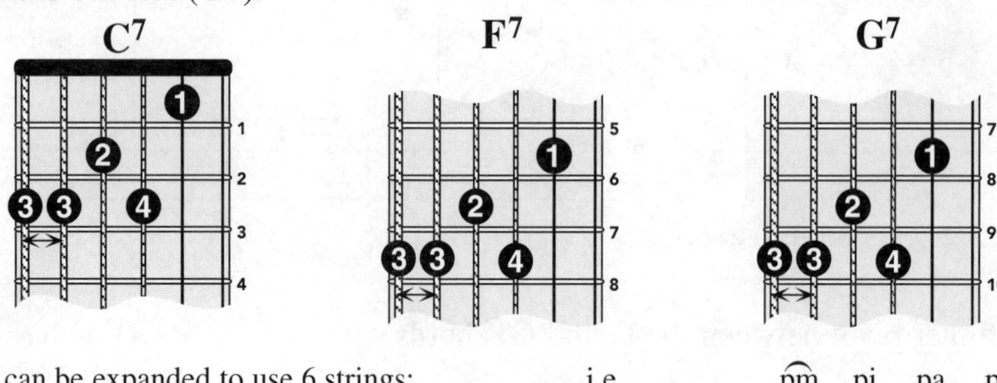

* This pattern can be expanded to use 6 strings:

i.e.	pm	pi	pa	pi
String No.	52	43	61	43
Count:	1	2+	3+	4+

Once again, the bass note is alternating between the 5th and 6th strings and is played in a staccato fashion. Bass note runs are used between the chord changes (refer to the tablature for the correct playing position of these runs).

Exercise 30

SECTION ONE SUMMARY

You have now completed Section One, and you should revise all of the fingerpicking patterns, applying them to songs and other progression. Also read Appendices Three and Four.

SONGS

The following songs make use of the picking patterns introduced in Section One. A suggested pattern has been given for each song, however any pattern (in the same time signature) can be used. Apply the picking patterns to other songs of your choice.

Aura Lee

PATTERN ONE

Suggested Pattern **p i m i**

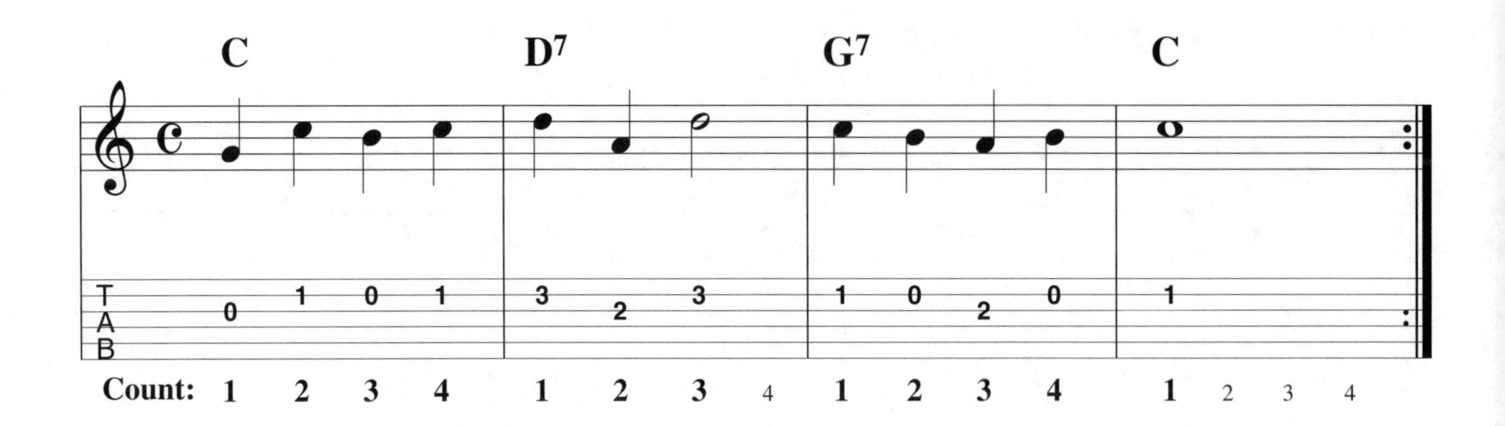

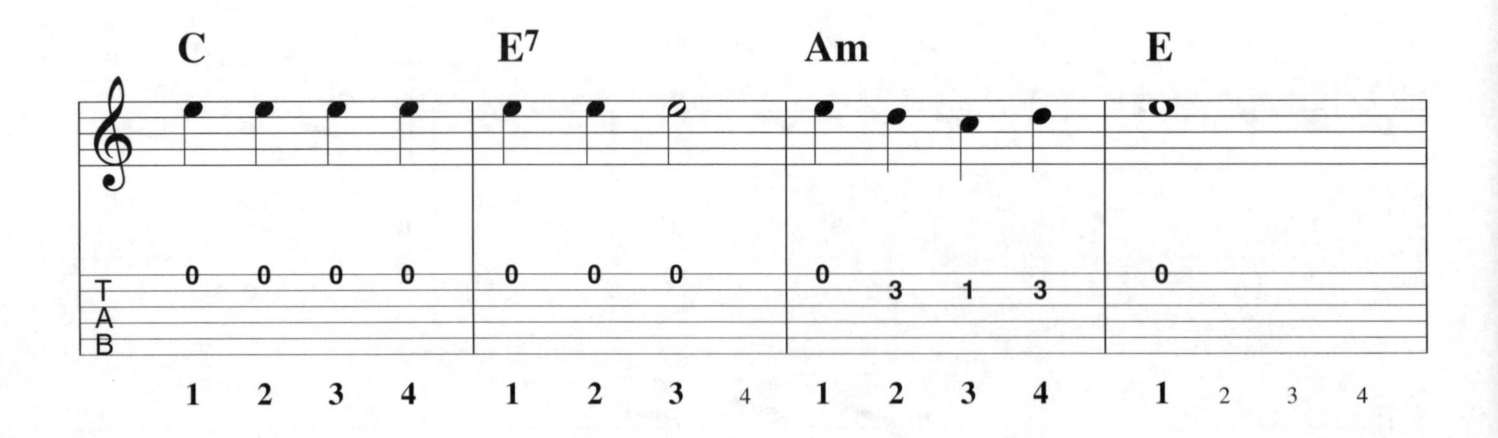

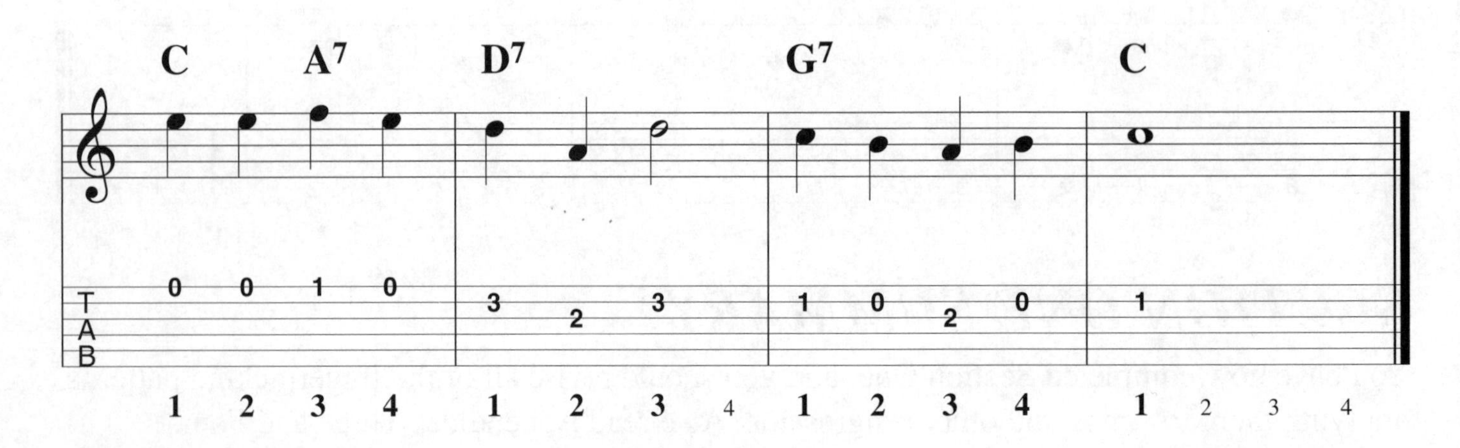

Auld Lang Syne

This song uses a **Lead-in** note which is a note (or notes) occurring before the first bar of music. In this case the lead-in note (A) is played on the 4th count (see tab) and the last bar contains only three counts (to balance out the four counts per bar).

PATTERN THREE

Suggested Pattern **p i m a**

Greensleeves

PATTERN SIX

Suggested Pattern 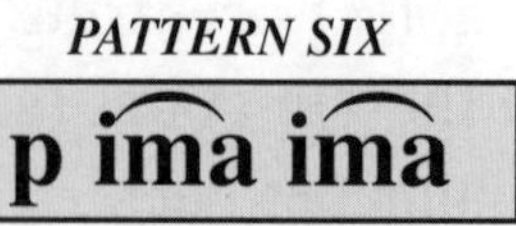

or *Suggested Pattern*

PATTERN SEVEN

p i m a m i

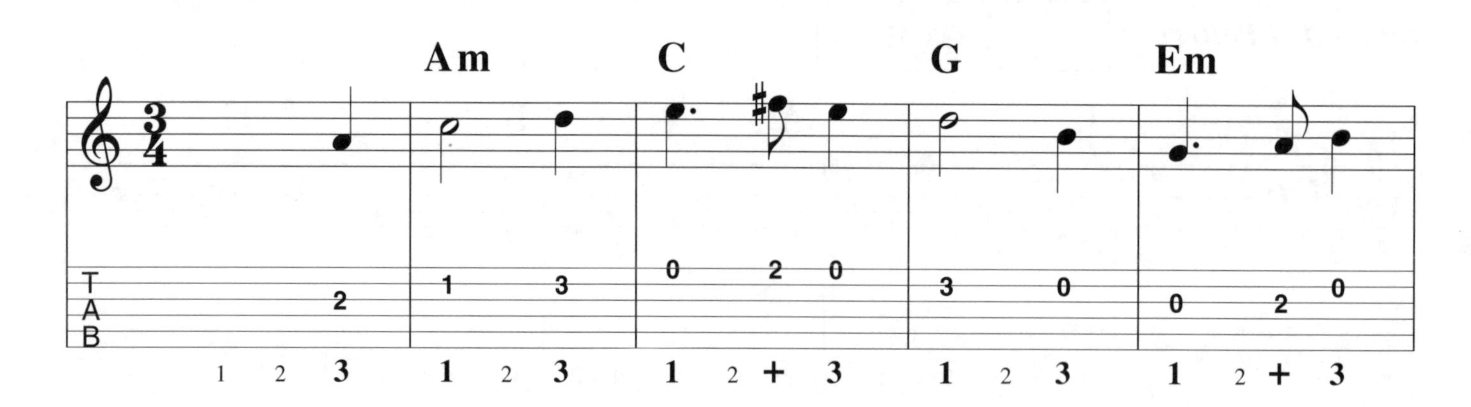

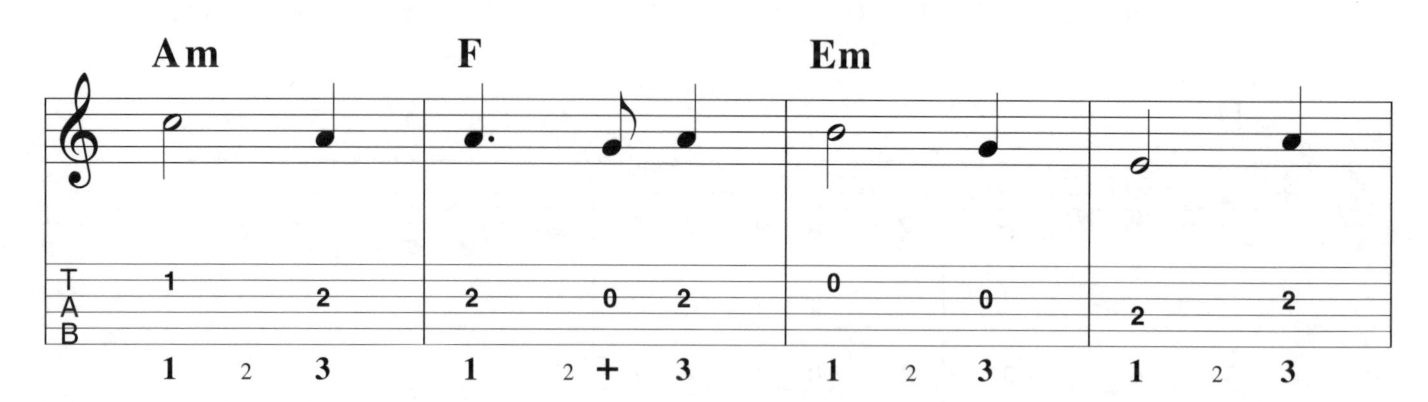

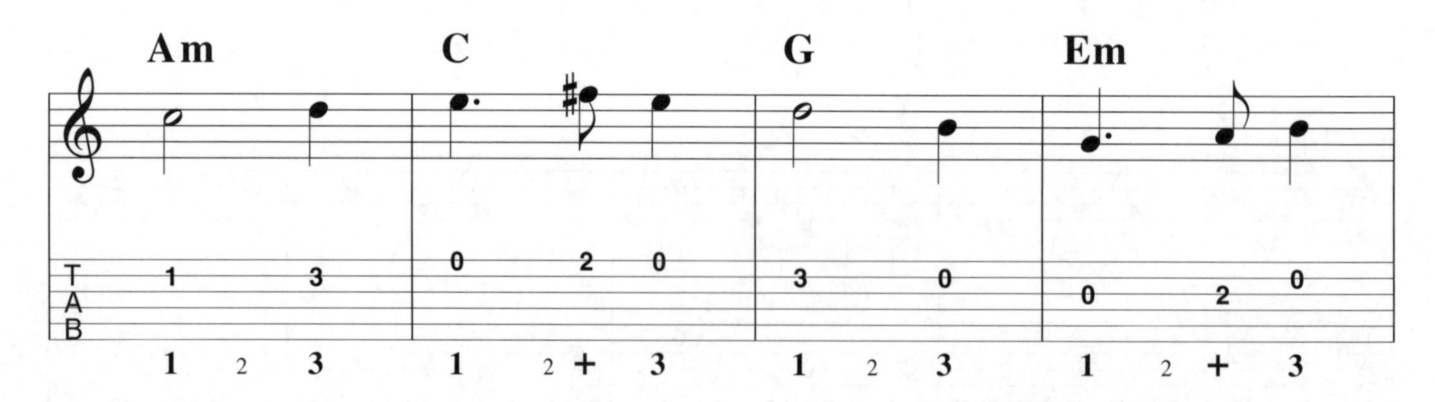

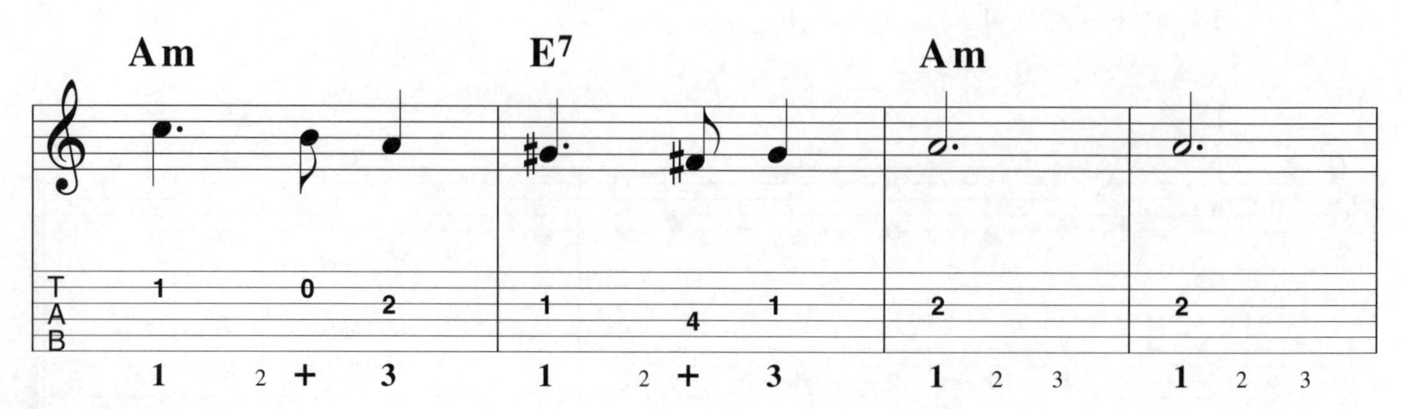

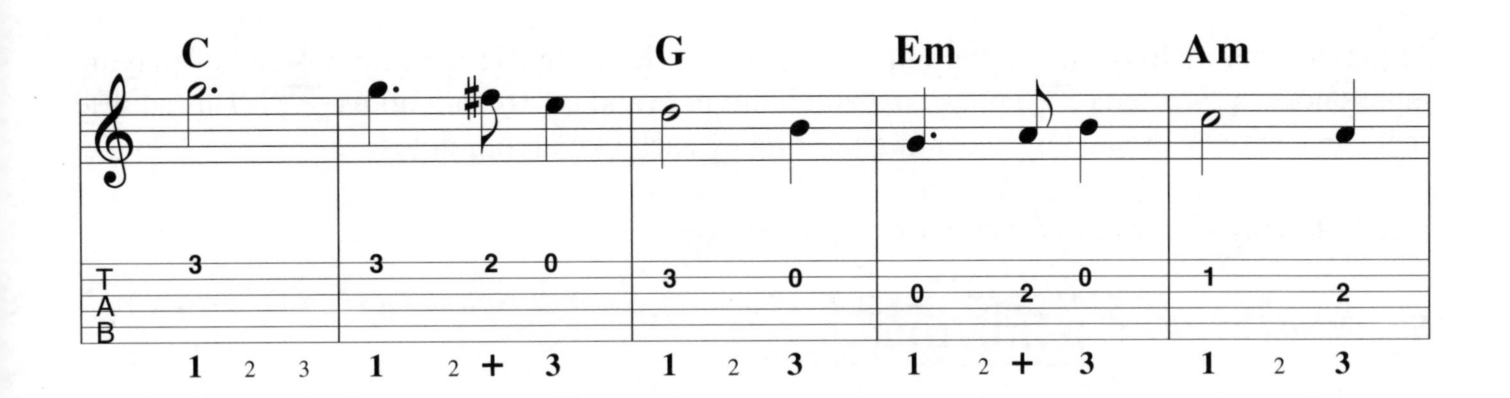
C G Em Am
T
A
B
1 2 3 1 2 + 3 1 2 3 1 2 + 3 1 2 3

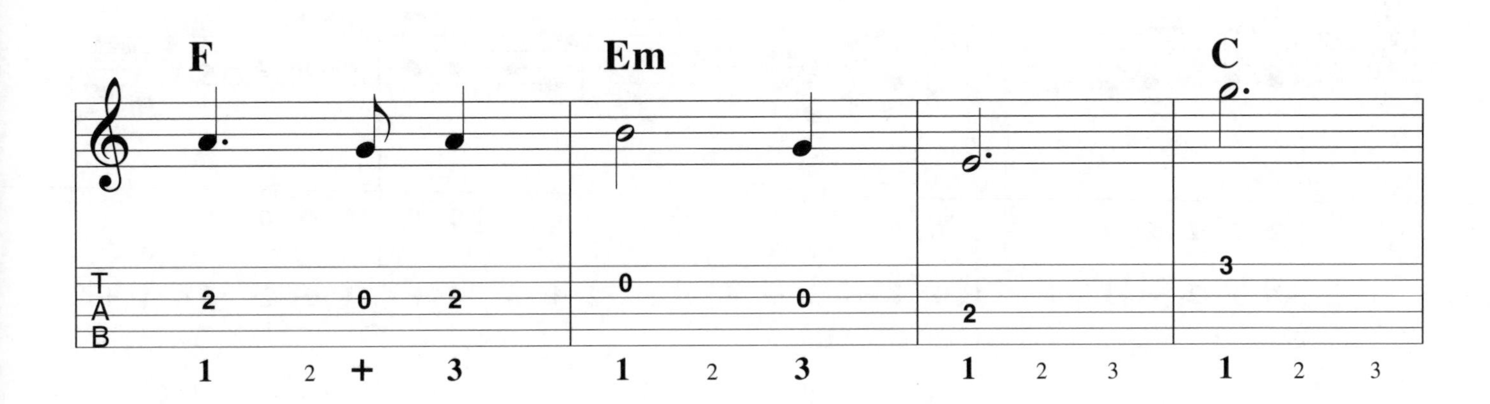
F Em C
T
A
B
1 2 + 3 1 2 3 1 2 3 1 2 3

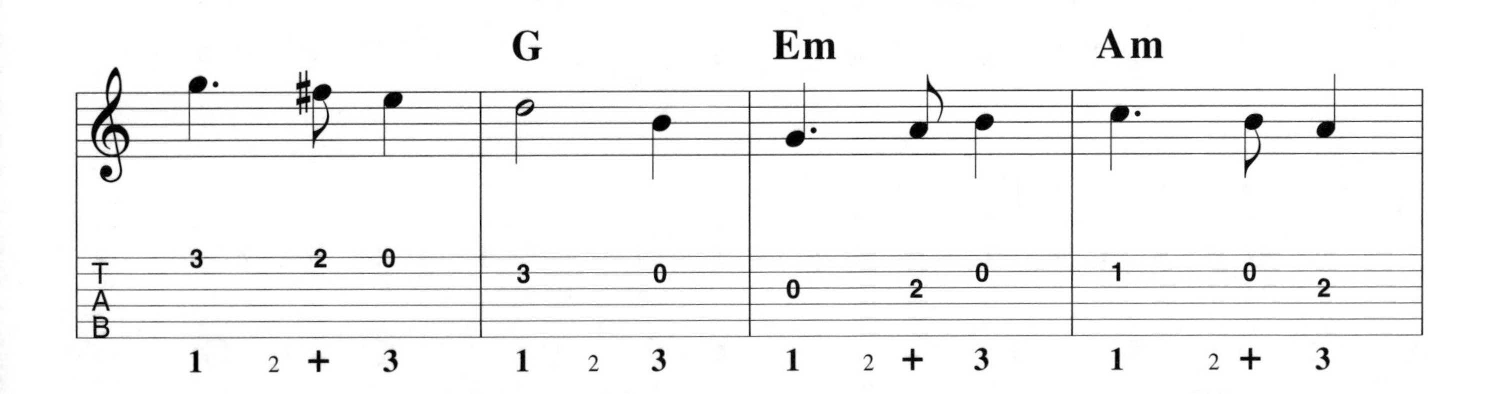
G Em Am
T
A
B
1 2 + 3 1 2 3 1 2 + 3 1 2 + 3

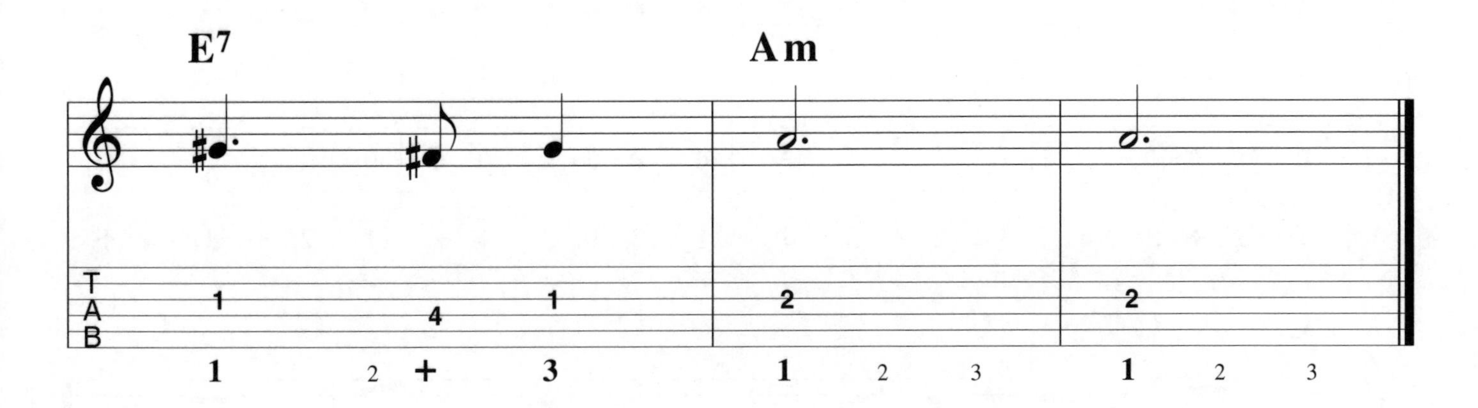
E7 Am
T
A
B
1 2 + 3 1 2 3 1 2 3

Waltzing Matilda

In playing the melody, the eighth notes are played with a shuffle feel, i.e. instead of playing eighth notes as written ([two eighth notes]) play a dotted eighth note and a sixteenth note ([dotted eighth and sixteenth]). This shuffle feel can easily be created by accenting the first of each two eighth notes.

The following pattern is a $\frac{4}{4}$ variation of **pattern 6**.

Suggested Pattern

Away in a Manger

PATTERN SEVEN-A

Suggested Pattern **p a m i m a**

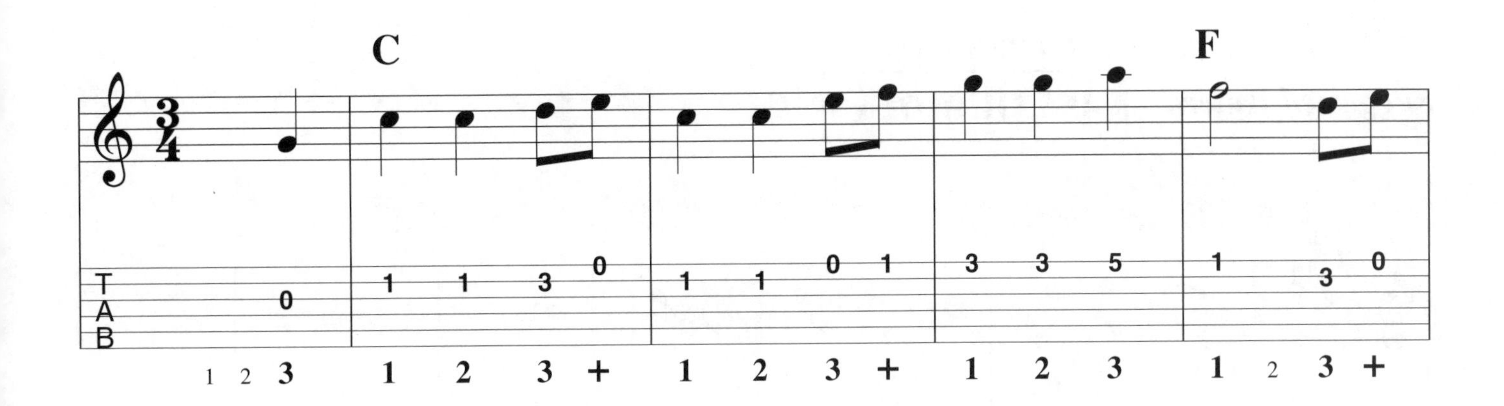

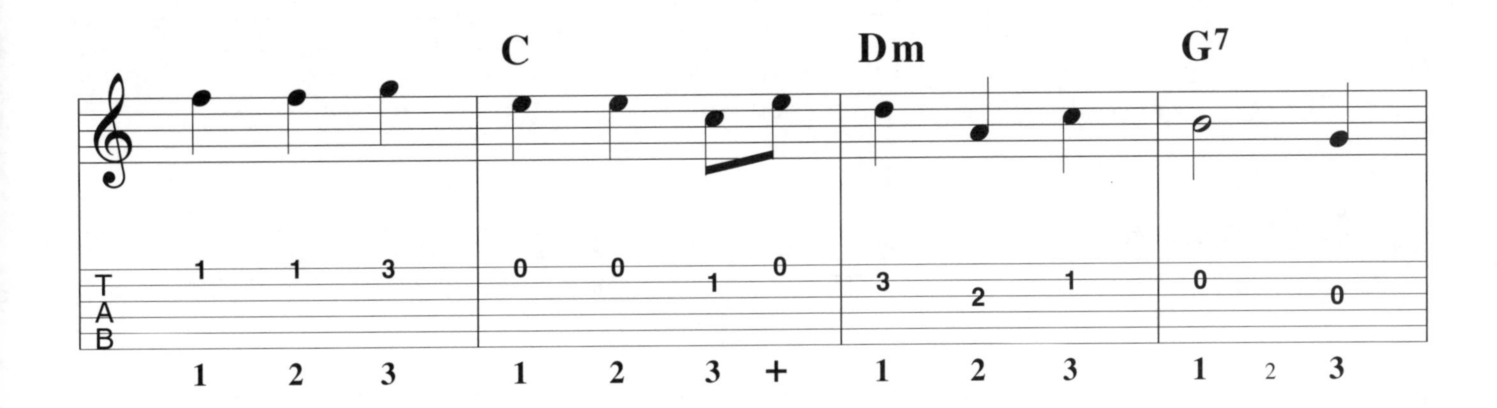

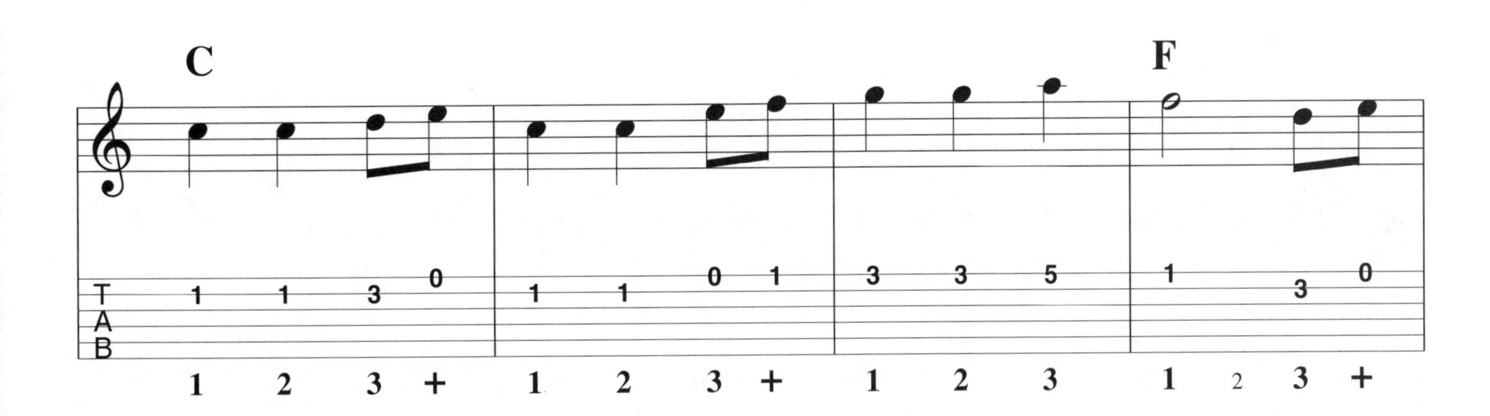

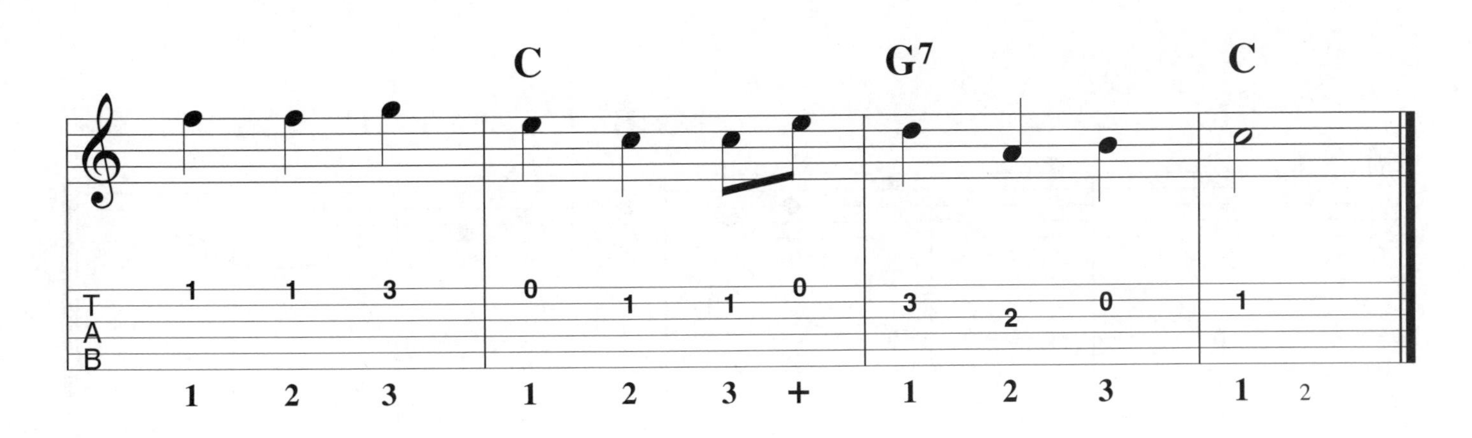

Silent Night

This song introduces the B7 chord:

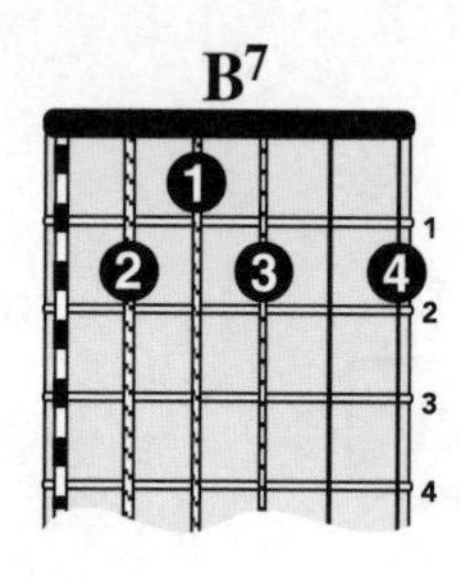

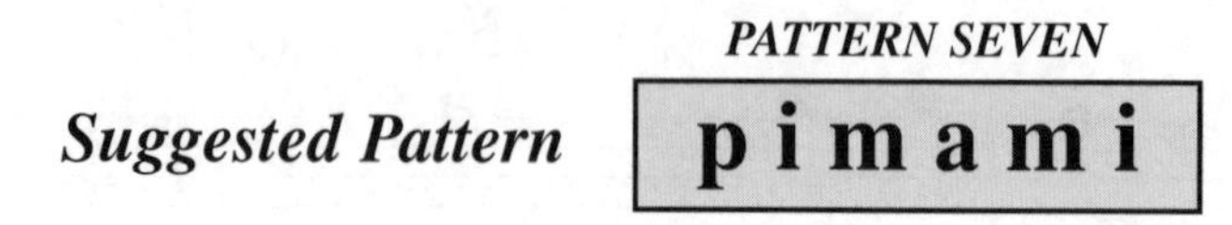

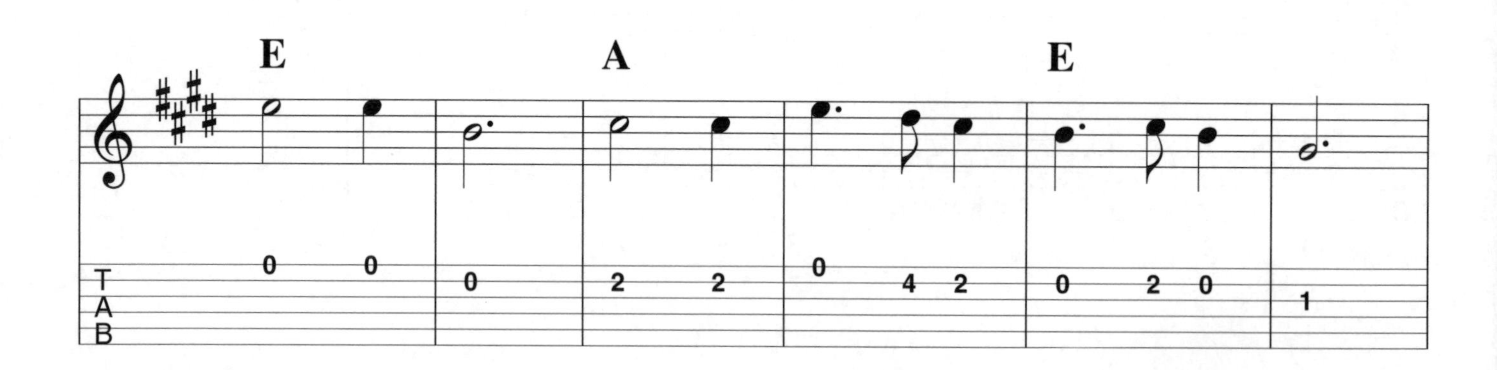

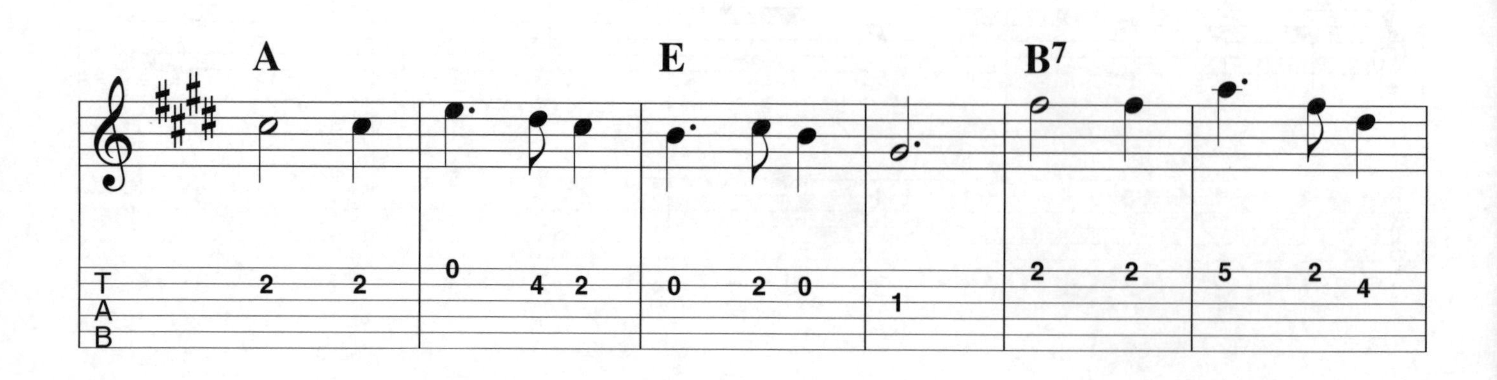

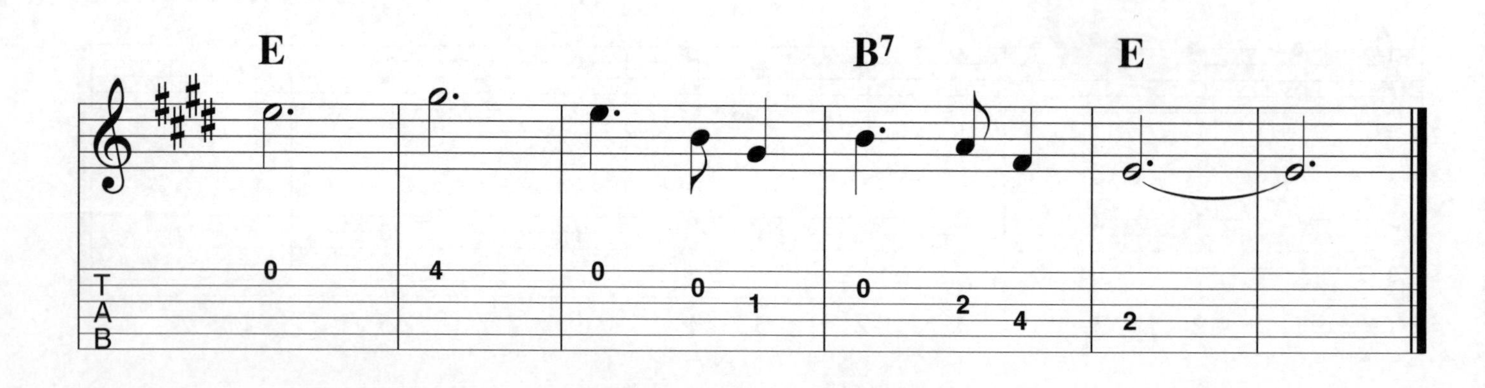

My Bonnie Lies Over the Ocean

PATTERN SEVEN

Suggested Pattern **p i m a m i**

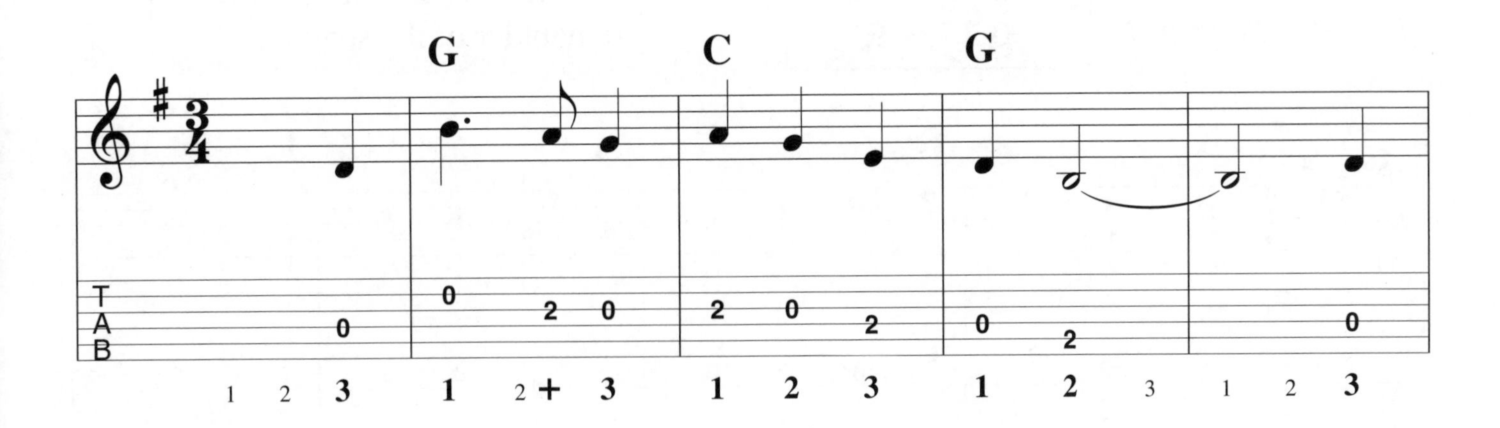

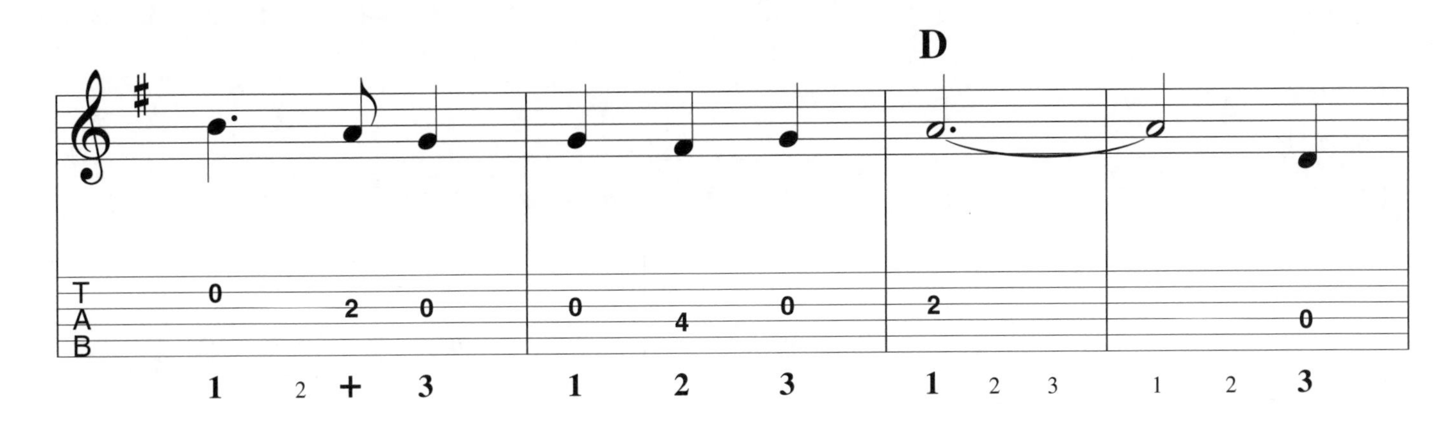

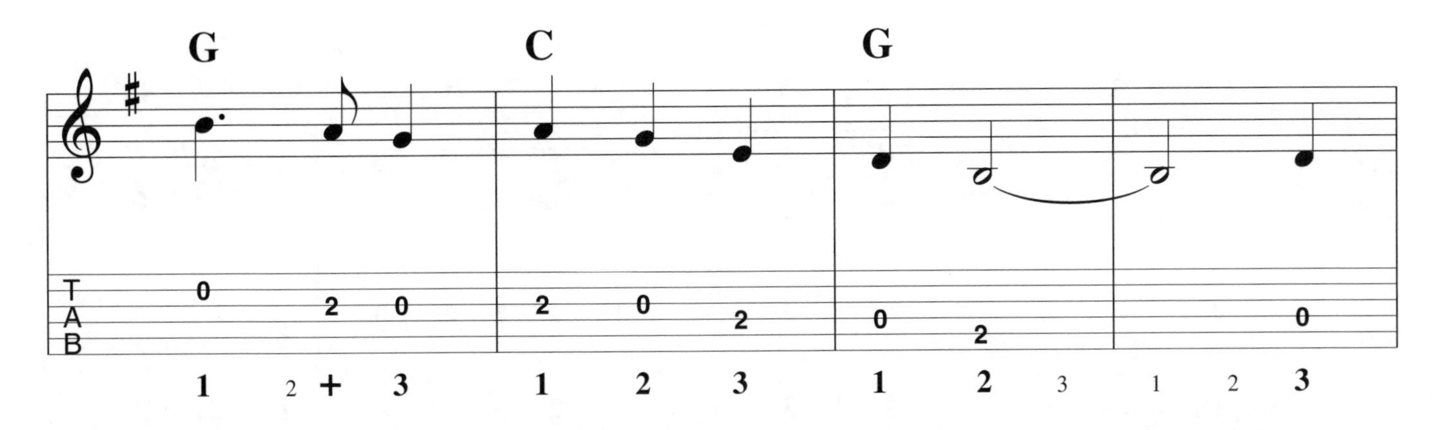

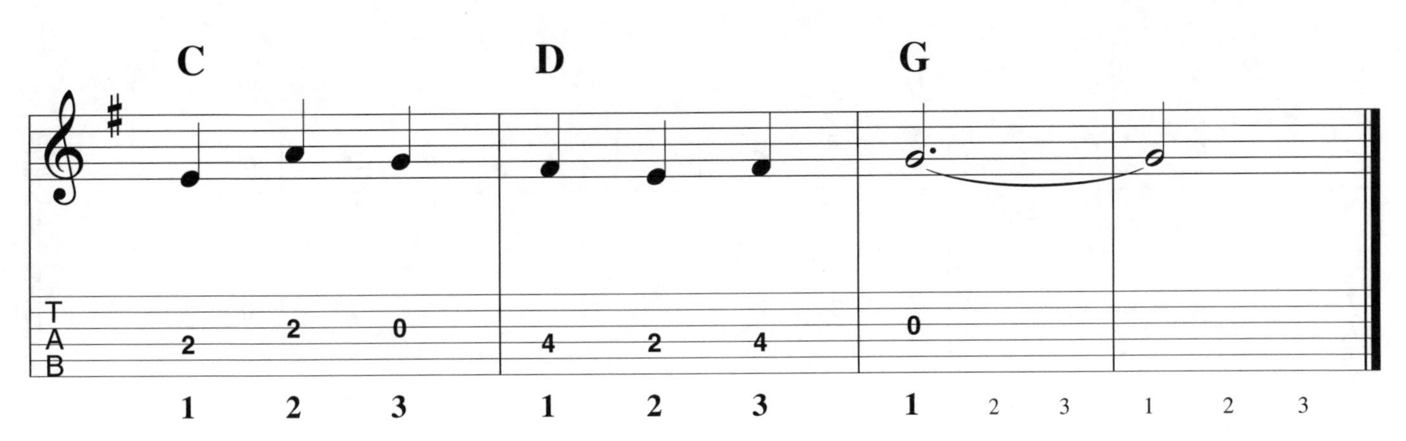

Song of Joy

PATTERN EIGHT

Suggested Pattern A **p i m a m i p i**

PATTERN THREE

Suggested Pattern B **p i m a**

In this song two suggested patterns have been given. The first pattern is played for the first seven bars and the second pattern is played for the remainder of the song.

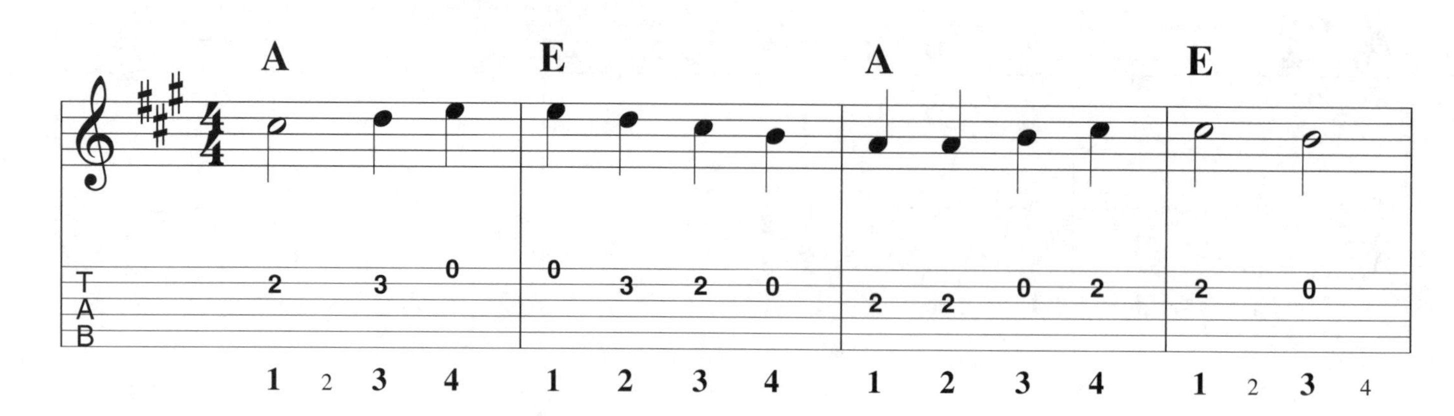

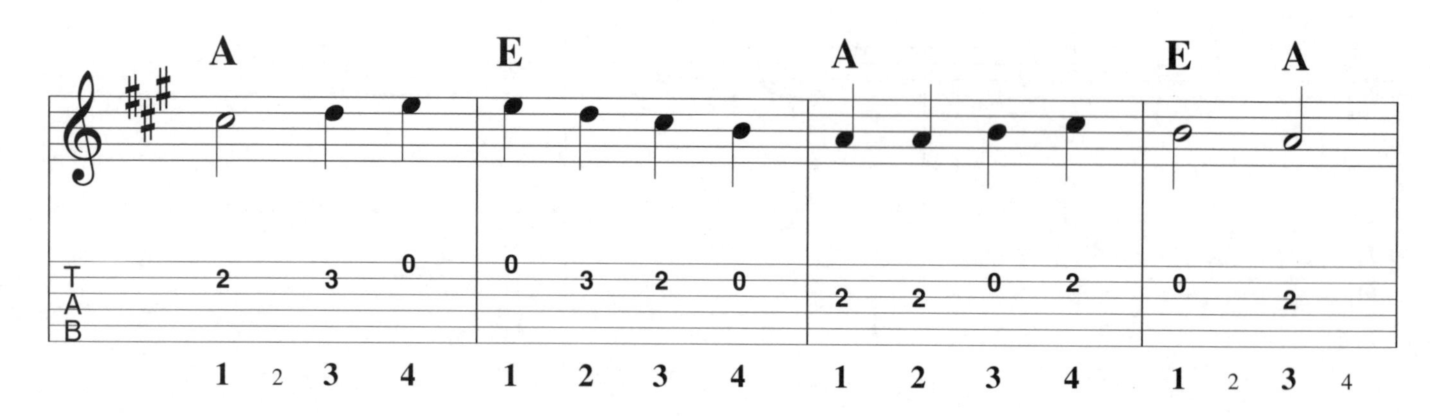

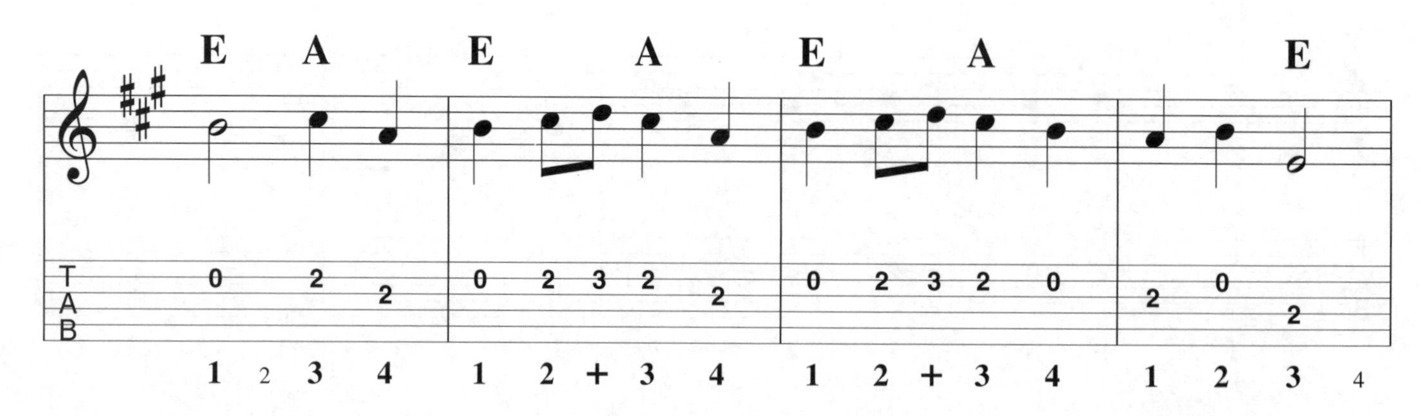

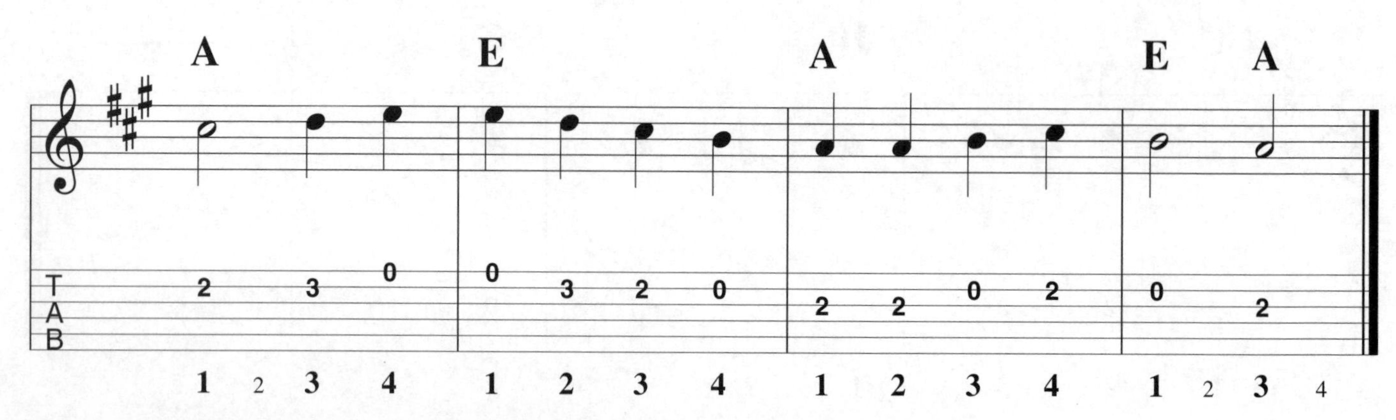

Amazing Grace

In this song the pattern used is a $\frac{3}{4}$ variation of **pattern 13**.

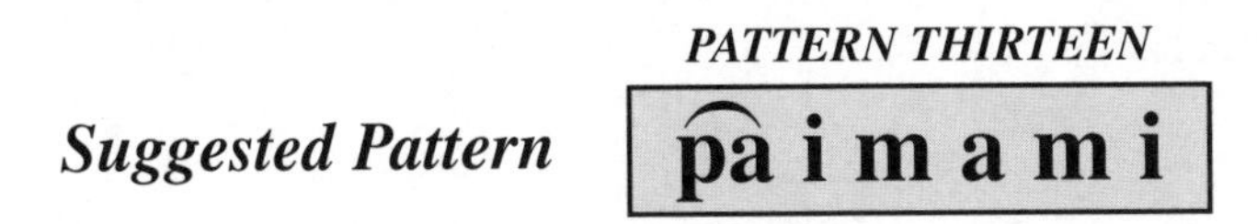

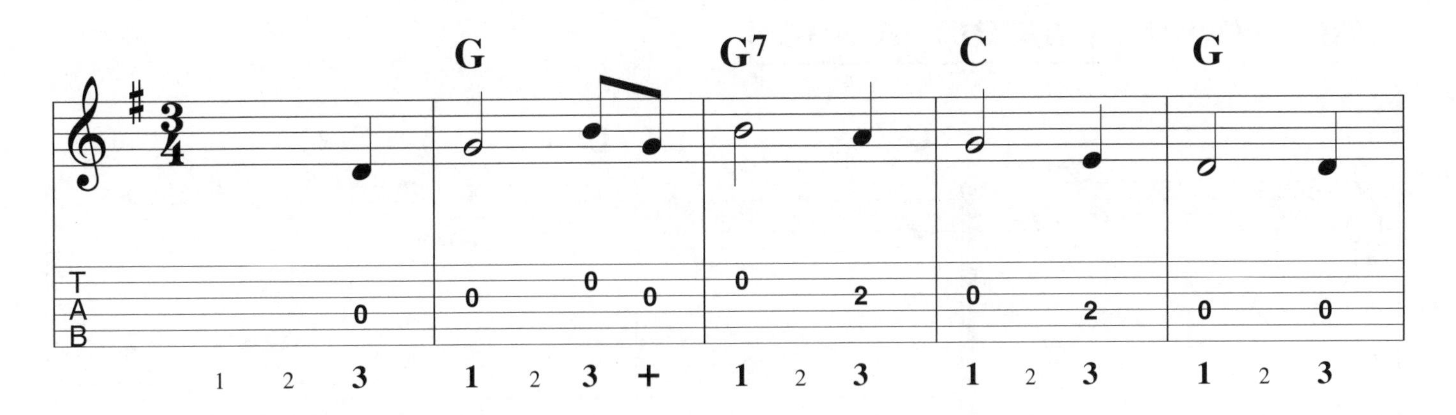

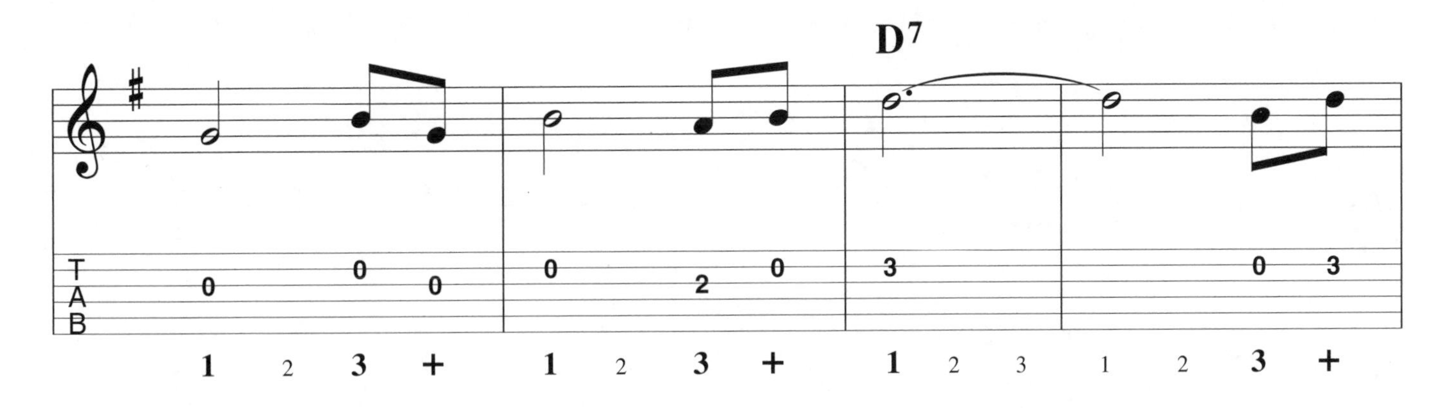

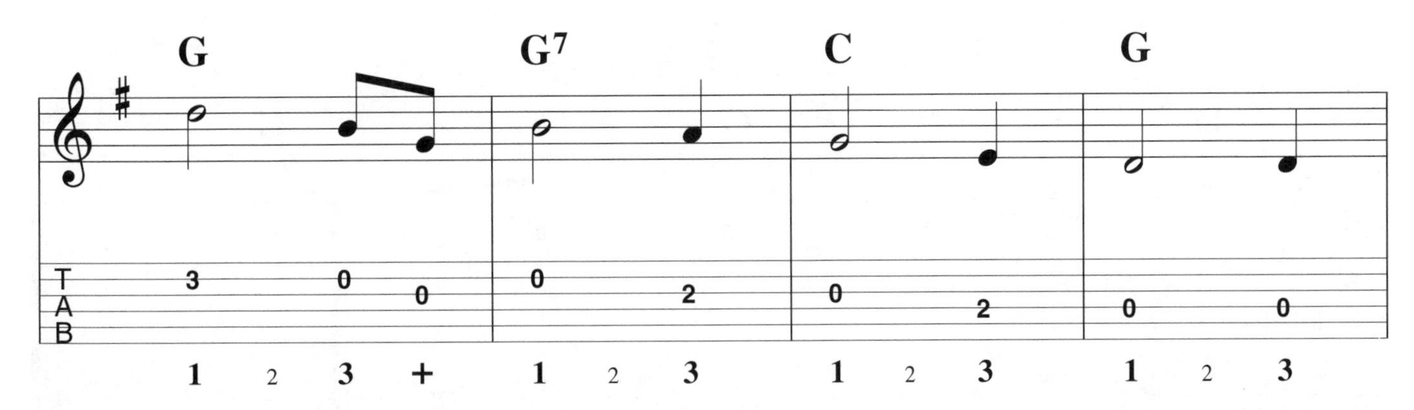

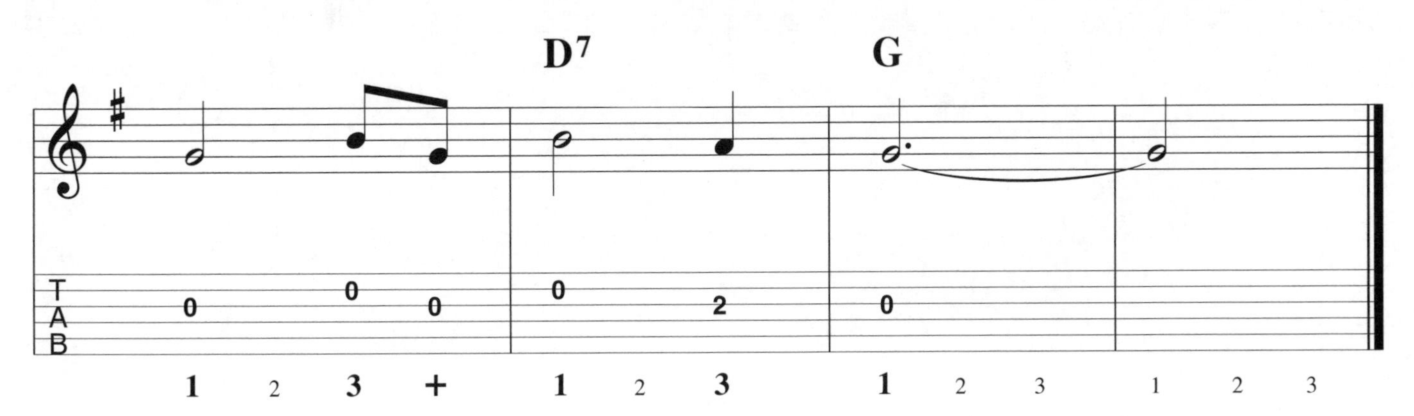

The First Noel

This song introduces First and Second Endings. On the first time through, ending one is played, then the progression is repeated (as indicated by the repeat sign), and ending two is played. Be careful not to play both endings together.

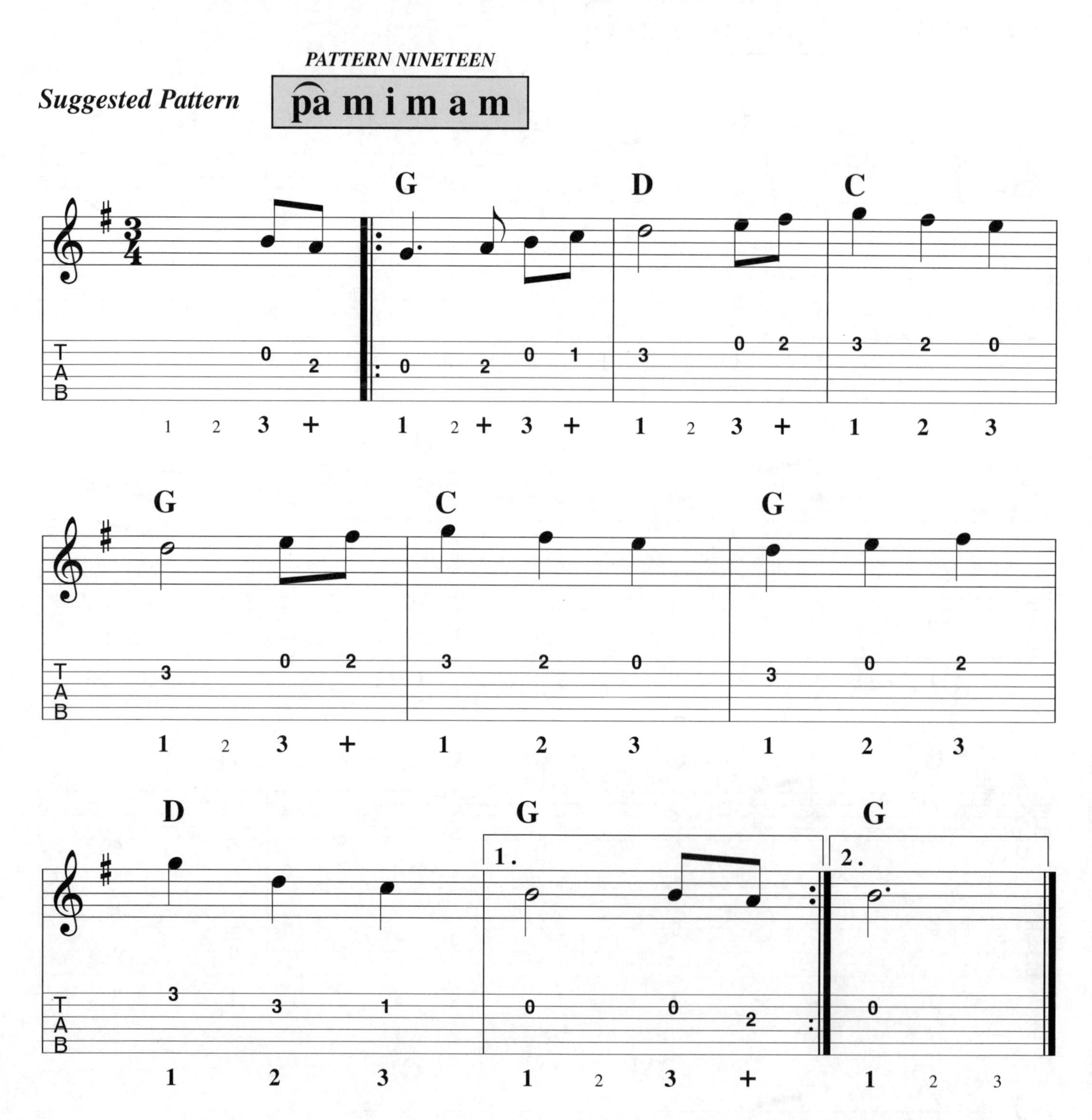

Scarborough Fair

PATTERN SEVEN

Suggested Pattern **p i m a m i**

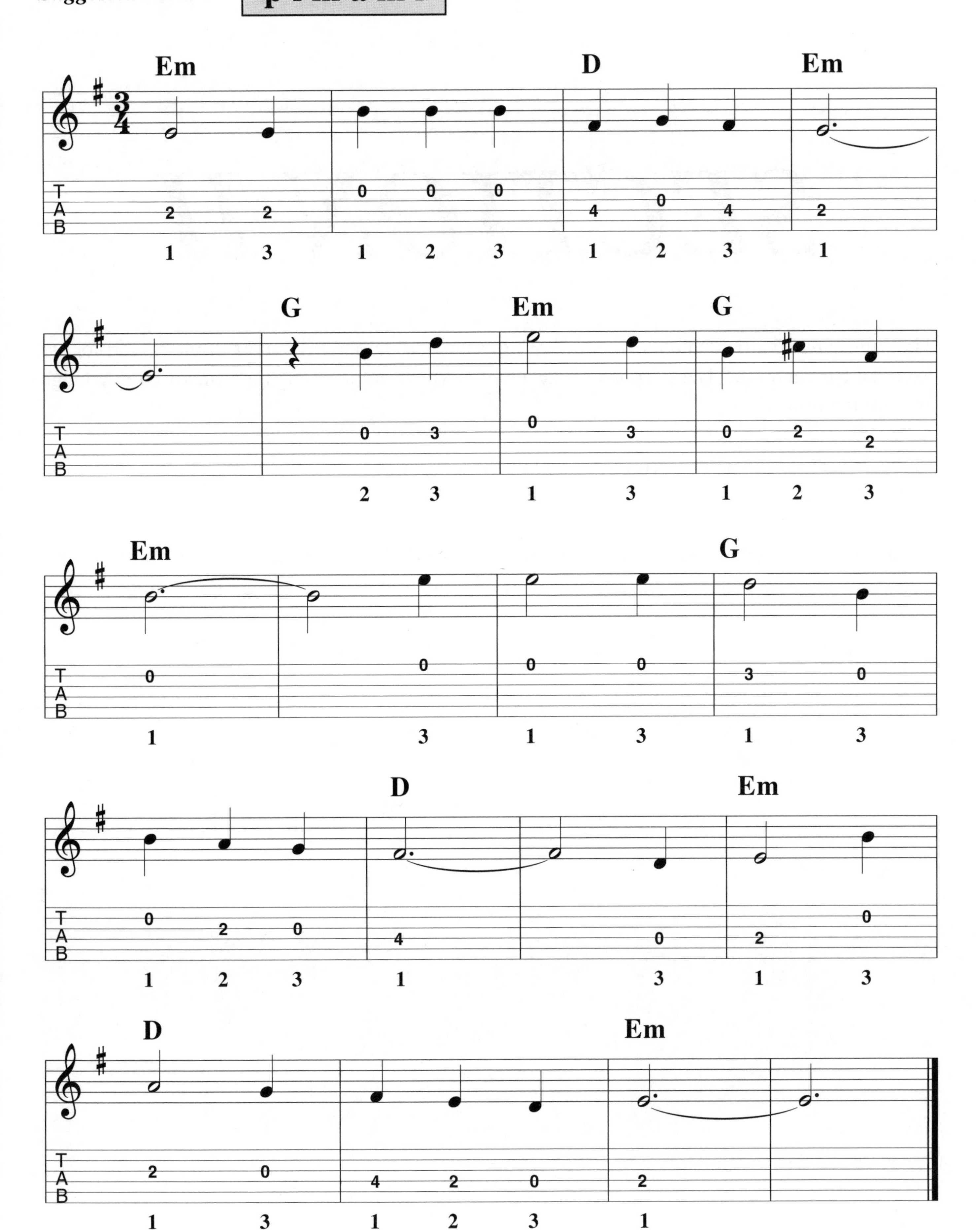

SECTION II

The following section contains 10 chord progressions, together with an example fingerpicking exercise for each one. The purpose of these is to expand upon your fingerpicking knowledge and application.

Many of the progressions feature unusual chord shapes, so you should follow the given diagrams carefully.

In each example music and tablature notation is provided, however it is possible to play each exercise simply by applying the given fingerpicking pattern to the chord progression.

PROGRESSION ONE

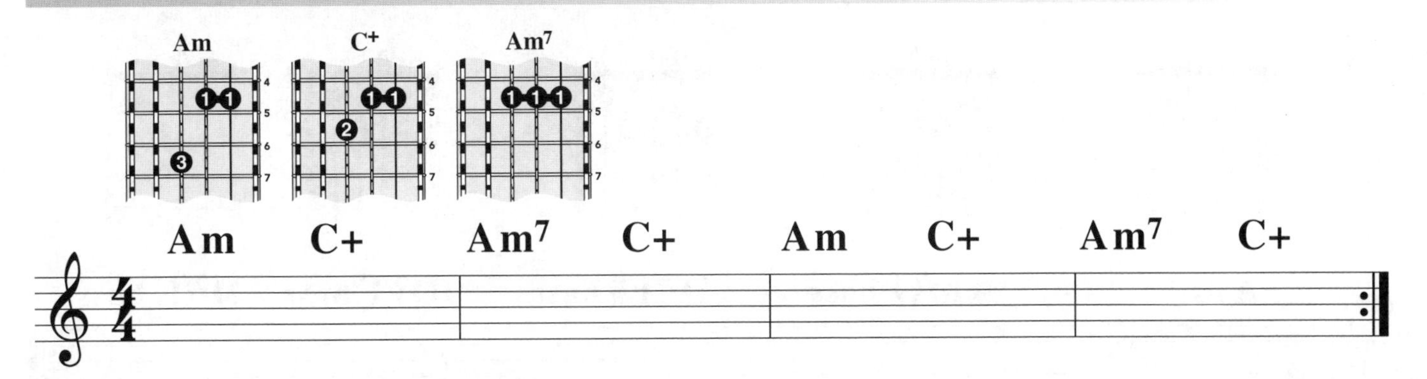

Each chord has a duration of two beats in this progression. It is played in the 5th position and may also be transposed to other positions; for example, the 3rd position:

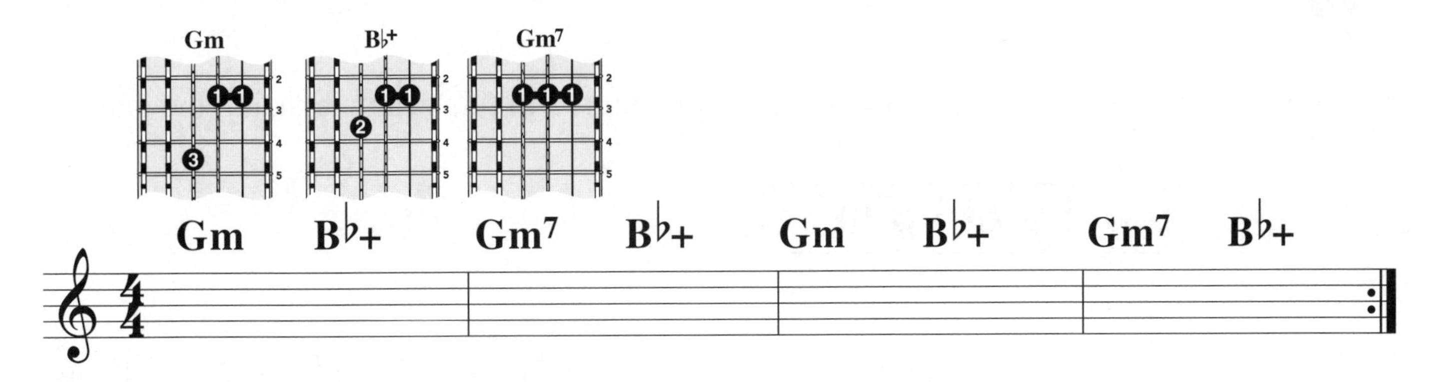

This exercise features a syncopated* bass and a descending bass line. The syncopated bass occurs on the **and** part of the 2nd and 4th beats (i.e. the **off** beat), involving the fingerpicking pattern **p i m p**.
The descending bass line uses the notes A - G♯ - G and then G - F♯ - F. For ease of playing, the first finger should bar across the 2nd, 3rd and 4th strings throughout the entire example.

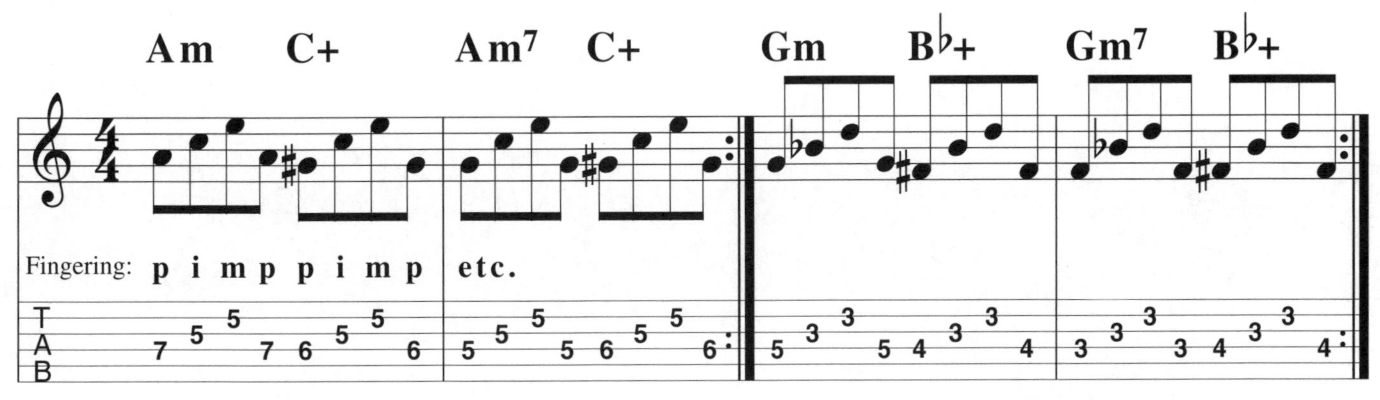

* Syncopation means an accent on the **off** beat.

PROGRESSION TWO

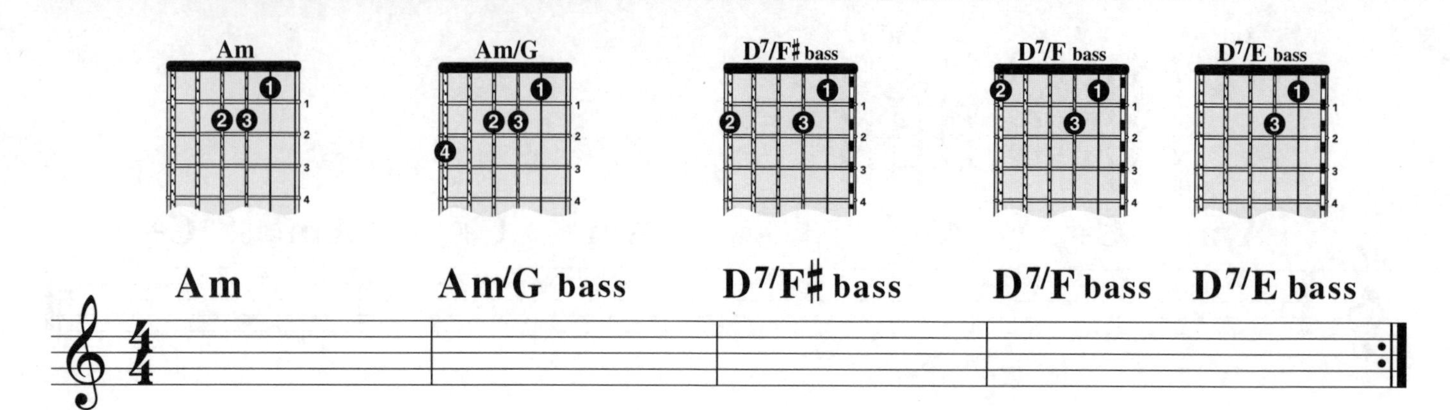

Syncopation and a descending bass line are again featured in this example, using the pattern:

p m i p m i p m

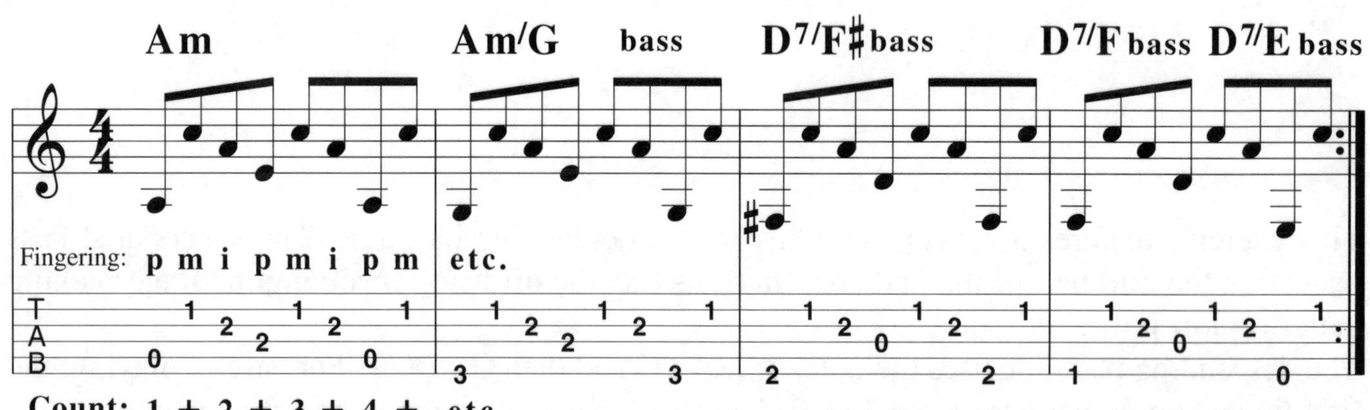

PROGRESSION THREE

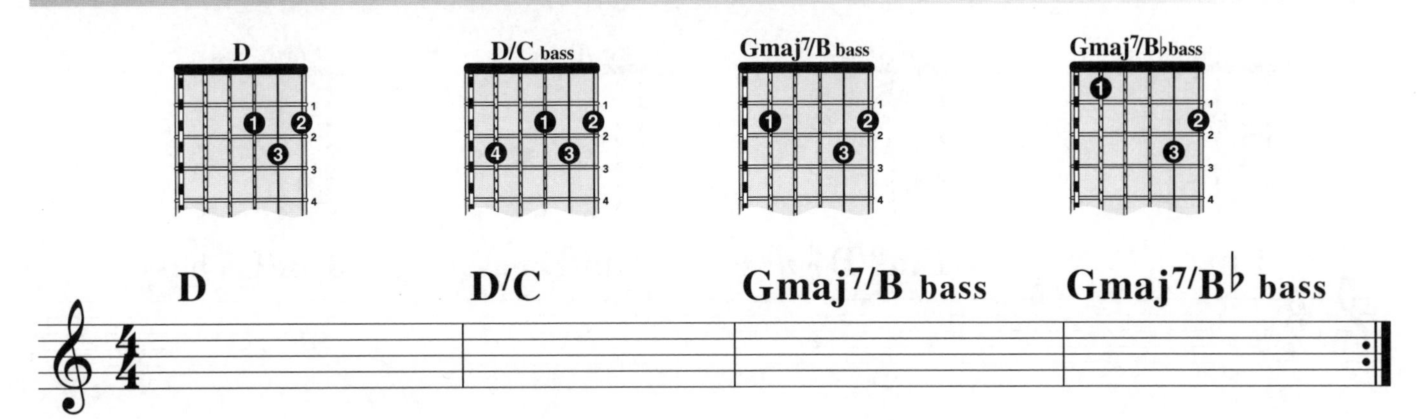

This example uses **pattern 17**, involving clawhammer with the pinch technique.

PATTERN 17 | pm p i p m p i |

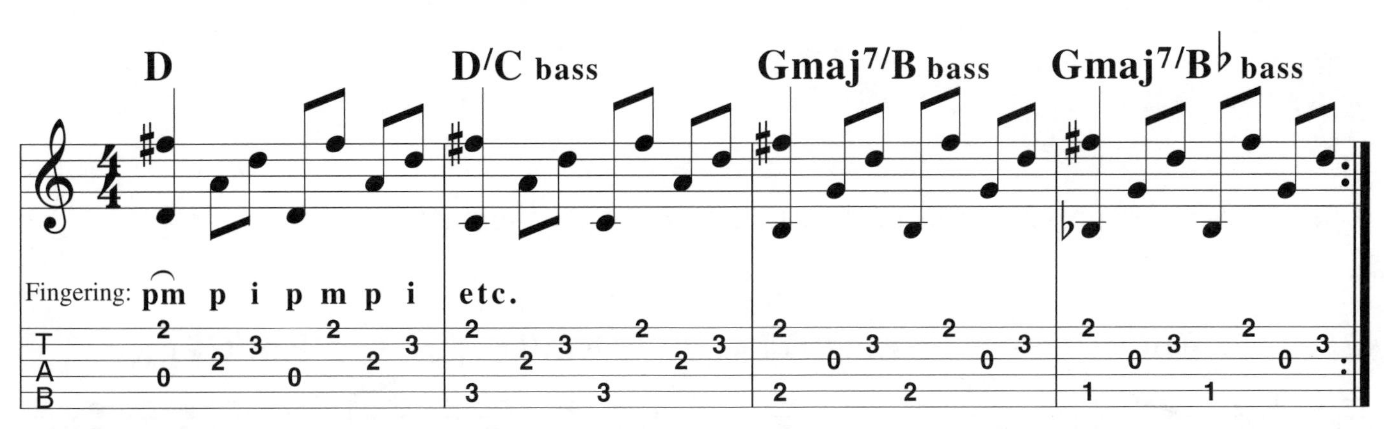

PROGRESSION FOUR

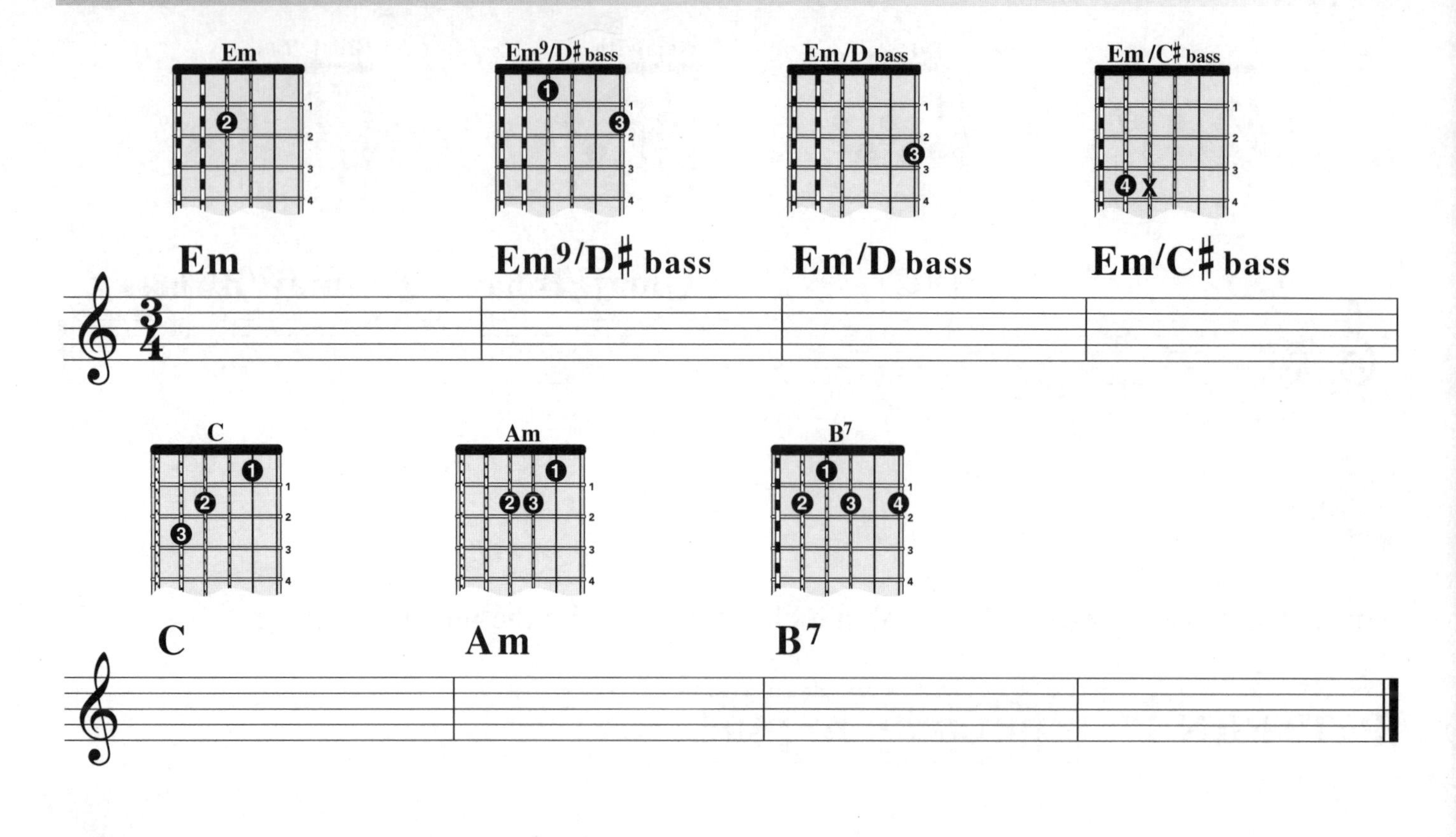

The following progression uses **patterns 6** and **7**, which alternate every bar.

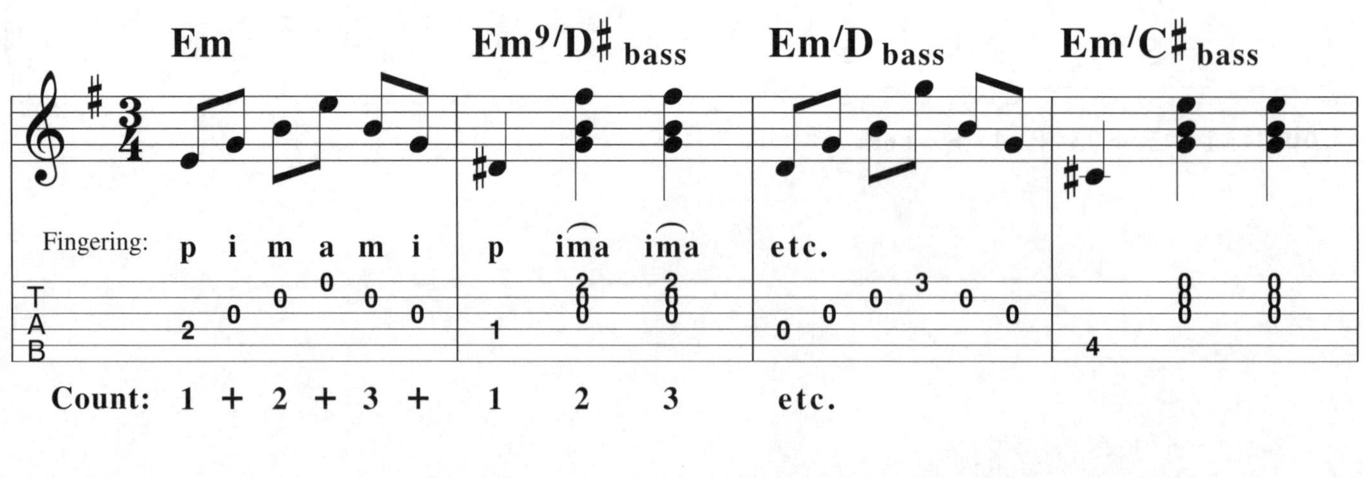

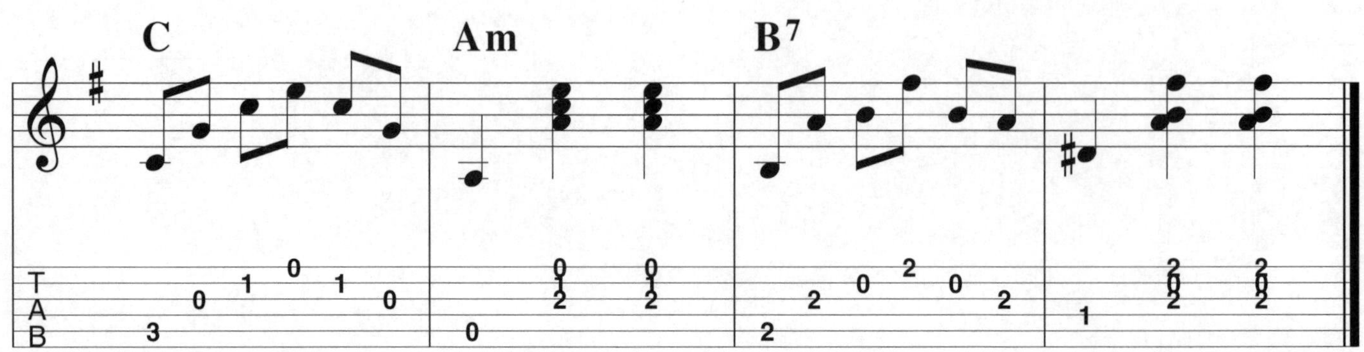

PROGRESSION FIVE

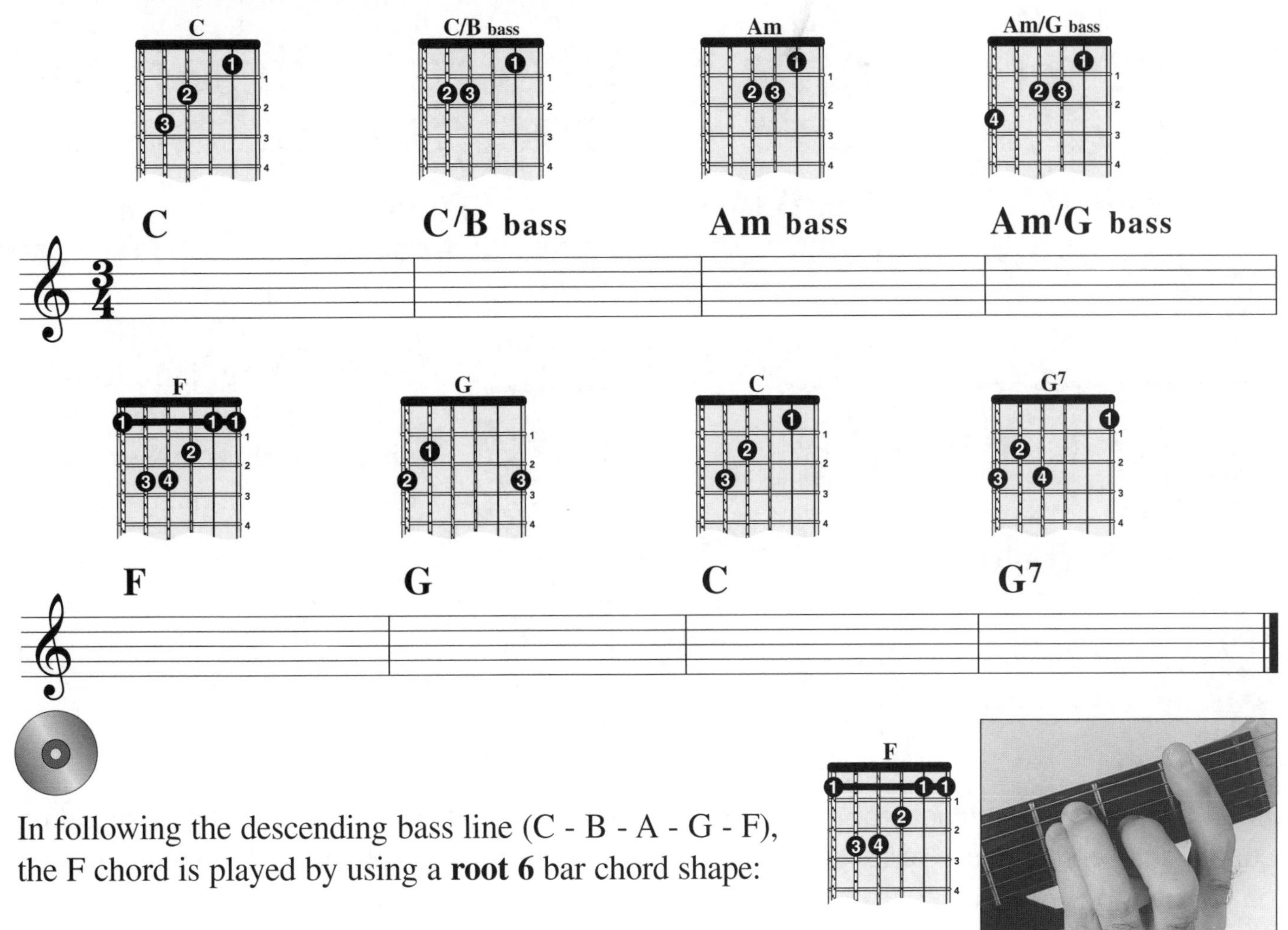

In following the descending bass line (C - B - A - G - F), the F chord is played by using a **root 6** bar chord shape:

For further information on bar chords, see ***Progressive Rhythm Guitar***. This book will also provide you with a large number of supplementary progressions for fingerpicking practice.

PATTERN 7 p i m a m i

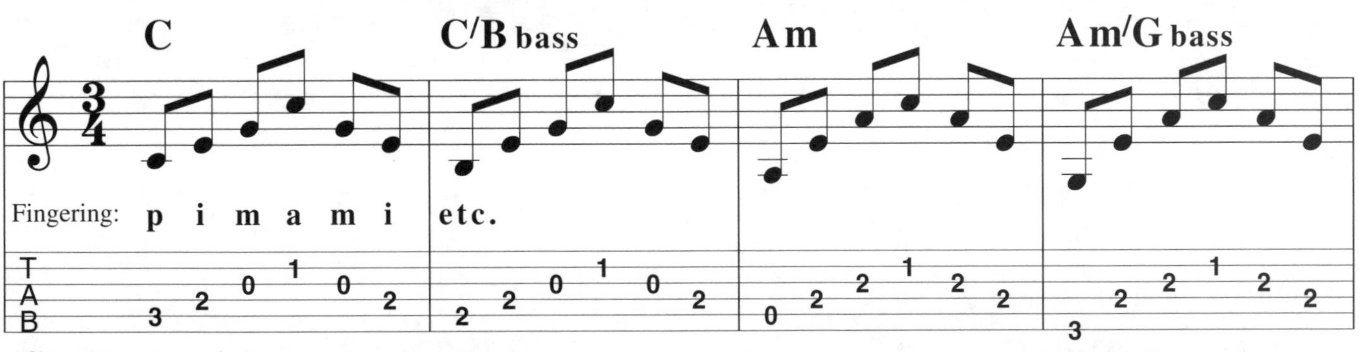

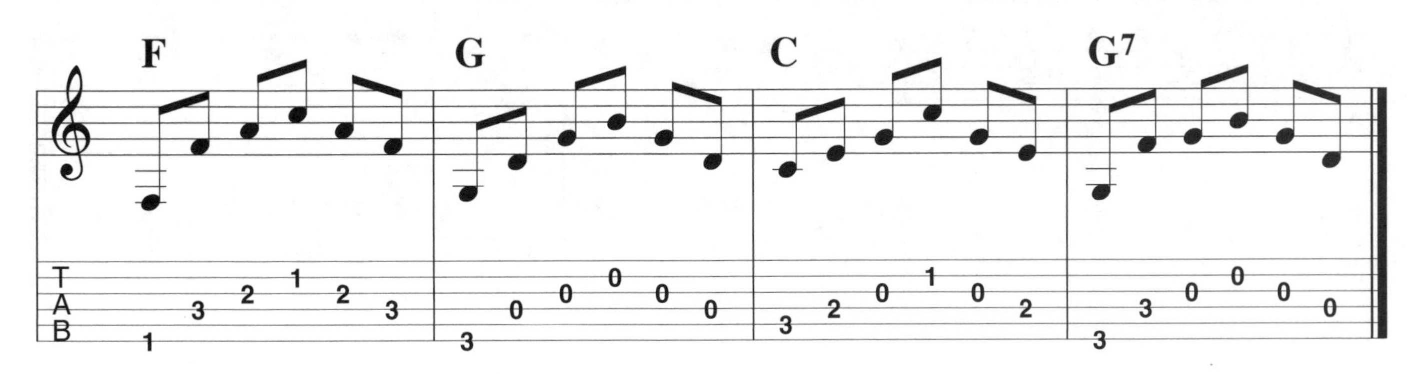

PROGRESSION SIX

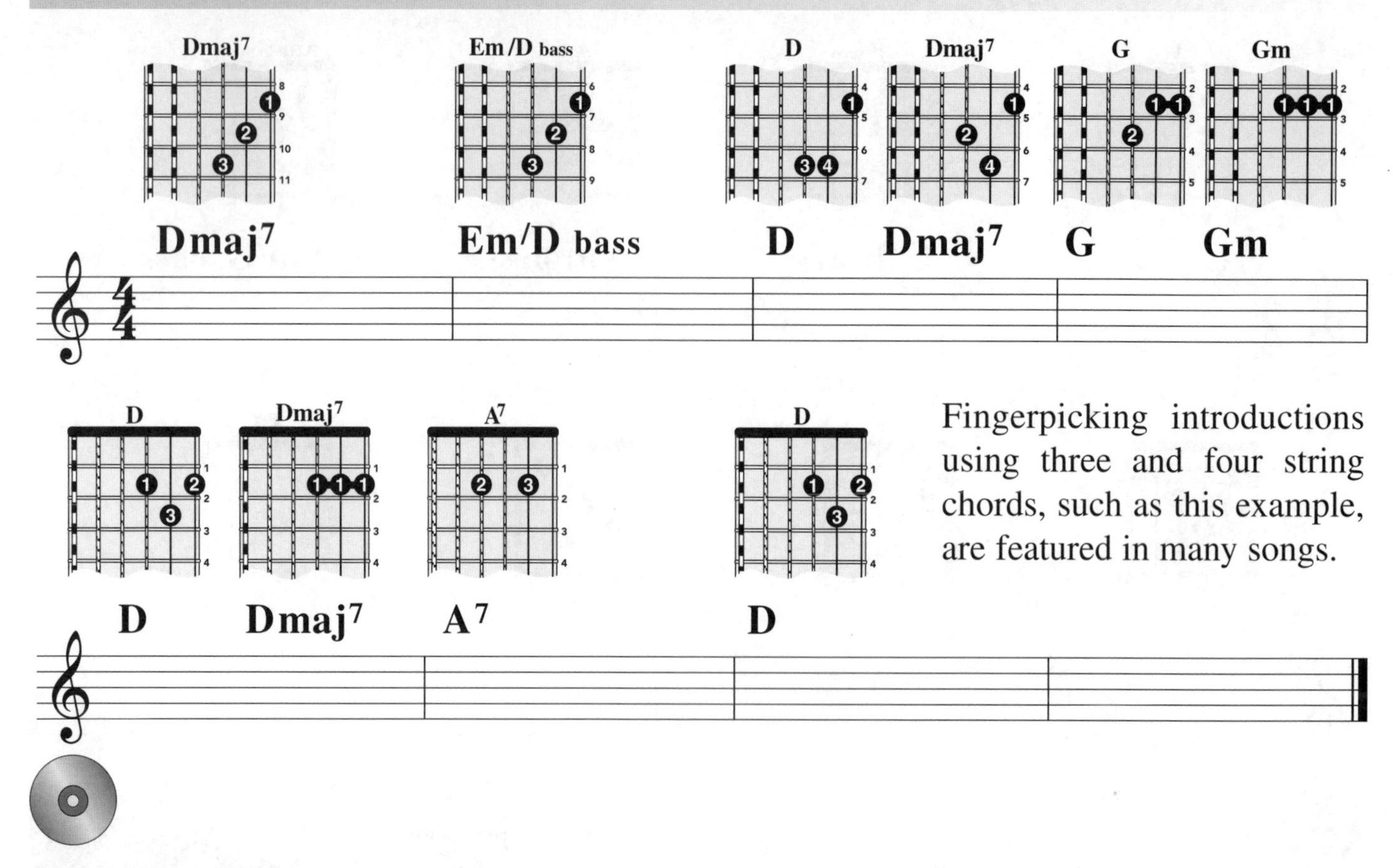

Fingerpicking introductions using three and four string chords, such as this example, are featured in many songs.

In this example the technique of a **droning** string is introduced. This involves a string sounding continuously throughout a series of chord changes. Use **pattern 13 (pa i m a)** throughout, played on the first four strings only (except for the A bass note in bars 6 and 7).

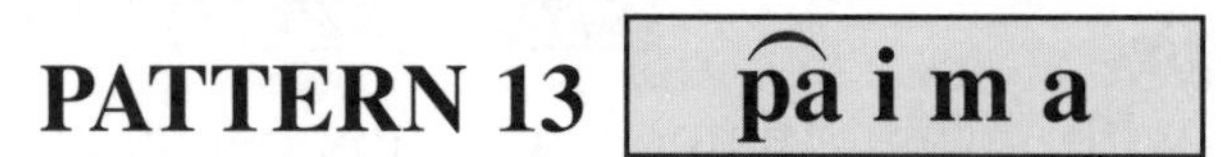

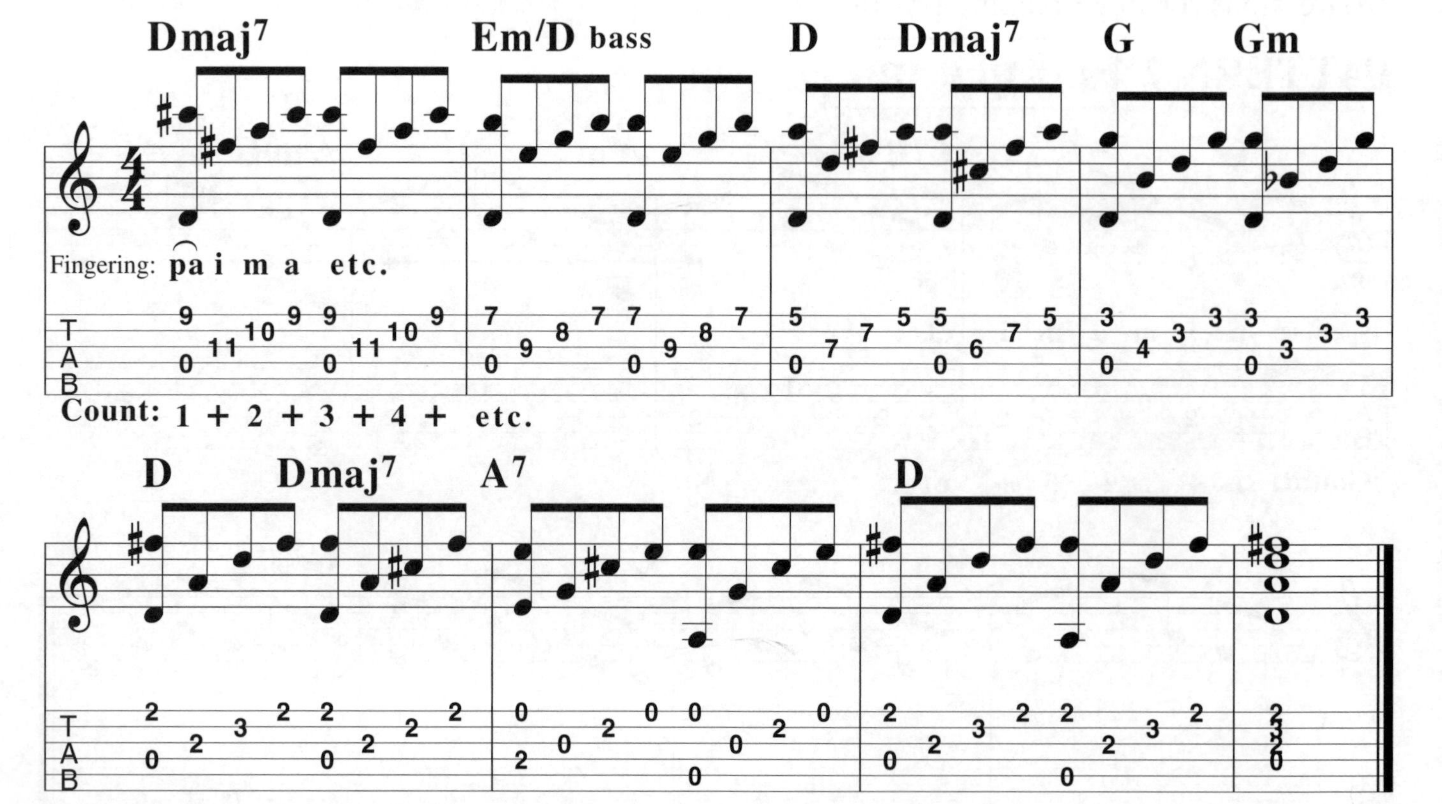

1 2 3 4

PROGRESSION SEVEN

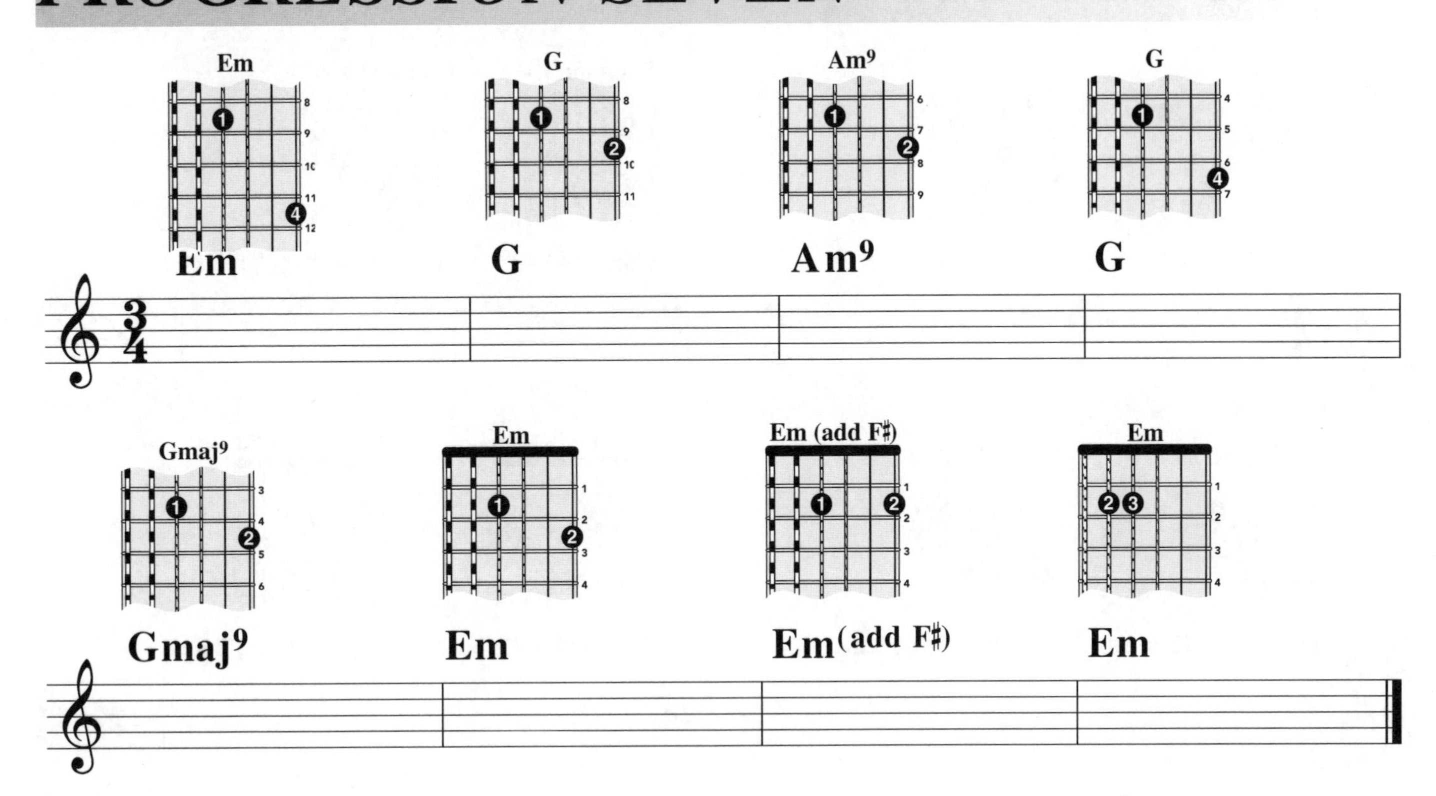

In this example the second and third strings are played open throughout. The fingerpicking pattern involves a combination of the pinch technique with **pattern 7**, giving the following:

pa i m a m i

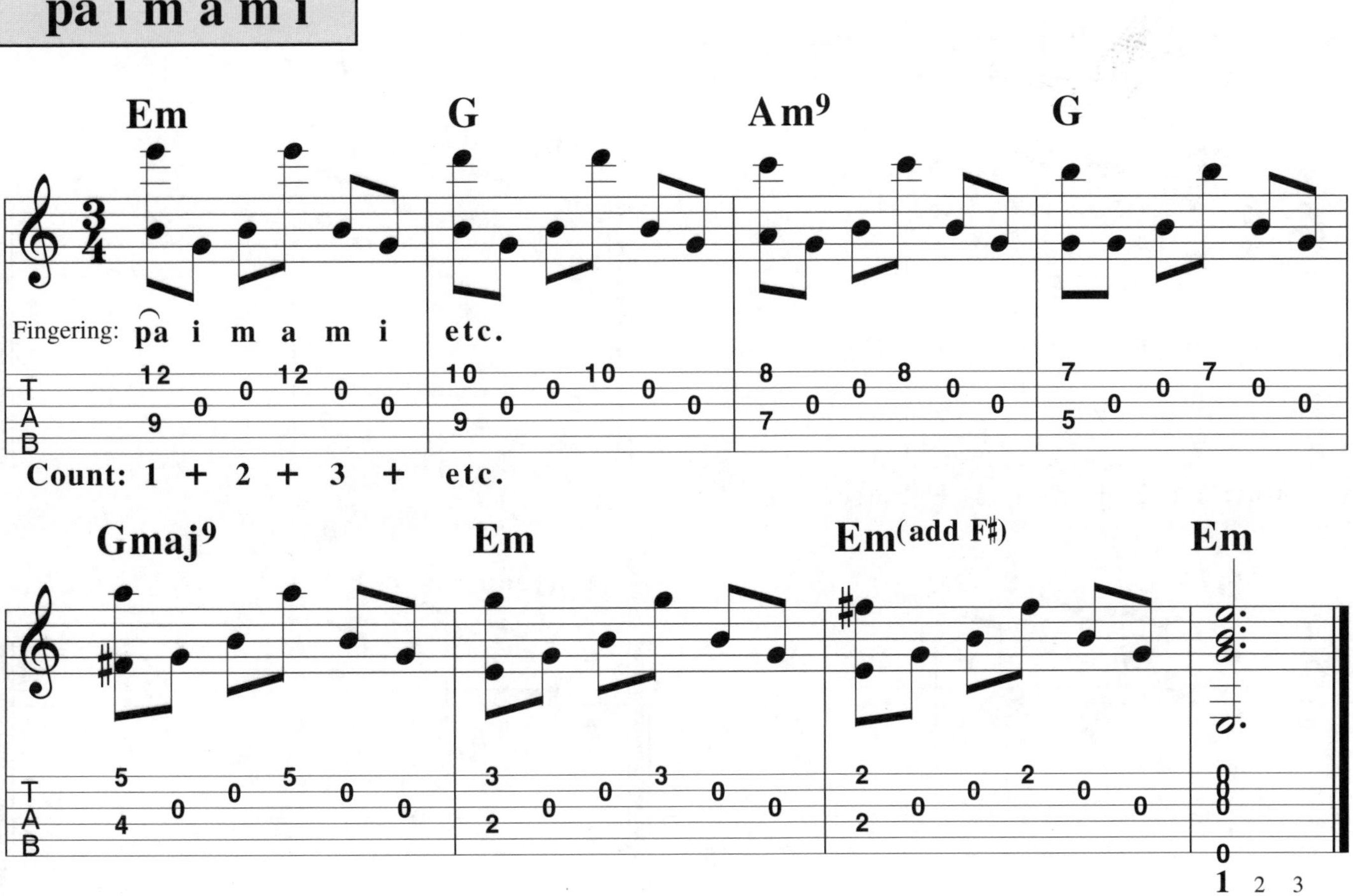

PROGRESSION EIGHT

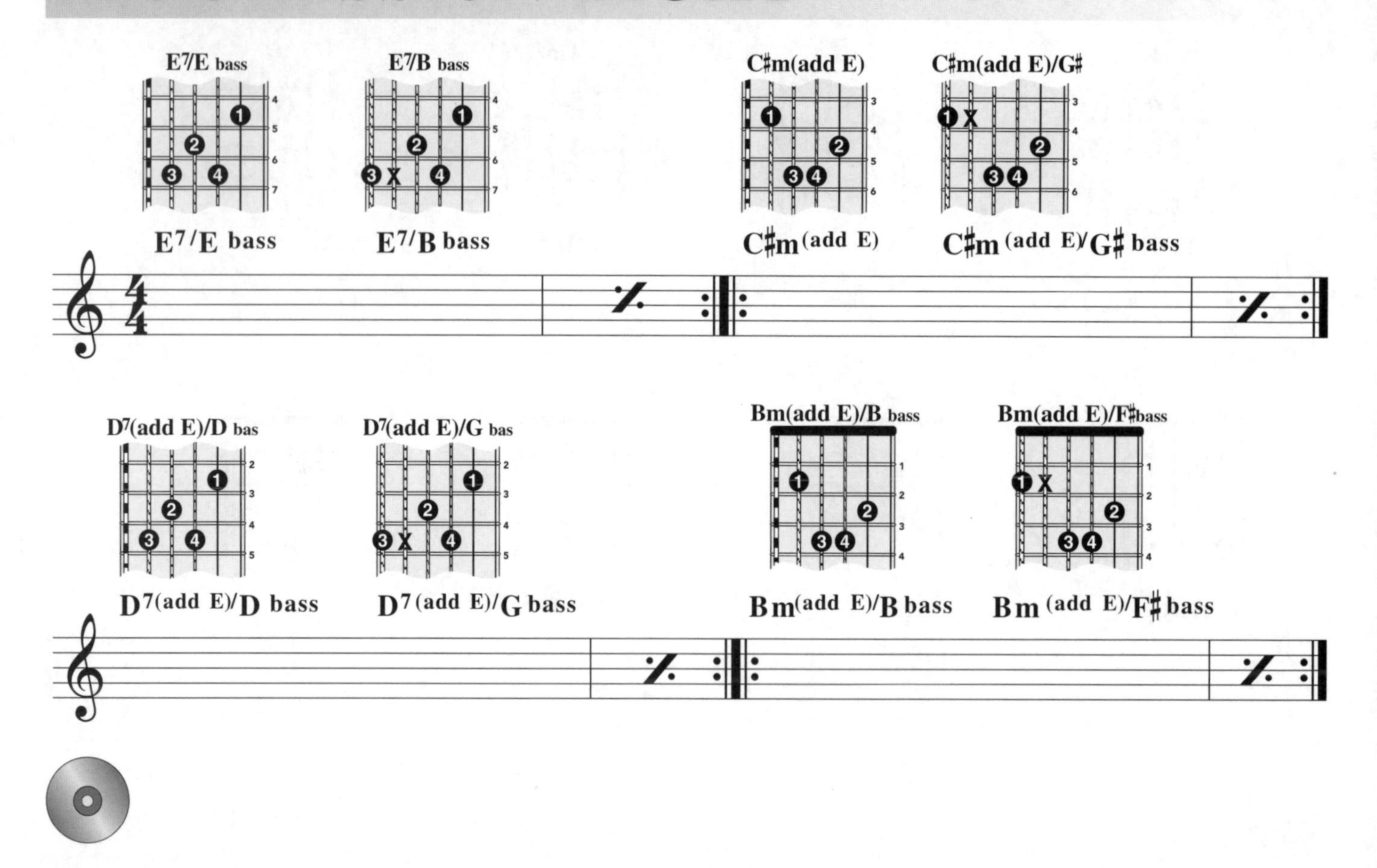

The following example uses the 6 string claw hammer (pattern 18), as studied in Lesson eighteen. It also involves a staccato bass (alternating between the 5th and 6th strings), as discussed in Lesson Twenty.

PATTERN 18 pm pi pa pi

PROGRESSION NINE

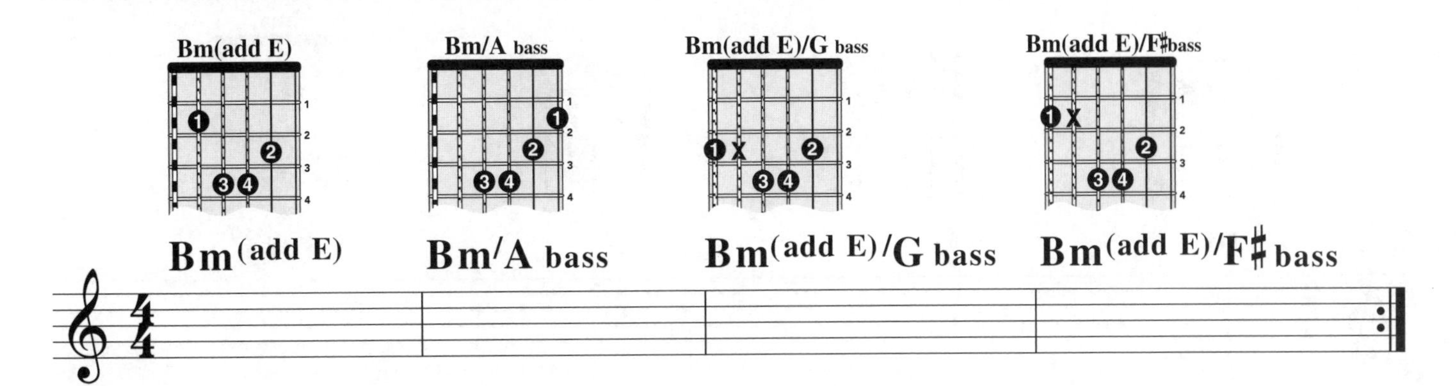

The following example continues with the use of pattern 18. Be sure to follow the correct bass notes (B - A - G - F♯).

PATTERN 18 **pm pi pa pi**

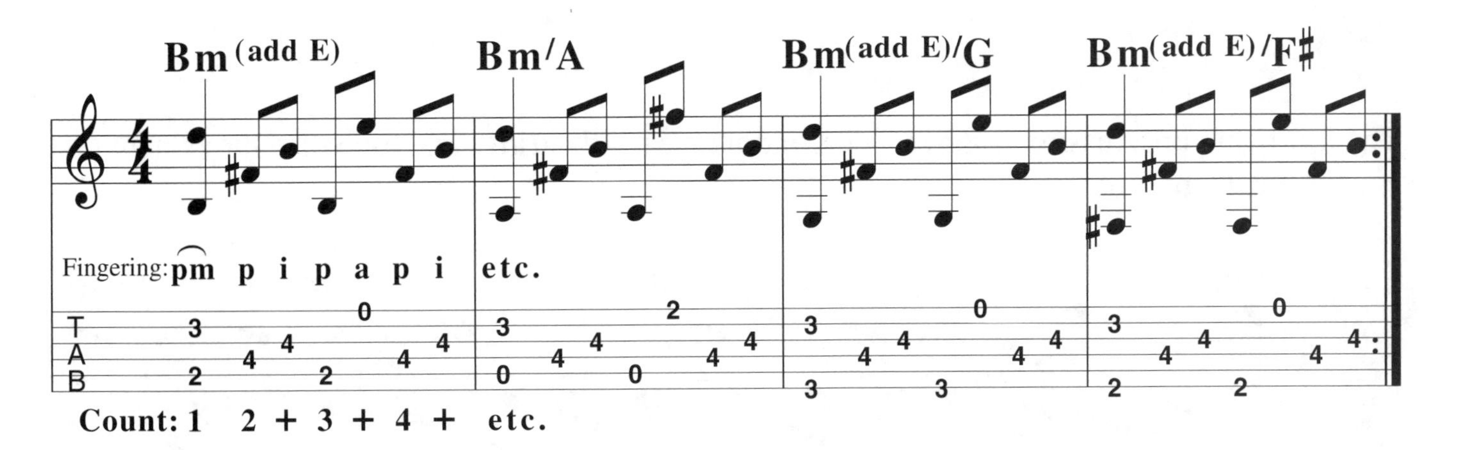

This example can be combined with example 8 to form one complete progression.

PROGRESSION TEN

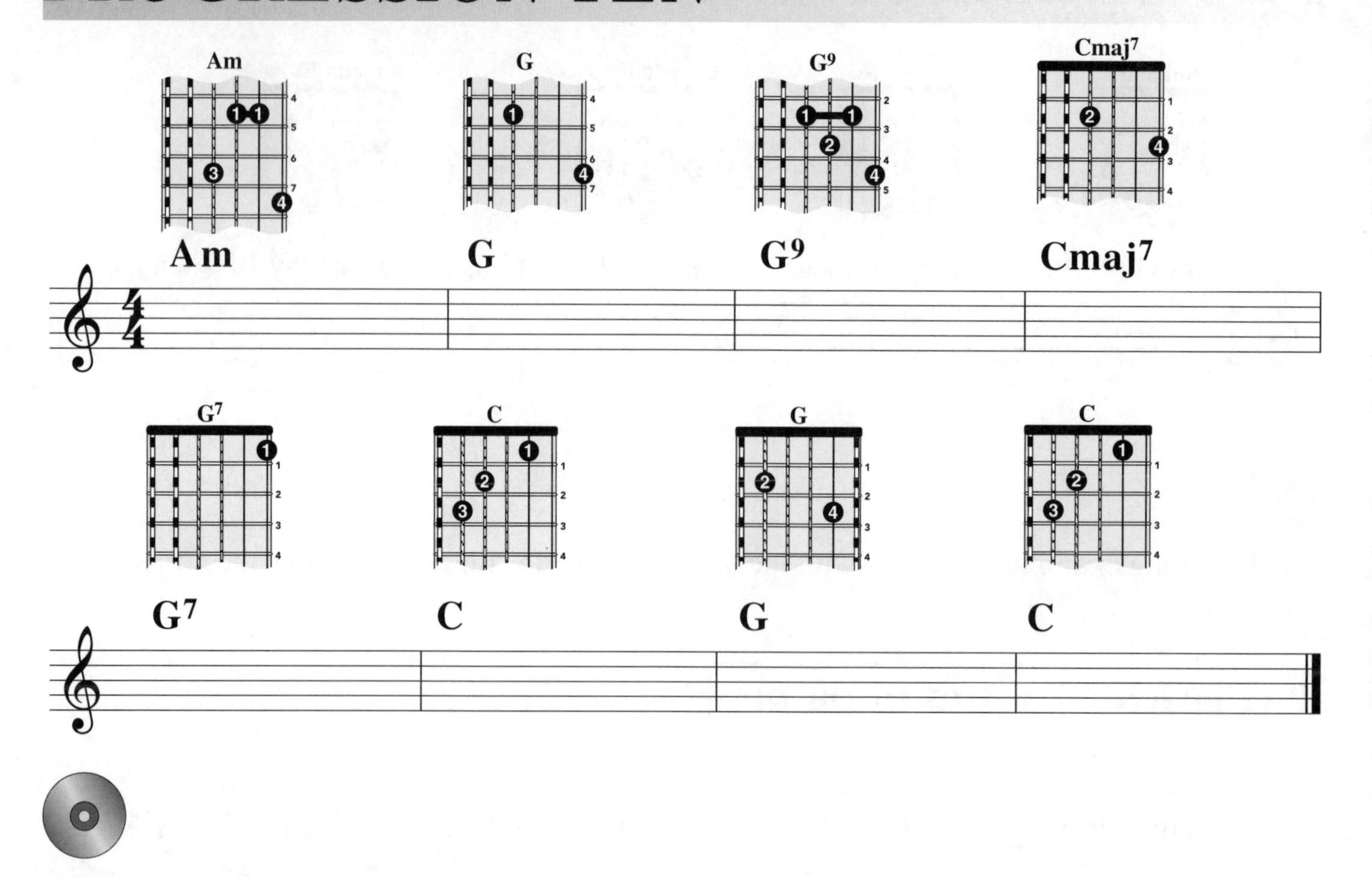

The following progression features a descending bass (4th string) and top voice movement (1st string). **Pattern 17** is used.

SECTION III

ARRANGEMENTS

An arrangement is the addition of harmony parts to accompany a melody. In this section **Greensleeves** has been presented to illustrate the most common steps involved in creating an arrangement for a melody. This involves a style of fingerpicking where you are no longer using set patterns.

The principles outlined within these steps can be applied to any melody and so you should experiment with other songs of your choice. Before you do this, it will be necessary to become familiar with the principles of chord construction, as outlined in ***Progressive Rhythm Guitar***.

STEP 1

WRITE DOWN THE MELODY

For the purpose of arranging, all melody notes are written.with the stems pointing upwards. This is done to visually distinguish the melody from the accompaniment, which has the stems pointing downwards.

The key of A minor has been selected for two reasons:

1. For ease of playing: a) All notes can be found in the first position.
   b) All chords can be played as open chords (i.e. open strings make arrangements easier to play).

2. For ease of arranging. Most of the melody notes are on the first three strings, leaving the other three strings available for bass notes and harmonies.

When you are doing your own arrangements make sure that the melody is in an easy key (e.g. C, G, Am, Em) and that most of the notes can be played on the first three strings.

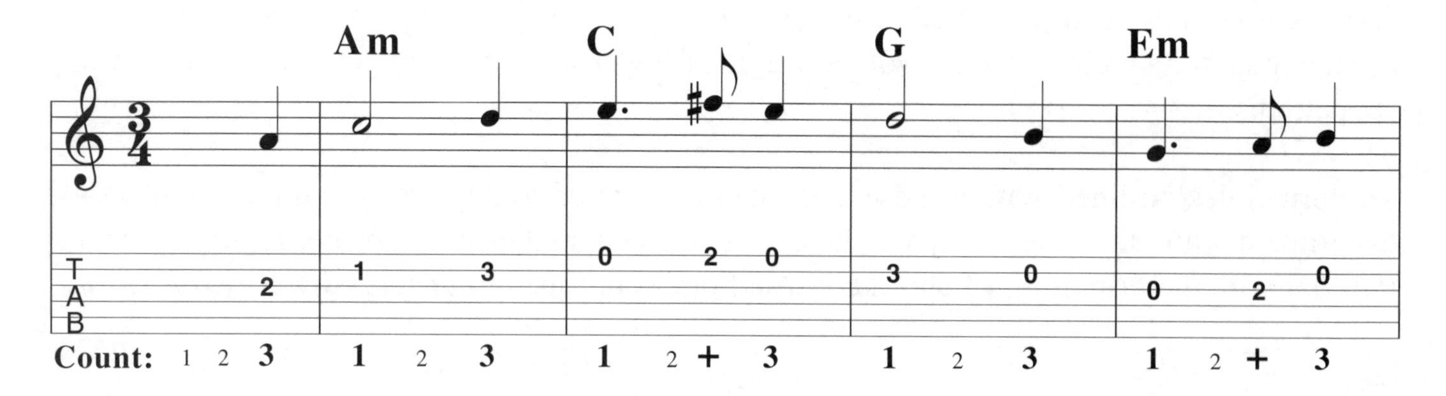

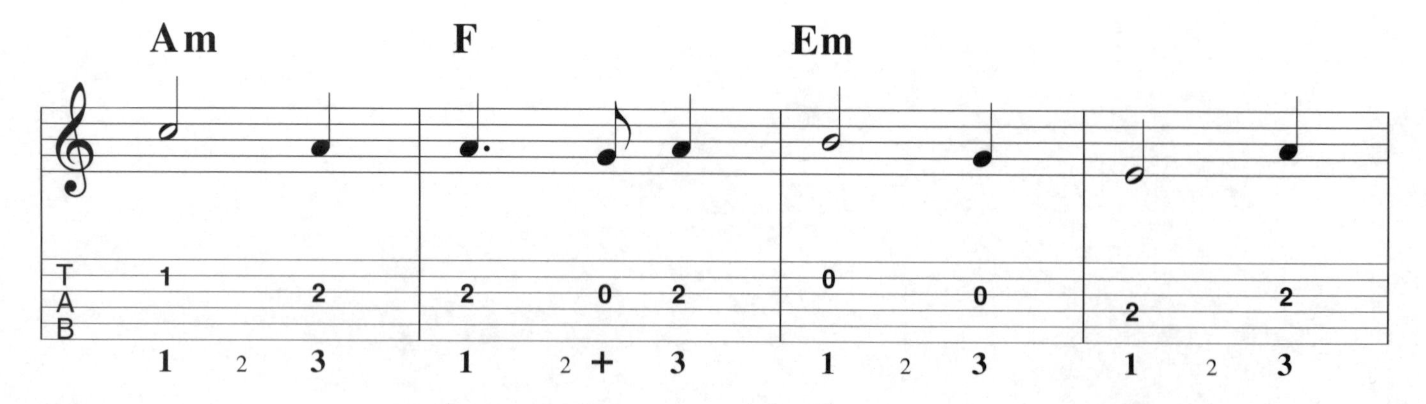

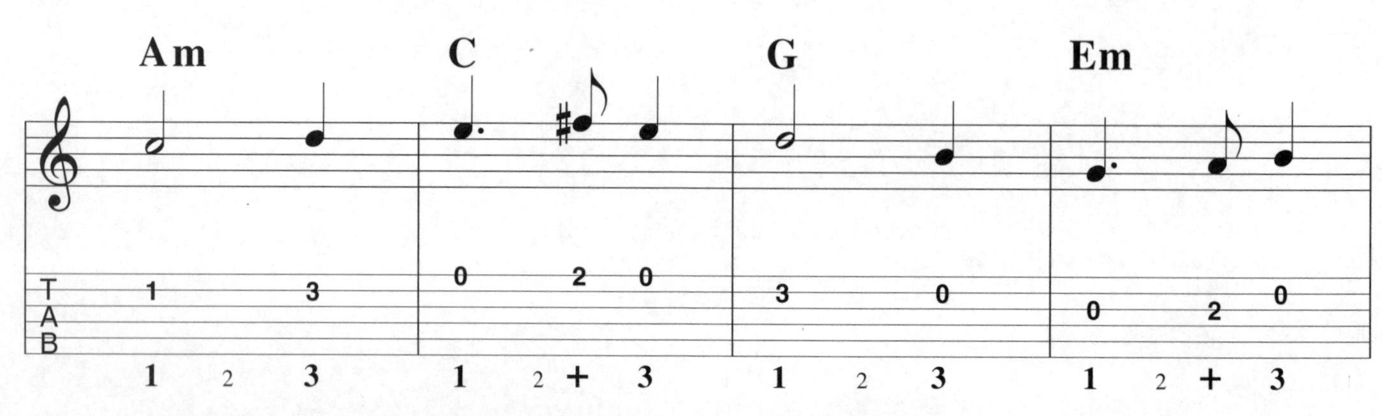

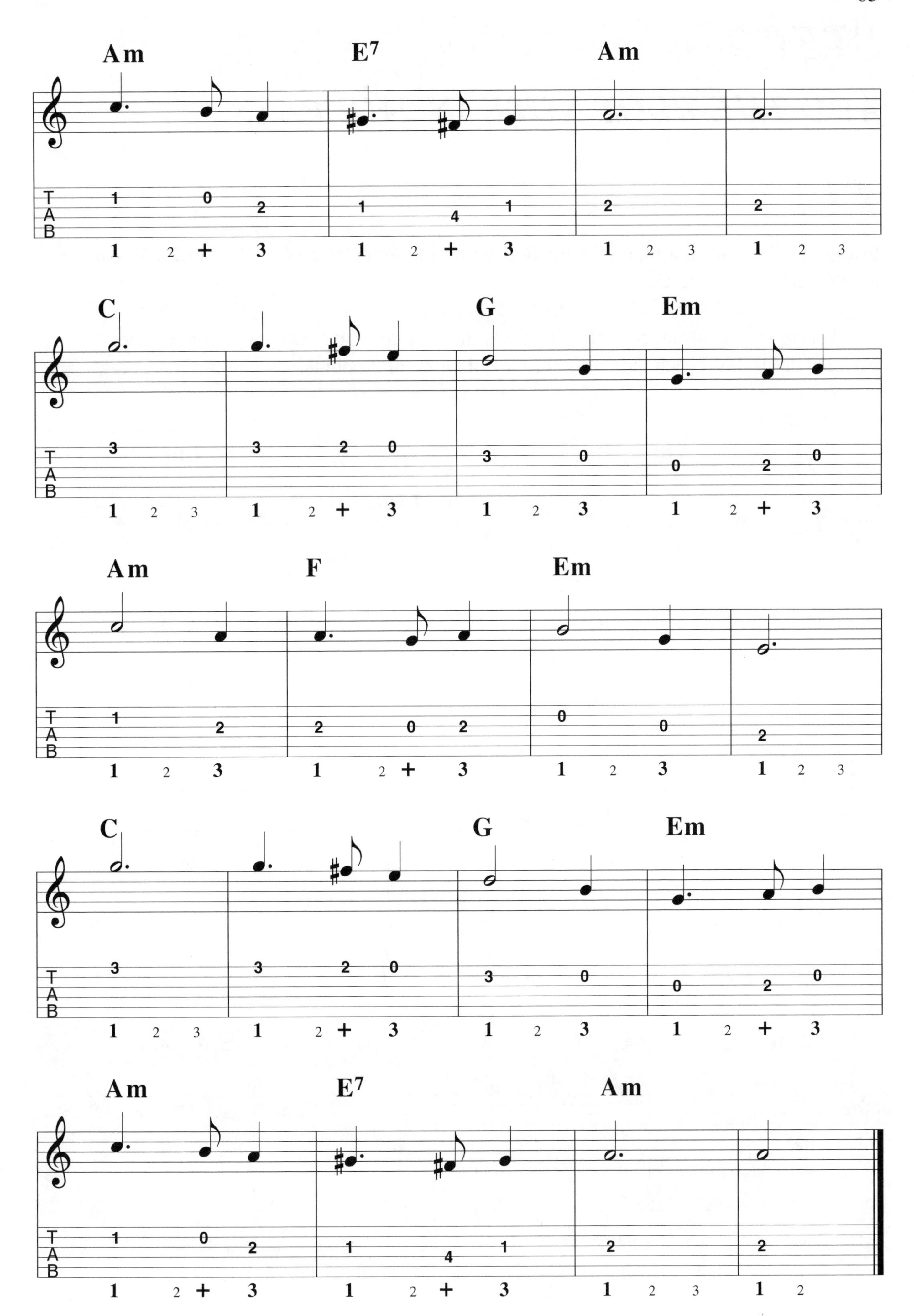
Am
E7
Am
T
A
B
1 0 2
1 4 1
2
2
1 2 + 3
1 2 + 3
1 2 3
1 2 3
C
G
Em
3
3 2 0
3 0
0 2 0
1 2 3
1 2 + 3
1 2 3
1 2 + 3
Am
F
Em
1 2
2 0 2
0 0
2
1 2 3
1 2 + 3
1 2 3
1 2 3
C
G
Em
3
3 2 0
3 0
0 2 0
1 2 3
1 2 + 3
1 2 3
1 2 + 3
Am
E7
Am
1 0 2
1 4 1
2
2
1 2 + 3
1 2 + 3
1 2 3
1 2

STEP 2

ADD THE ROOT NOTE IN THE BASS

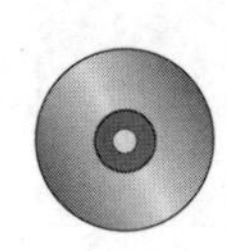

In Lesson One the root note is defined as being the letter note of each chord, e.g. Am - root note A; G7 - root note G.

For this step of the arrangement, write down the root note (in the bass) on the first beat of each bar. Be sure to hold each bass note for its full value of 3 counts.

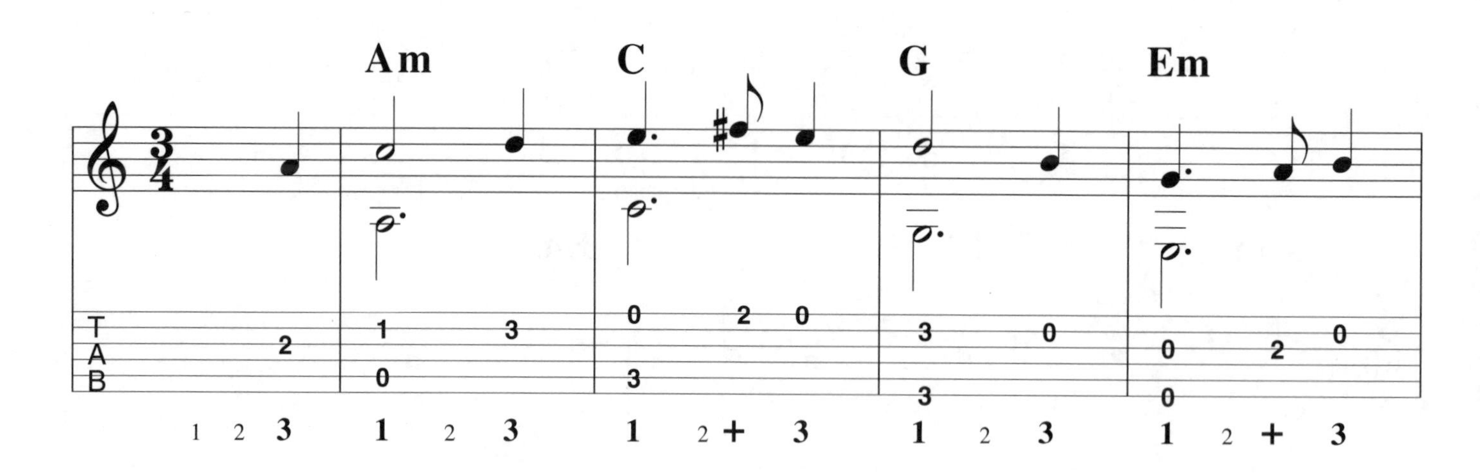

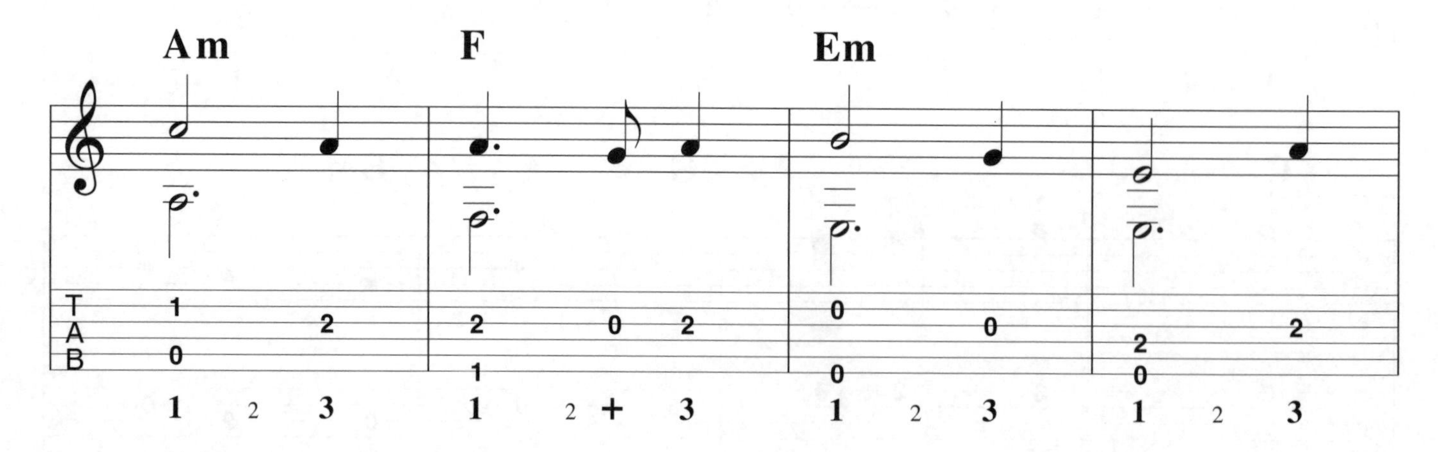

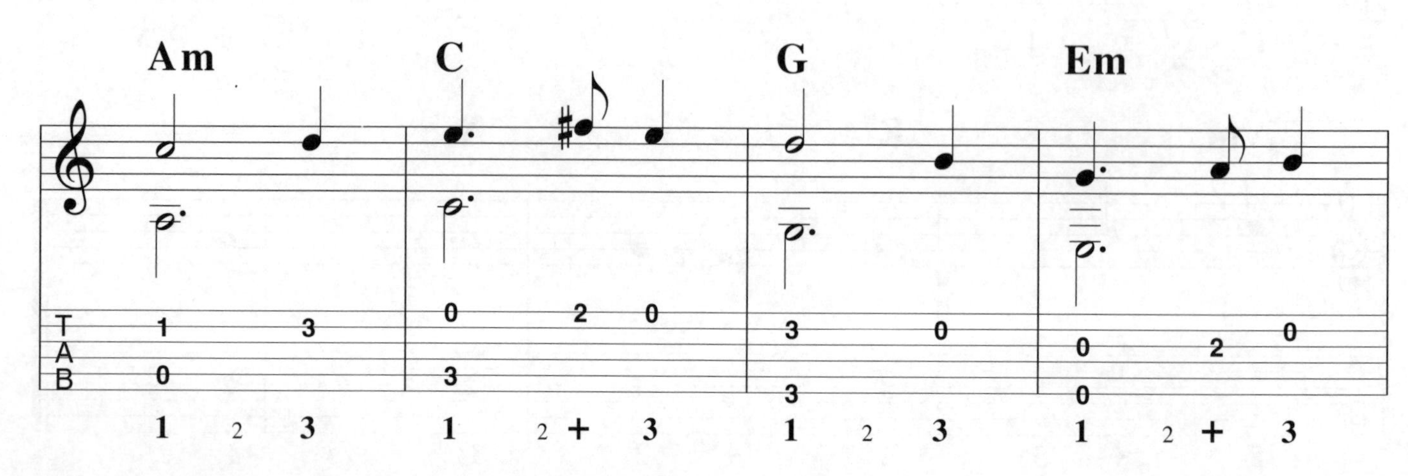

This step of the arrangement illustrates and example of two part writing. Other examples of two part writing can be found in the Supplementary List (e.g. Silent Night page 109, The First Noel page 107, etc.)

STEP 3

ADD A HARMONY* NOTE TO THE BASS (A MIDDLE VOICE)

The simplest way to add a harmony note to the bass is to select a note from the given chord. For example, in bar 1 the notes of the Am chord are A, C and E, so any of these could be used to harmonise the A bass note. Your choice of note will depend on the overall sound of the various combinations (e.g. in bar 4 the E note is used in preference to the B note). In some cases it may also depend on the ease of playing.
The notes that you are adding in this step of the arrangement can be referred to as a **middle voice** because they occur between the bass and melody lines.

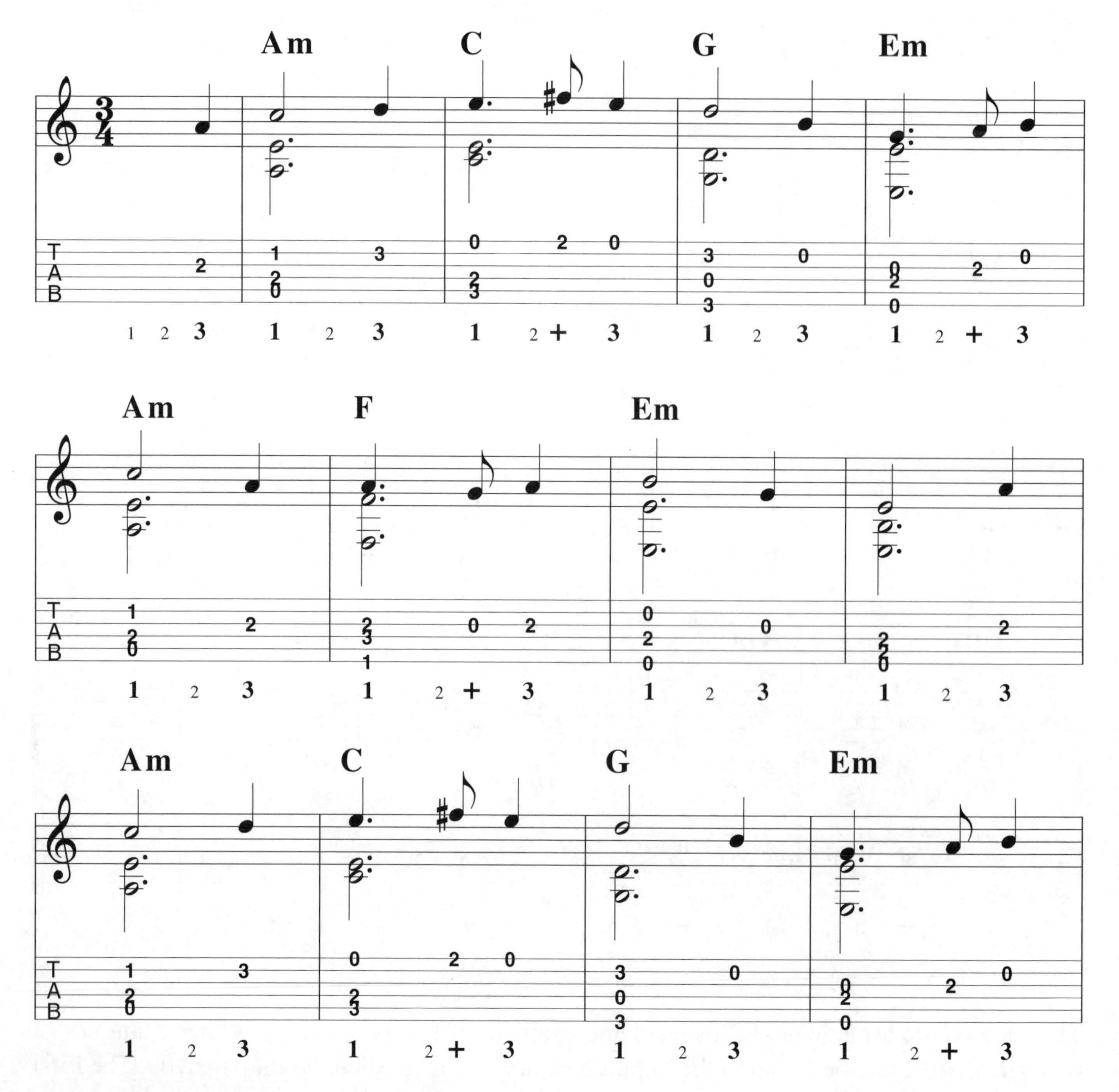

* **Harmony** can be defined as the simultaneous sounding of two or more different notes.

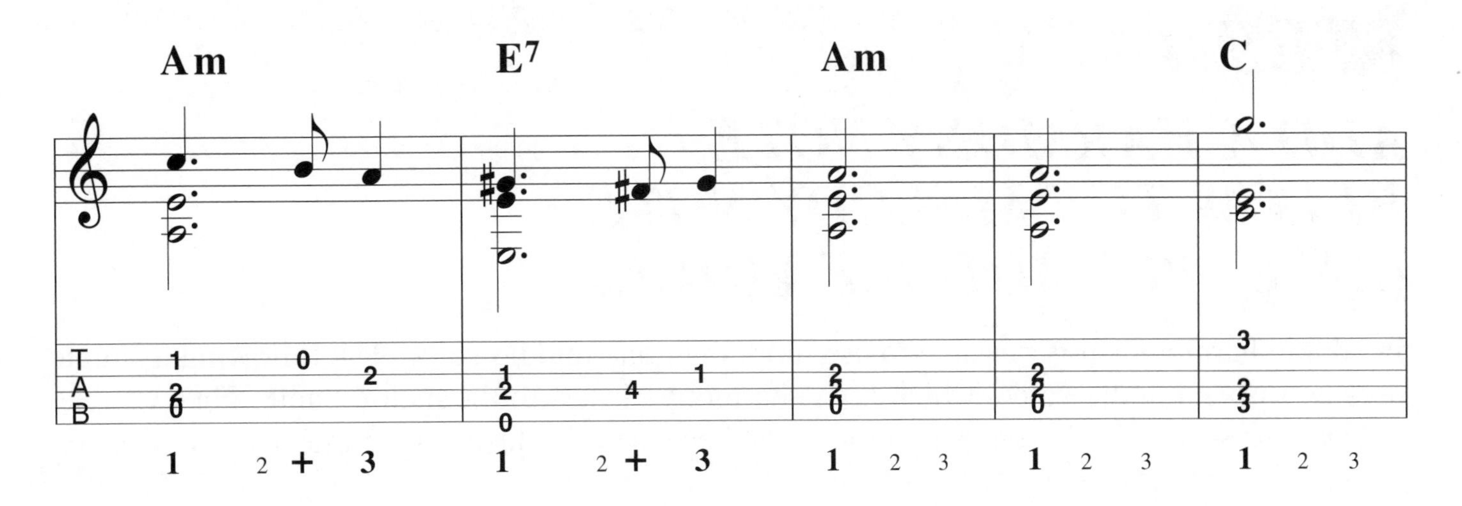
Am
E7
Am
C
T
A
B
1 2 + 3
1 2 + 3
1 2 3
1 2 3
1 2 3

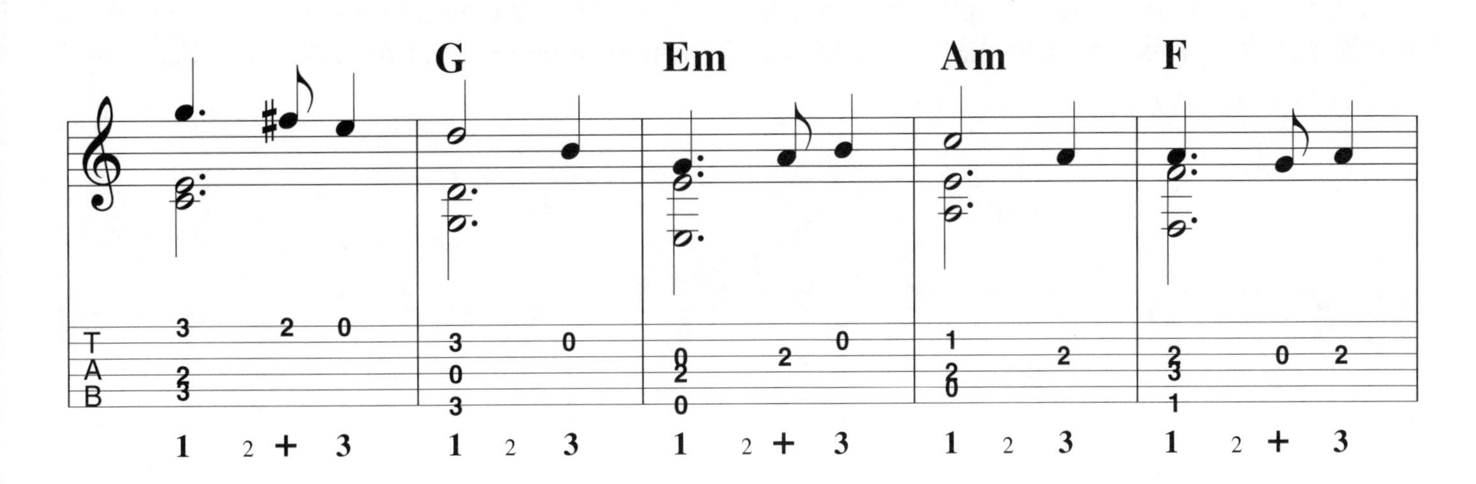
G
Em
Am
F
T
A
B
1 2 + 3
1 2 3
1 2 + 3
1 2 3
1 2 + 3

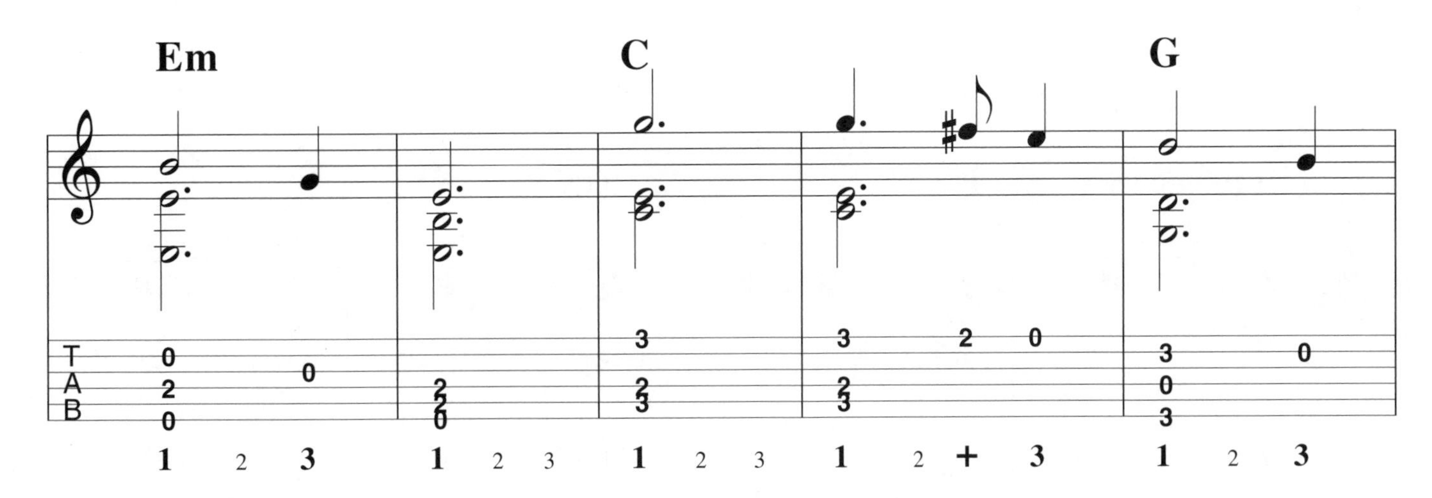
Em
C
G
T
A
B
1 2 3
1 2 3
1 2 3
1 2 + 3
1 2 3

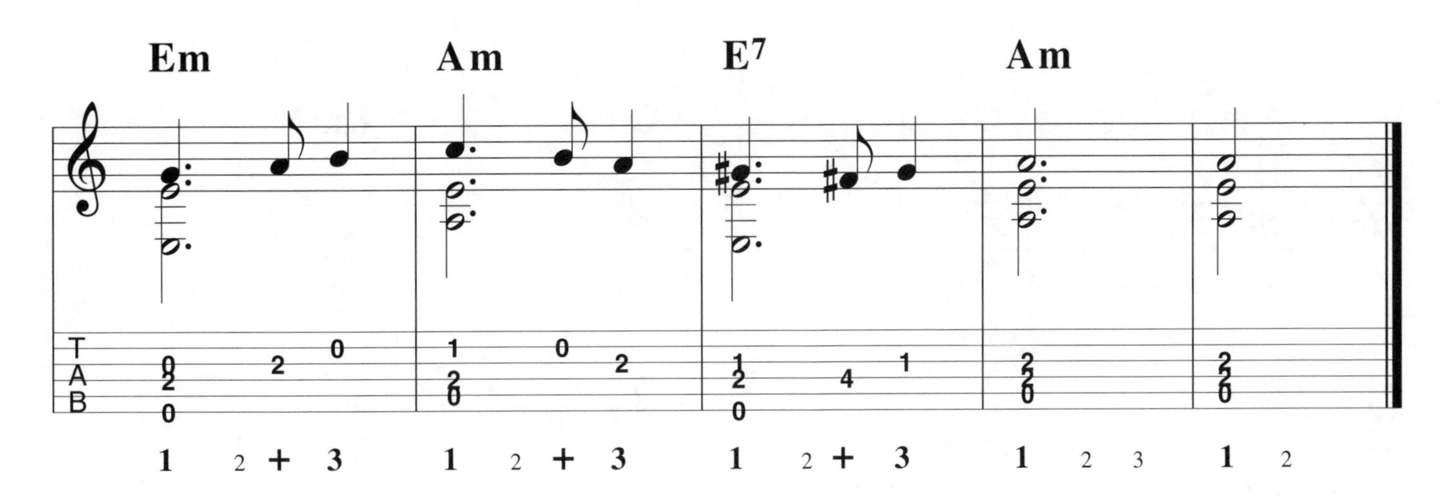
Em
Am
E7
Am
T
A
B
1 2 + 3
1 2 + 3
1 2 + 3
1 2 3
1 2

STEP 4

ADD A HARMONY NOTE BELOW THE MELODY NOTE (AN UPPER MIDDLE VOICE)

In adding harmonies it is possible to use more than one middle voice. The following example uses an **upper** middle voice, which is the harmony closest to the melody note. For example, in bar 1 the A note is chosen as harmony note because it is closer to the melody than C or E.

You will notice that in bar 4 the same note (E) is used in both of the middle voice arrangements. It is quite acceptable in harmony to overlap the voices in this manner. Also notice the ② symbol next to the E note in bar 17, which indicates that the note is to be played on the second string.

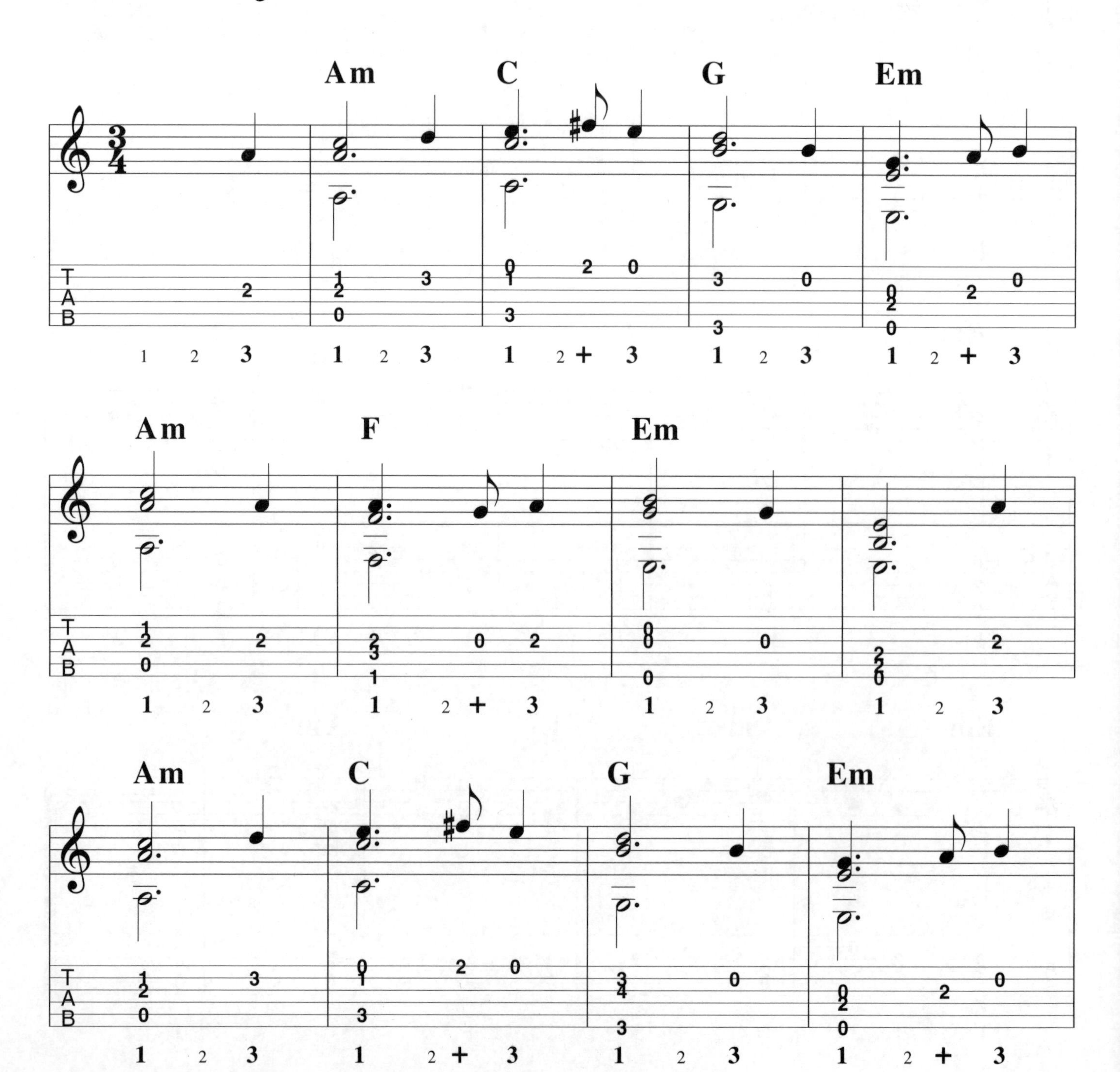

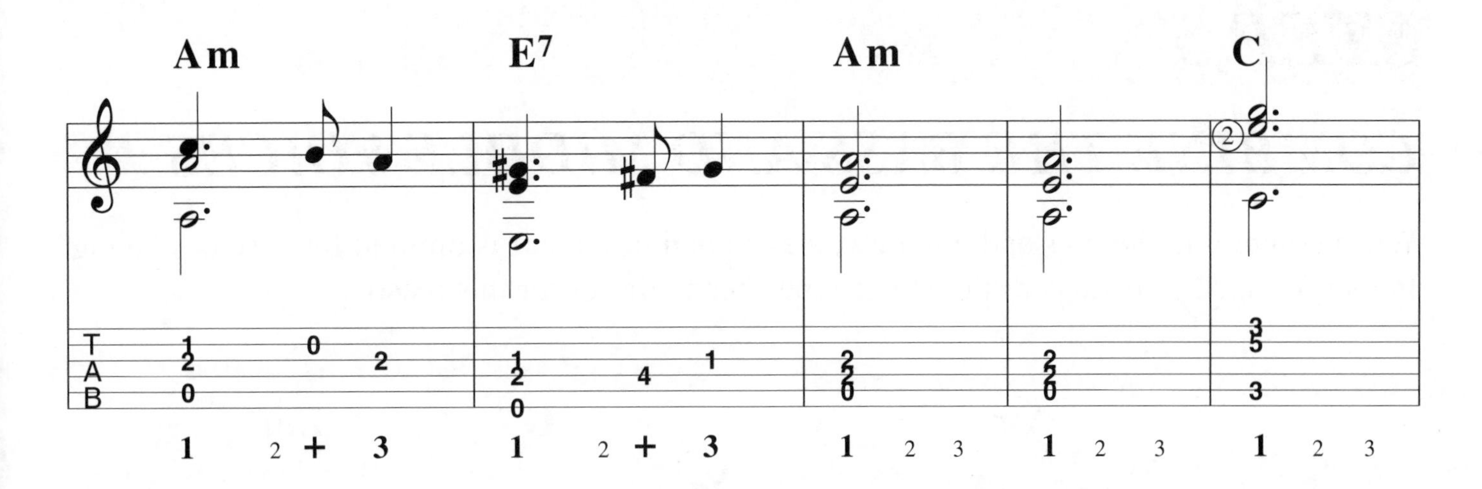
Am
E7
Am
C
1 2 + 3
1 2 + 3
1 2 3
1 2 3
1 2 3

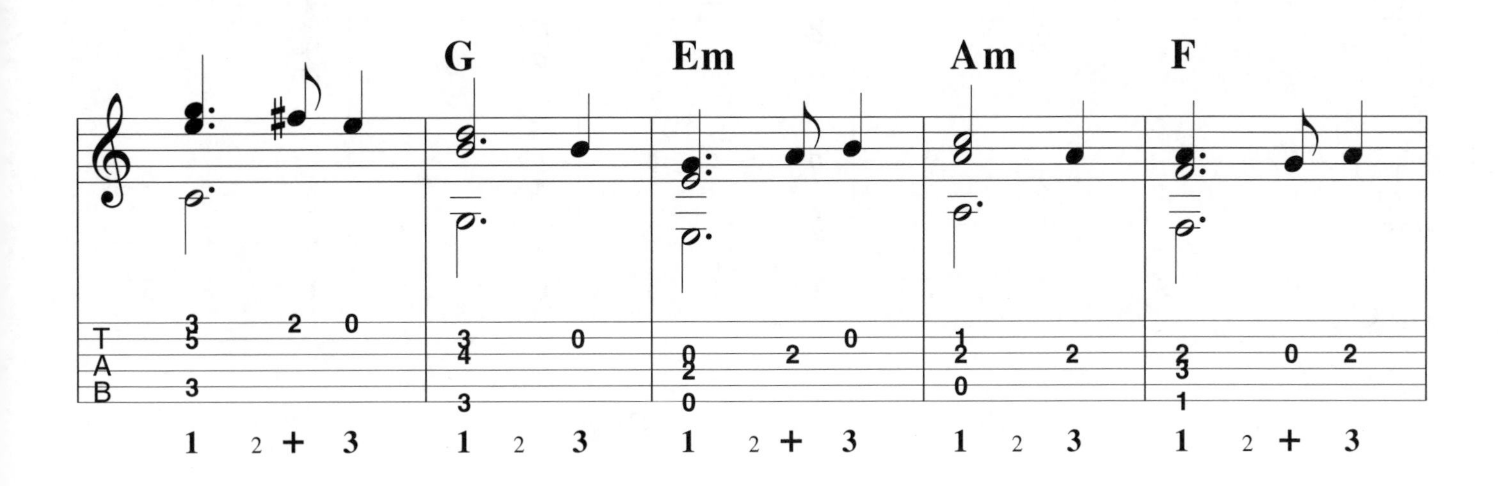
G
Em
Am
F
1 2 + 3
1 2 3
1 2 + 3
1 2 3
1 2 + 3

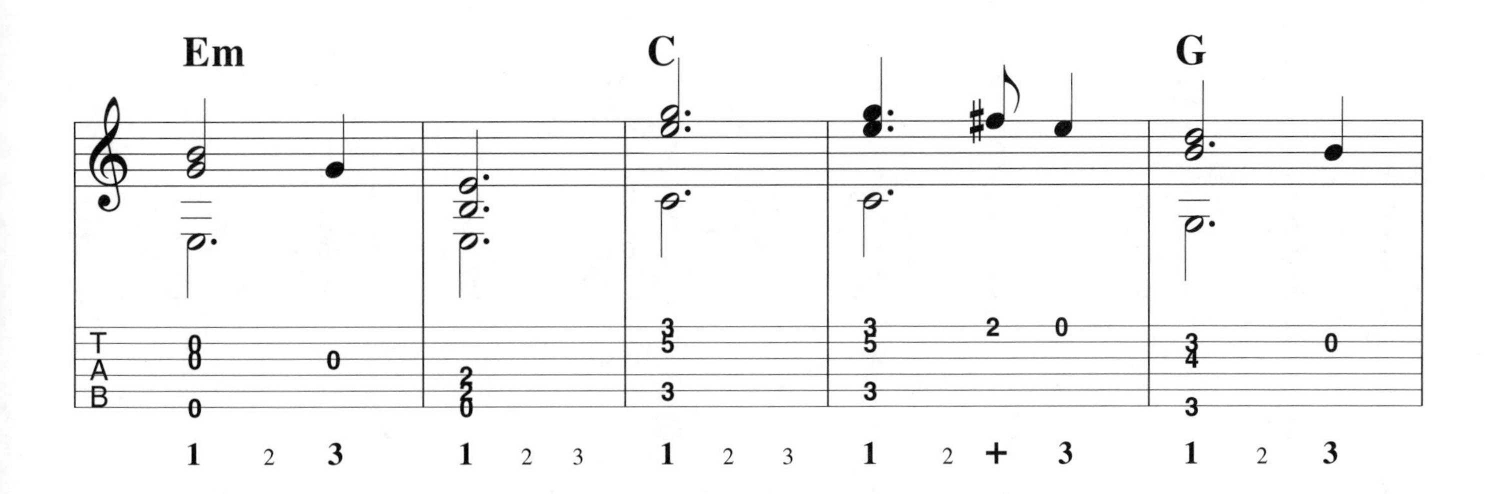
Em
C
G
1 2 3
1 2 3
1 2 3
1 2 + 3
1 2 3

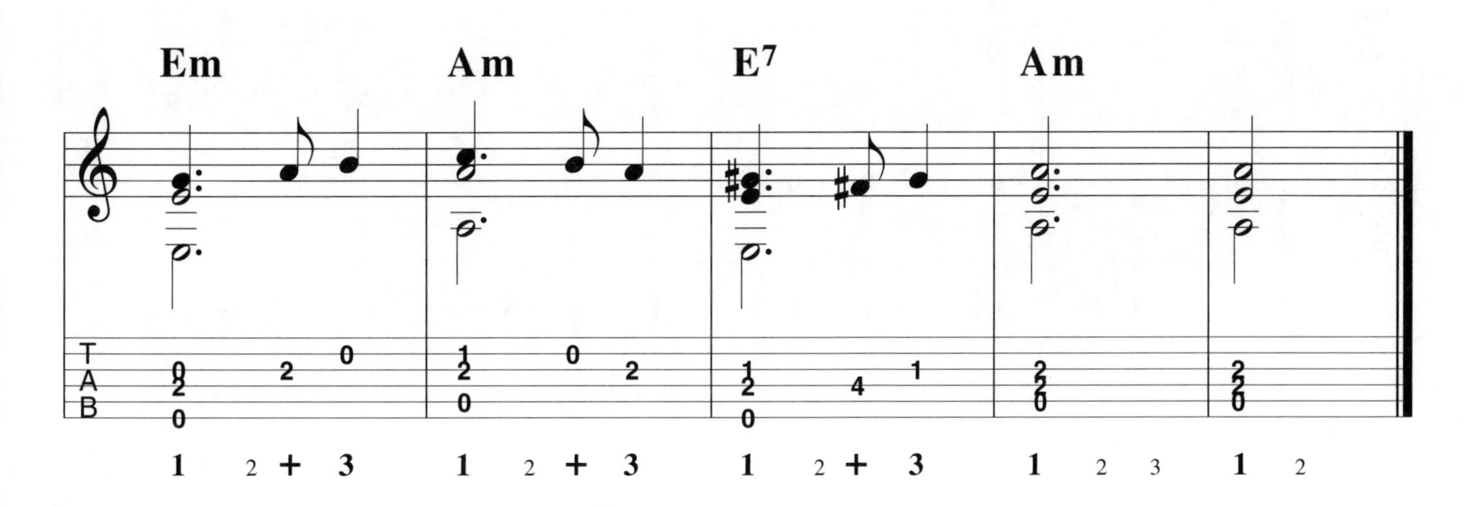
Em
Am
E7
Am
1 2 + 3
1 2 + 3
1 2 + 3
1 2 3
1 2

STEP 5

COMBINE THE BASS AND MIDDLE VOICES

When combining the bass and middle voices sometimes a part is omitted for ease of playing. In bars 17 and 25 the upper middle voice has been left out for this reason.

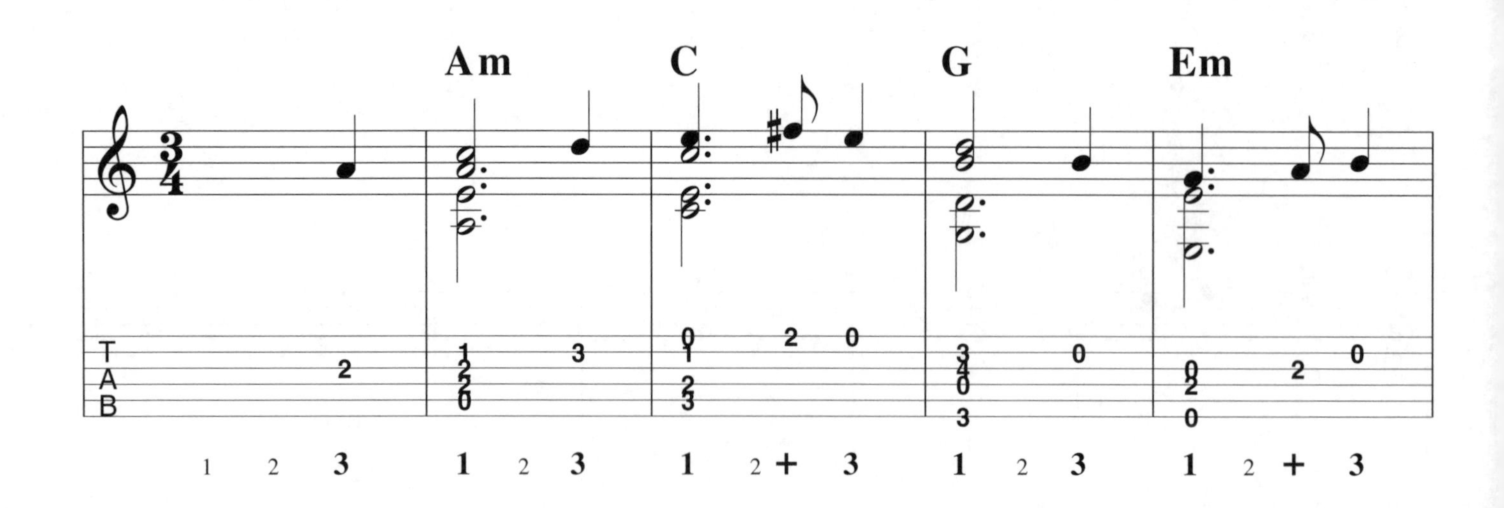

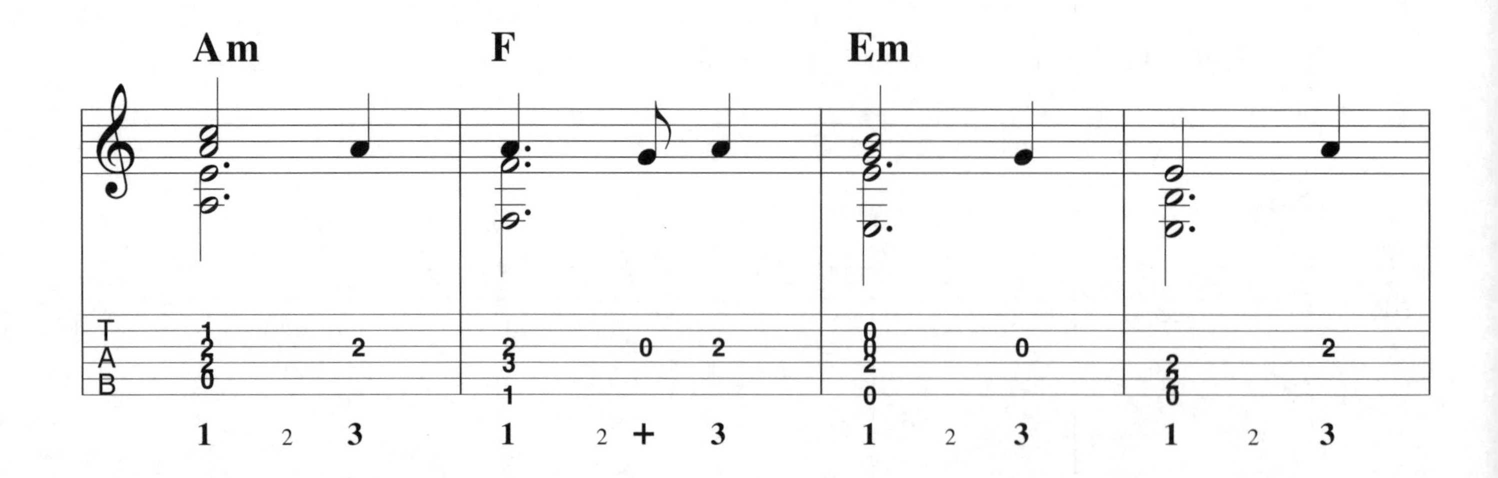

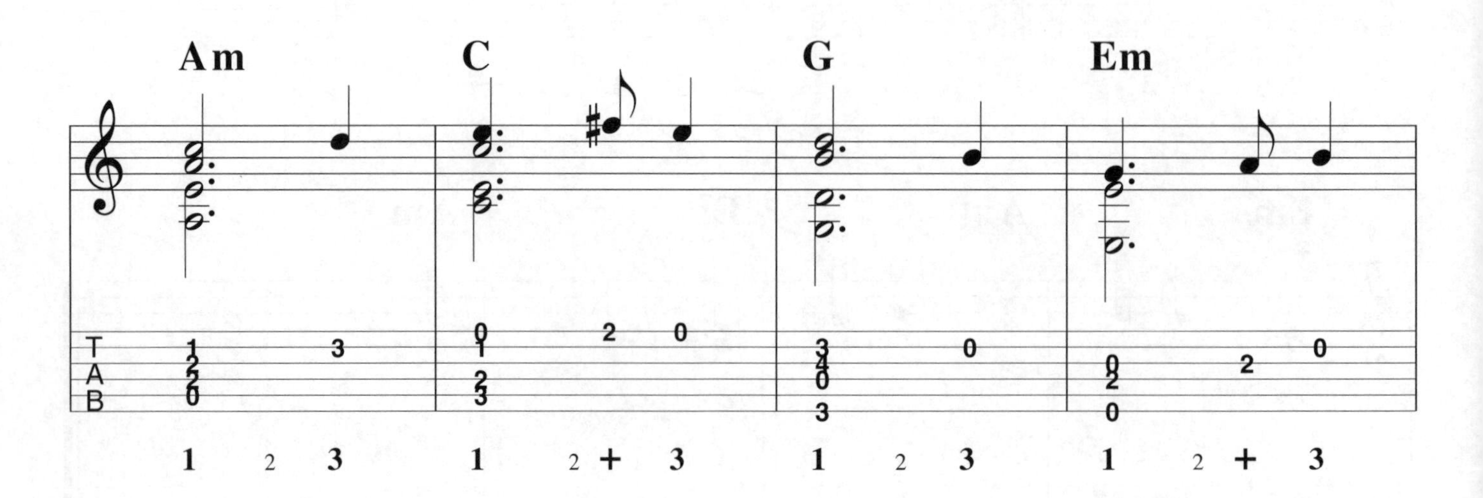

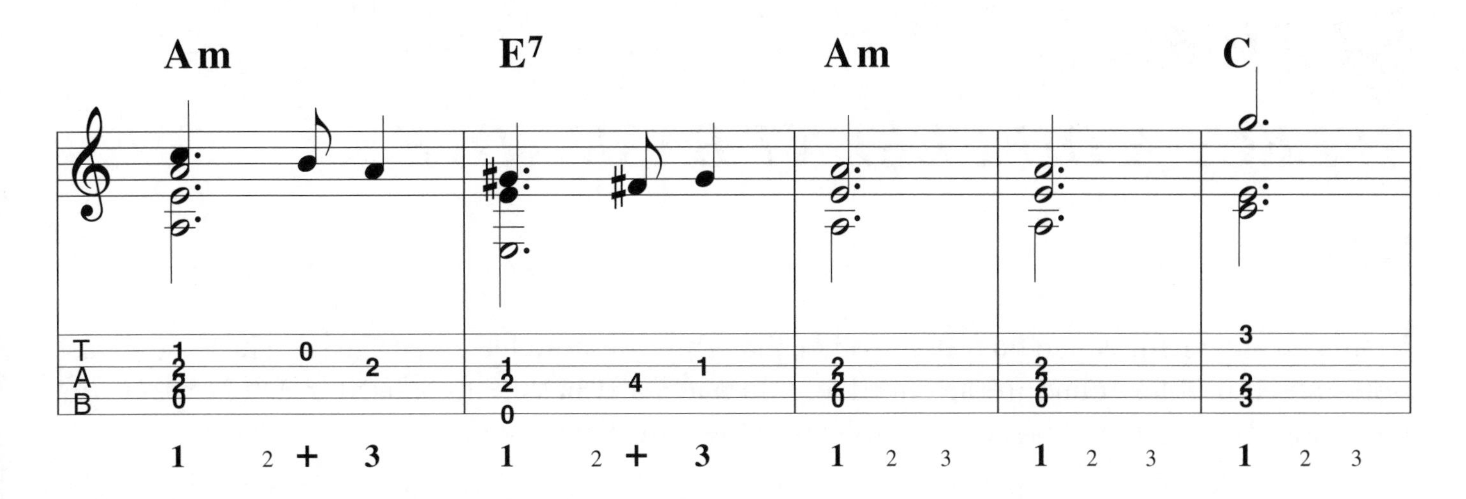
Am
E7
Am
C

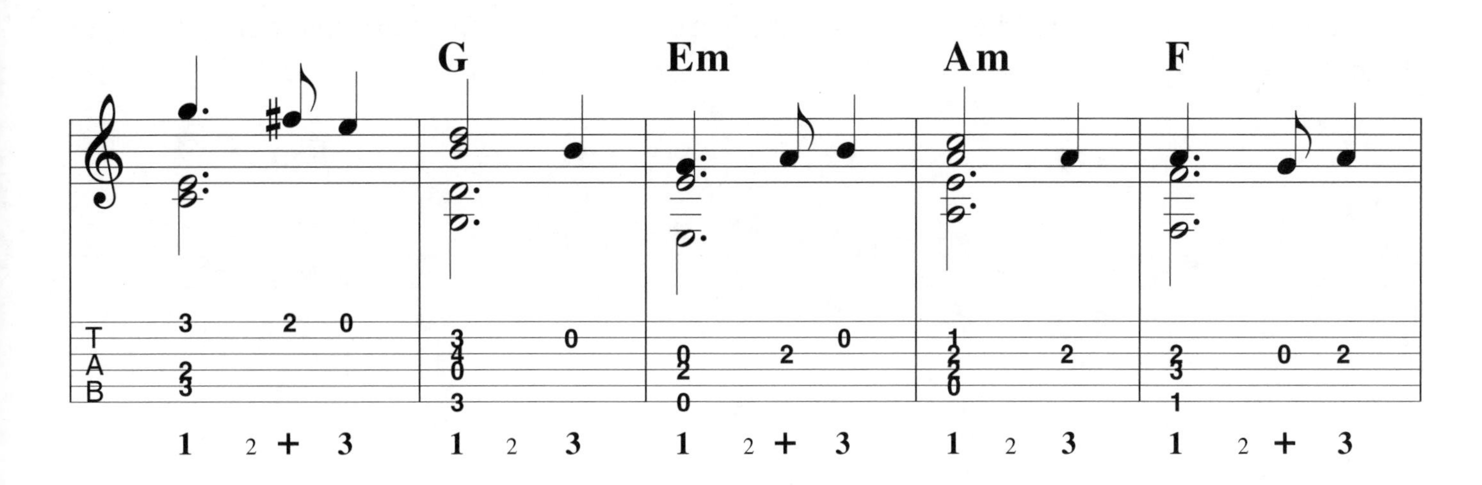
G
Em
Am
F

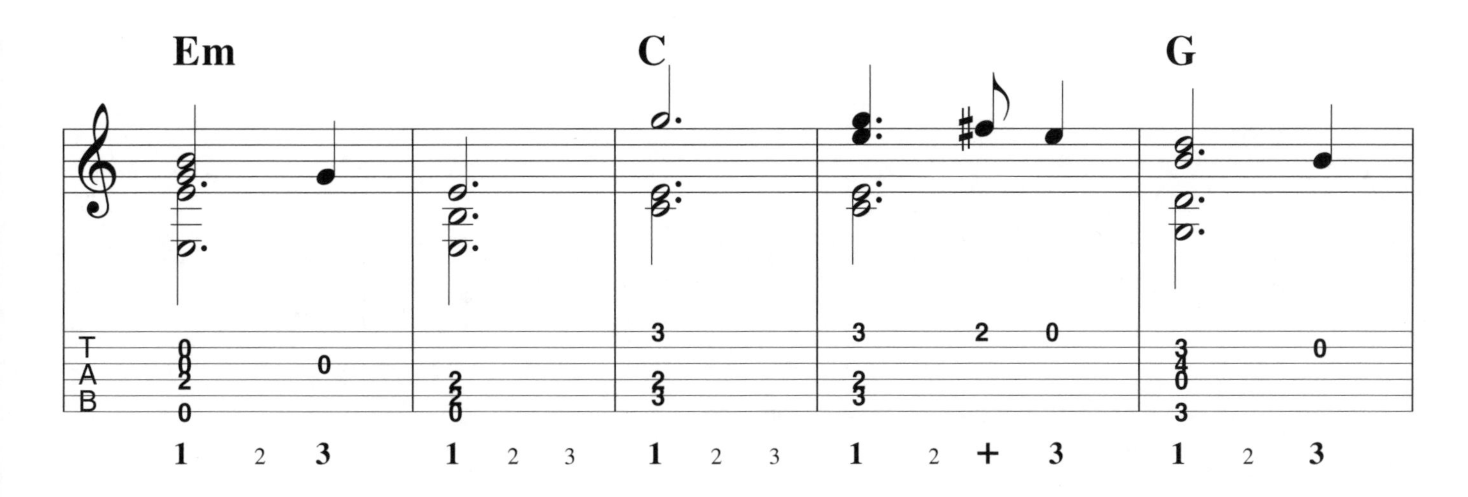
Em
C
G

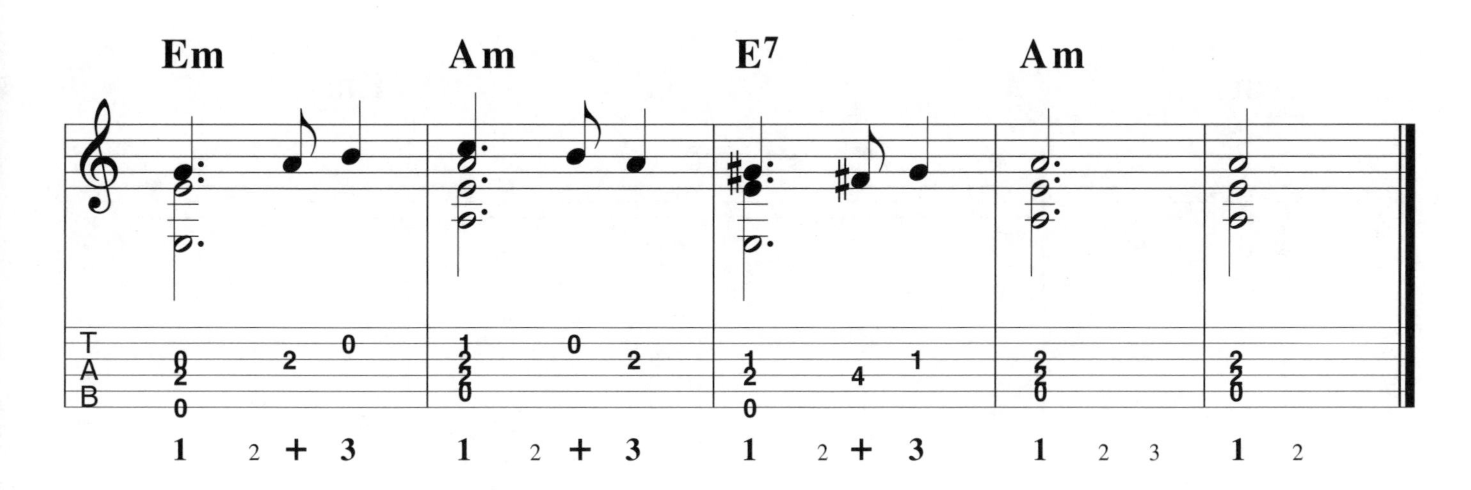
Em
Am
E7
Am

STEP 6

SELECT A DIFFERENT BASS NOTE

In this arrangement, some bass notes other than the root note have been used. These new bass notes are still notes found in the chord. e.g. in bar 3 a B bass note is used instead of a G root bass note. Bass note runs (see Lesson Nine) have also been used.

For arrangements in $\frac{4}{4}$ time it is common practice to alternate from the root note to another bass note on the 1st and 3rd beats (e.g. see the Turnaround and Blues arrangements on pages 91 and 92).

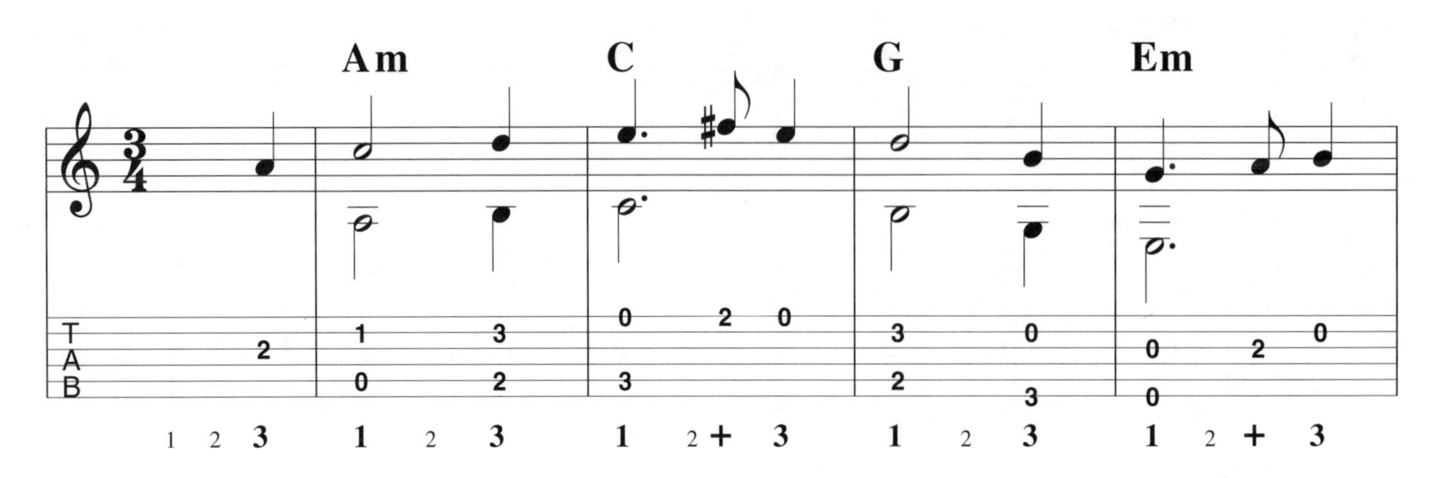

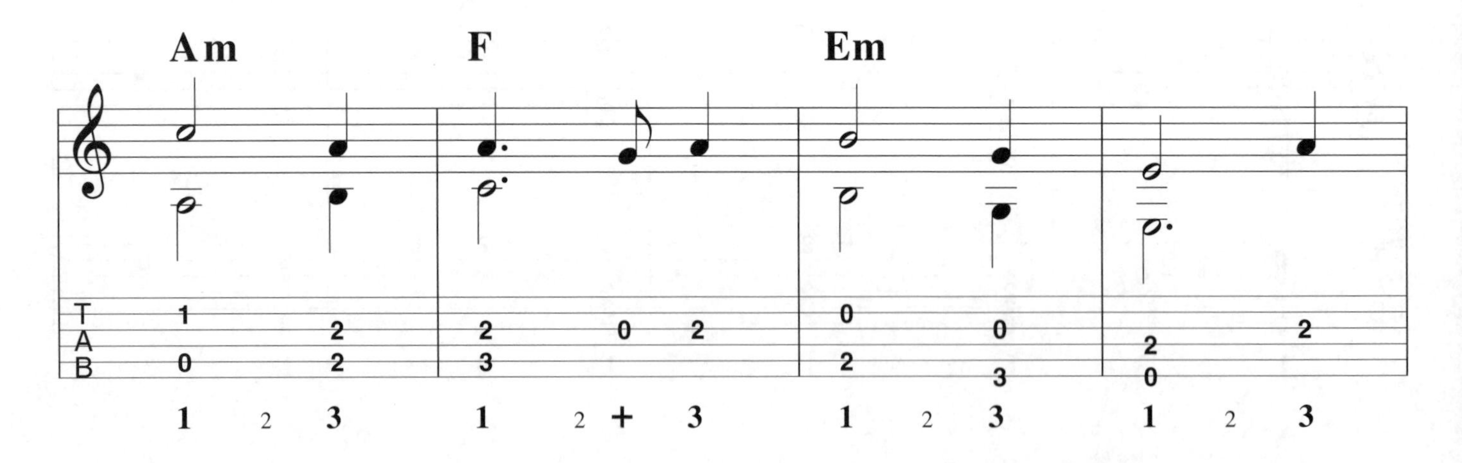

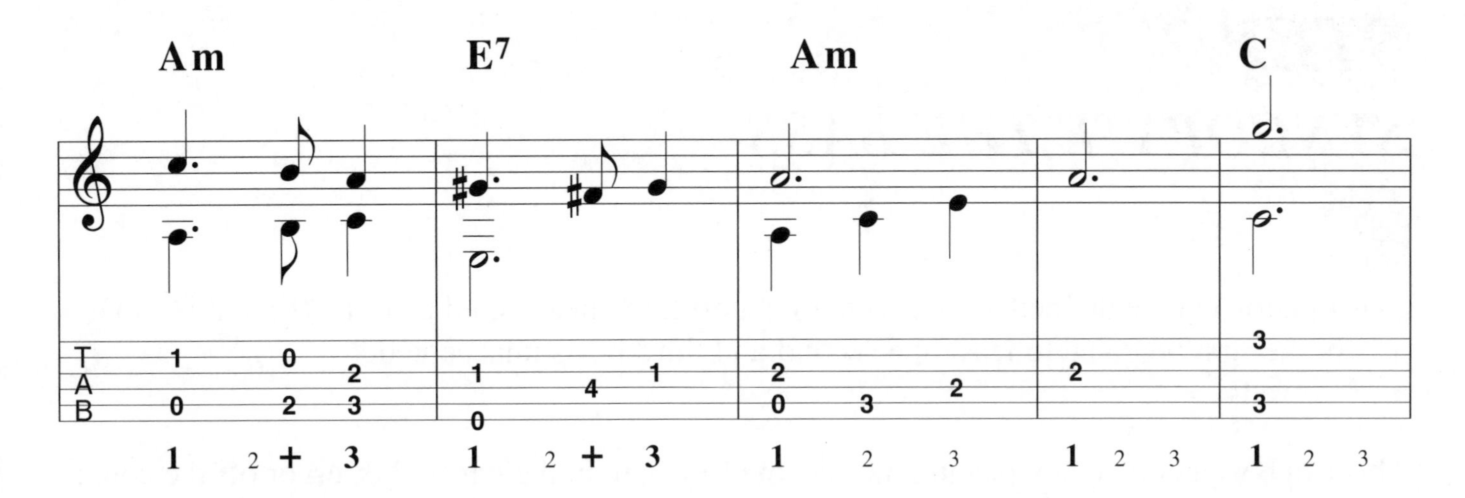
Am
E7
Am
C

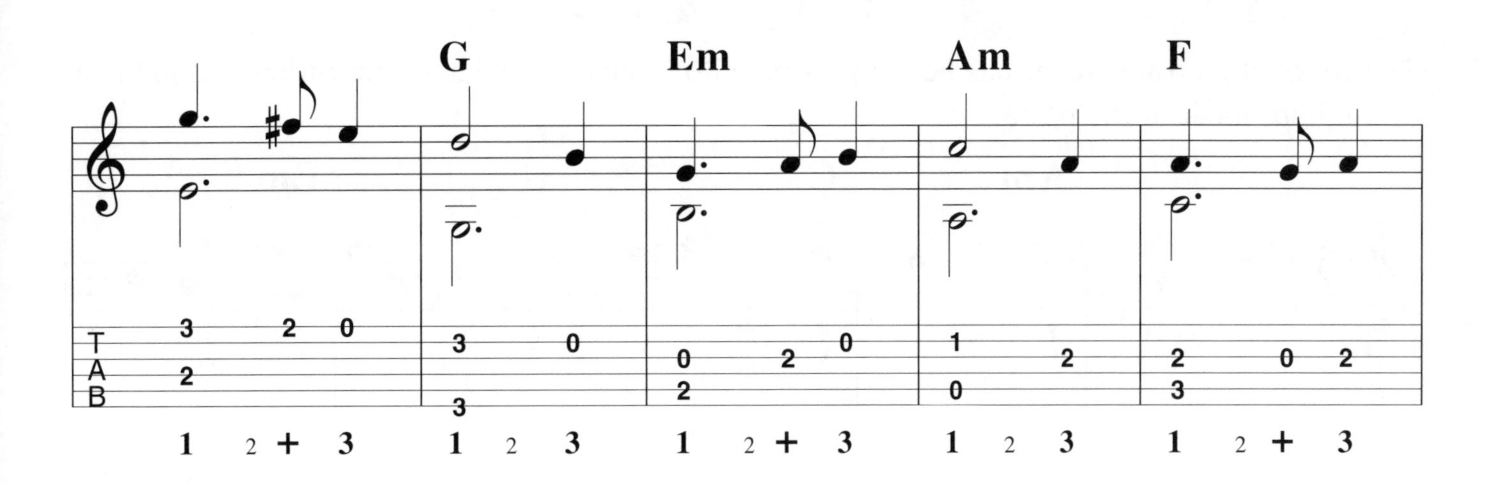
G
Em
Am
F

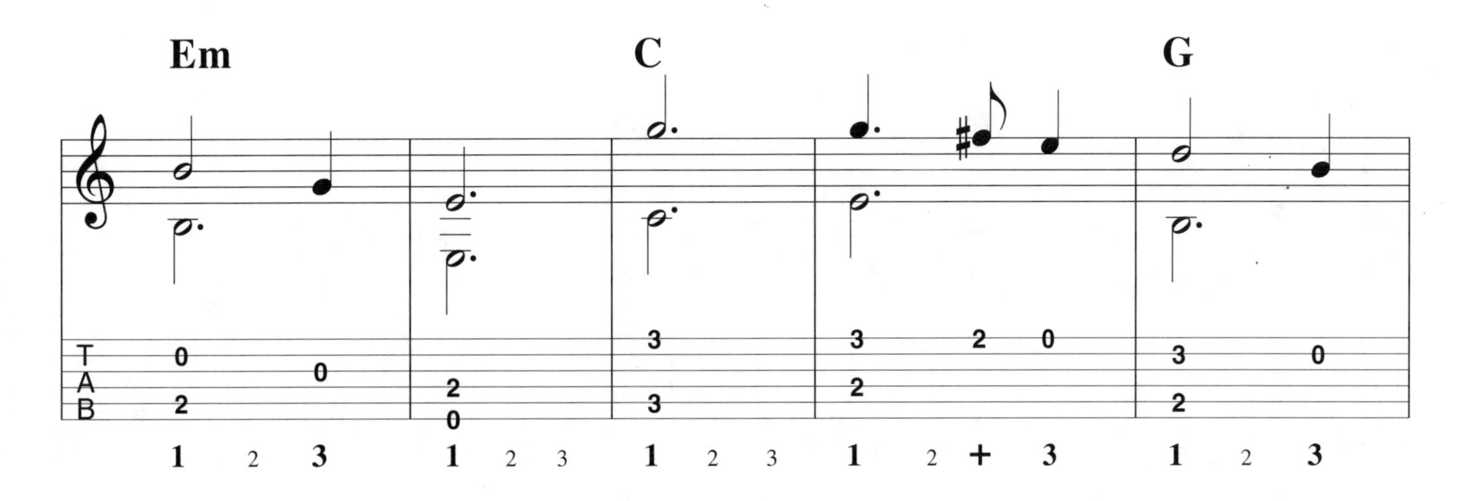
Em
C
G

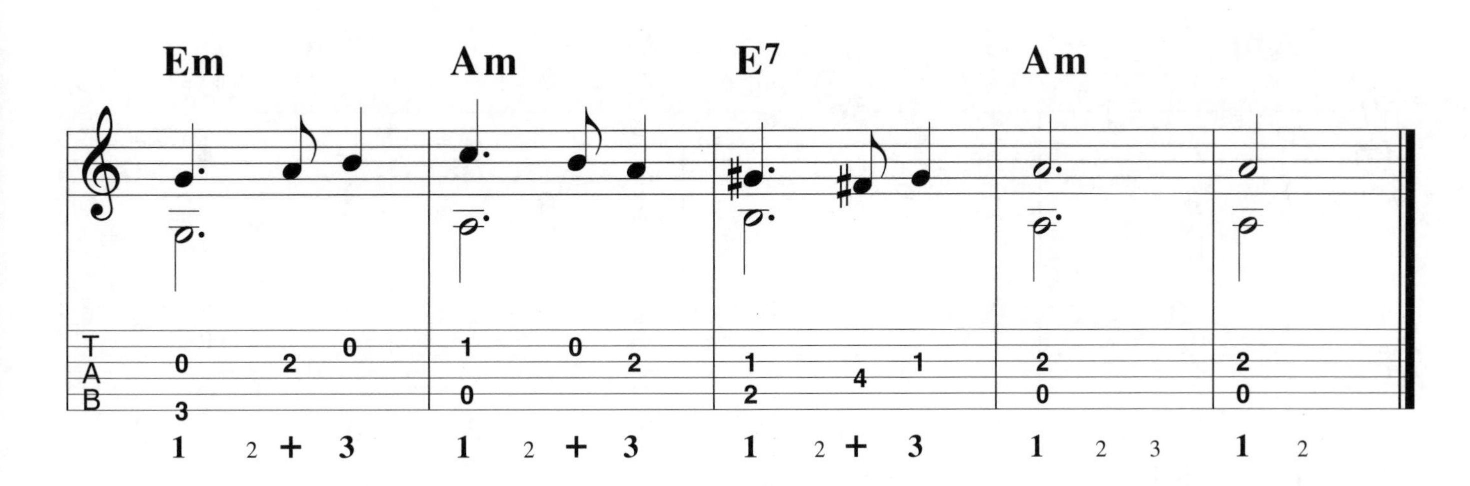
Em
Am
E7
Am

STEP 7

SYNCOPATE THE BASS

Syncopation can be defined as an accent on a normally unaccented beat. In $\frac{3}{4}$ time it is usual to accent the first beat and to leave the second and third beats unaccented:*

$\frac{3}{4}$ 1̂ 2 3 (accent on 1)

This can be syncopated by placing the accent elsewhere in the bar (either **on** or **off** the count):

$\frac{3}{4}$ 1 2 3 (accent on 2) $\frac{3}{4}$ 1 2 3 (accents on 2 and 3) $\frac{3}{4}$ 1 + 2 + 3 + (accents on + after 2 and + after 3)

The following arrangement has been syncopated by placing the bass note on the second beat throughout most of the piece.

* In $\frac{4}{4}$ time it is usual to accent the first and third beats.

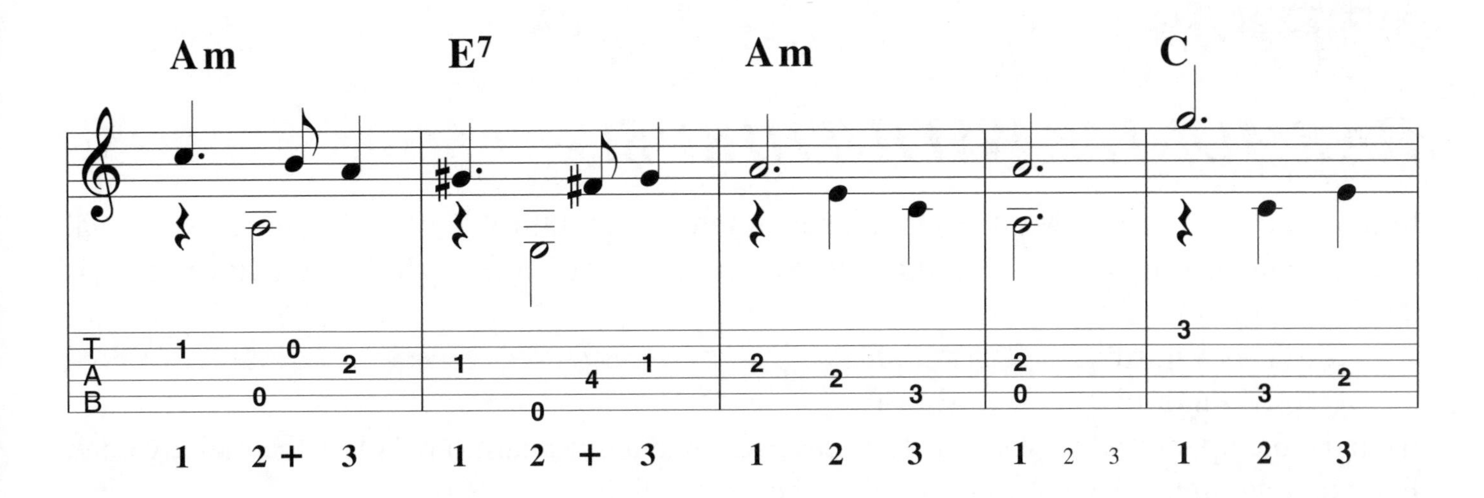
Am
E7
Am
C
T
A
B
1 2 + 3 1 2 + 3 1 2 3 1 2 3 1 2 3

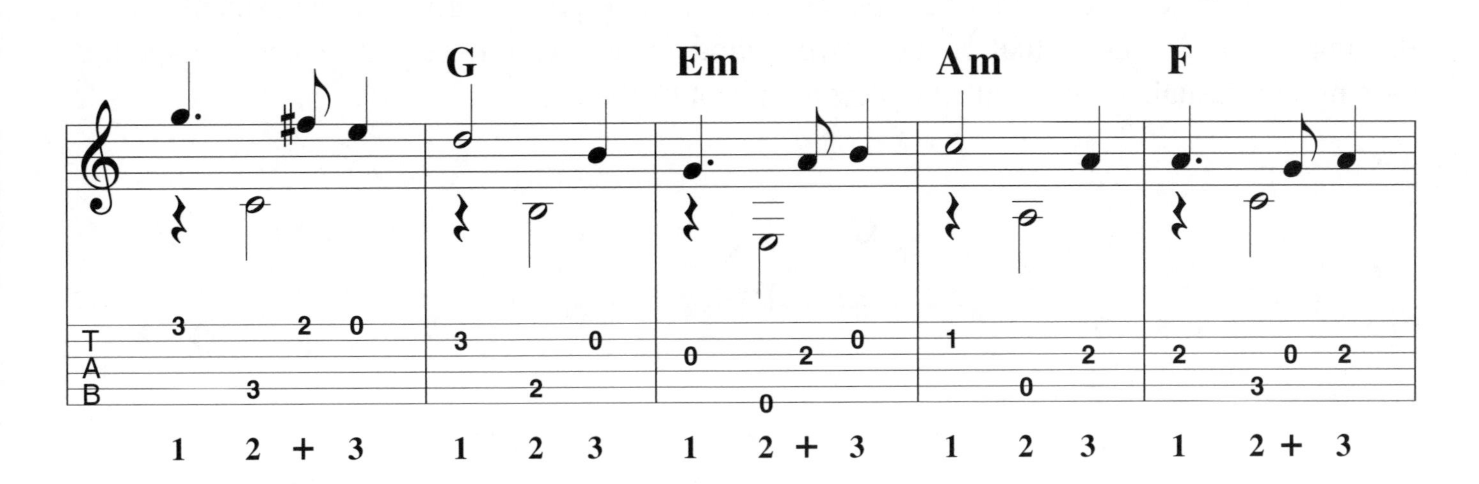
G
Em
Am
F
T
A
B
1 2 + 3 1 2 3 1 2 + 3 1 2 3 1 2 + 3

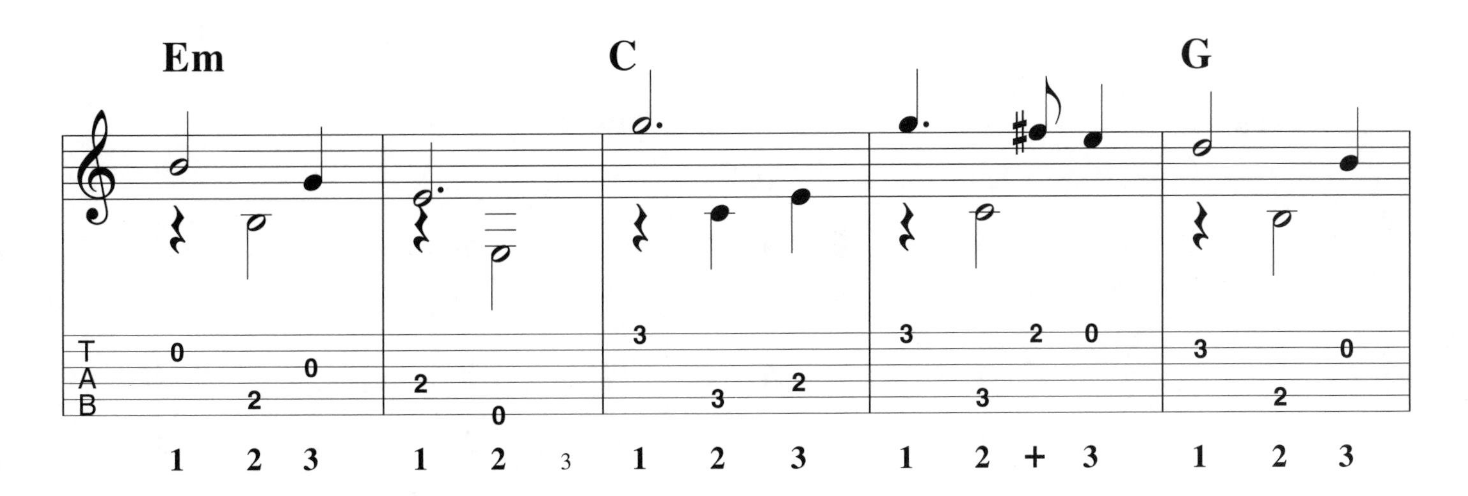
Em
C
G
T
A
B
1 2 3 1 2 3 1 2 3 1 2 + 3 1 2 3

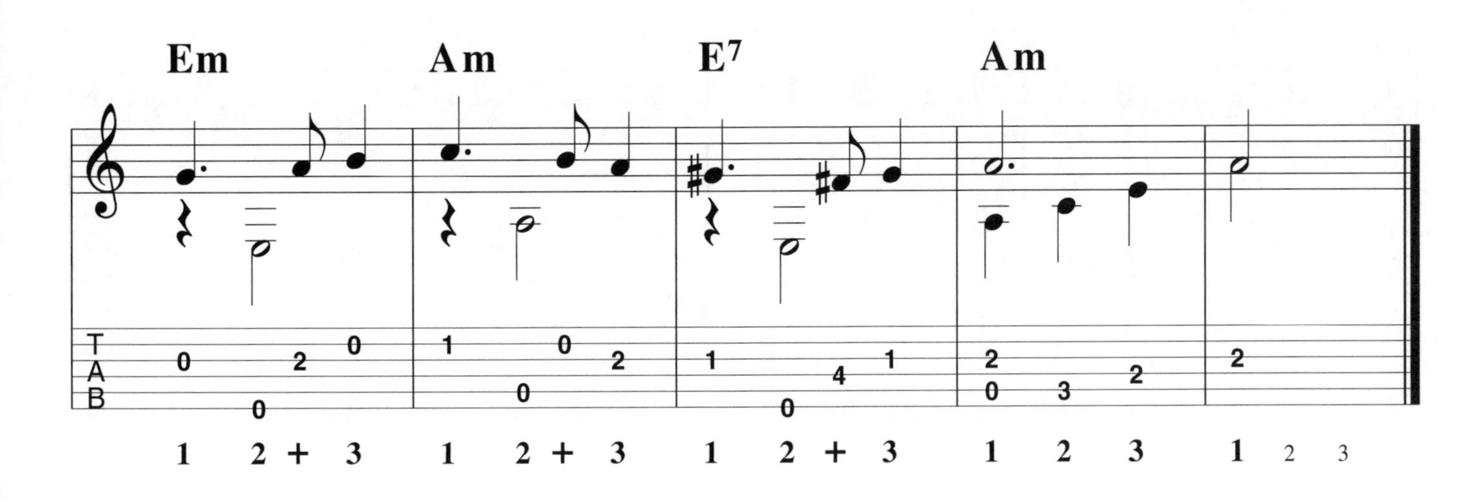
Em
Am
E7
Am
T
A
B
1 2 + 3 1 2 + 3 1 2 + 3 1 2 3 1 2 3

STEP 8

HARMONIZE WITH THIRDS:

In music, a third is any two notes that have an interval of a third between them. This interval can be calculated by counting up three notes from the lower note, including the lower note as the first of the three, e.g.

C to E is a third*: C D E
D to F is a third*: D E F

In step 4 the upper middle voice in most cases created a third harmony below the melody note. For example, in bar 1 the A note is a third below the C note - A B C.

The use of thirds can be extended to apply to passing notes, as illustrated in the example below. Passing notes are notes that connect two melody notes which are a third or less apart. A passing note usually occurs on an unaccented beat of the bar.

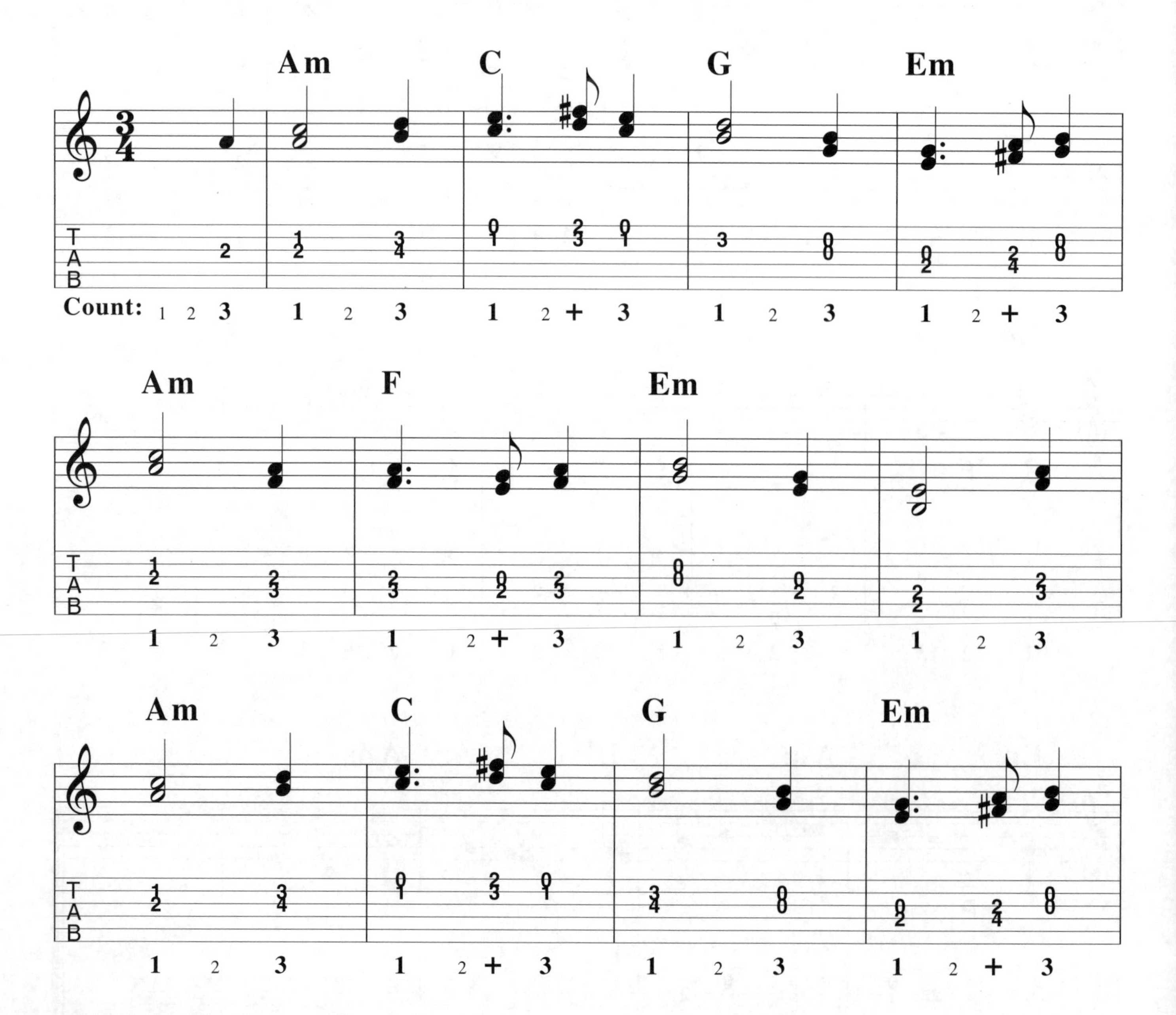

* C to E is technically referred to as a Major 3rd because the distance between them is 2 tones (4 frets). D to F is a Minor 3rd because the distance between them is 1½ tones (3 frets).

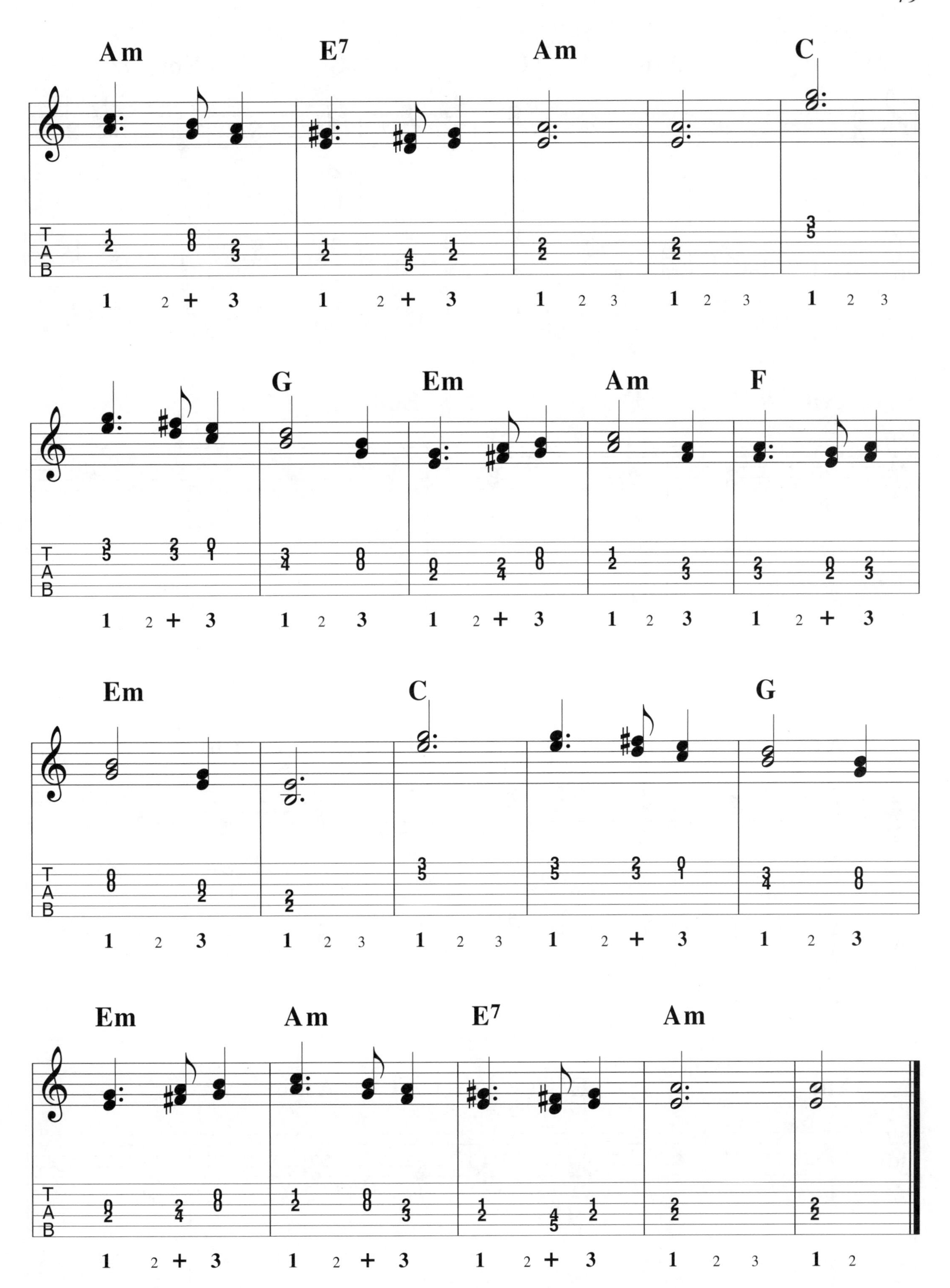

In adding other parts to this arrangement (e.g. a root bass note) you will need to take into consideration the overall sound of the arrangement and the ease of playing. Try the following:

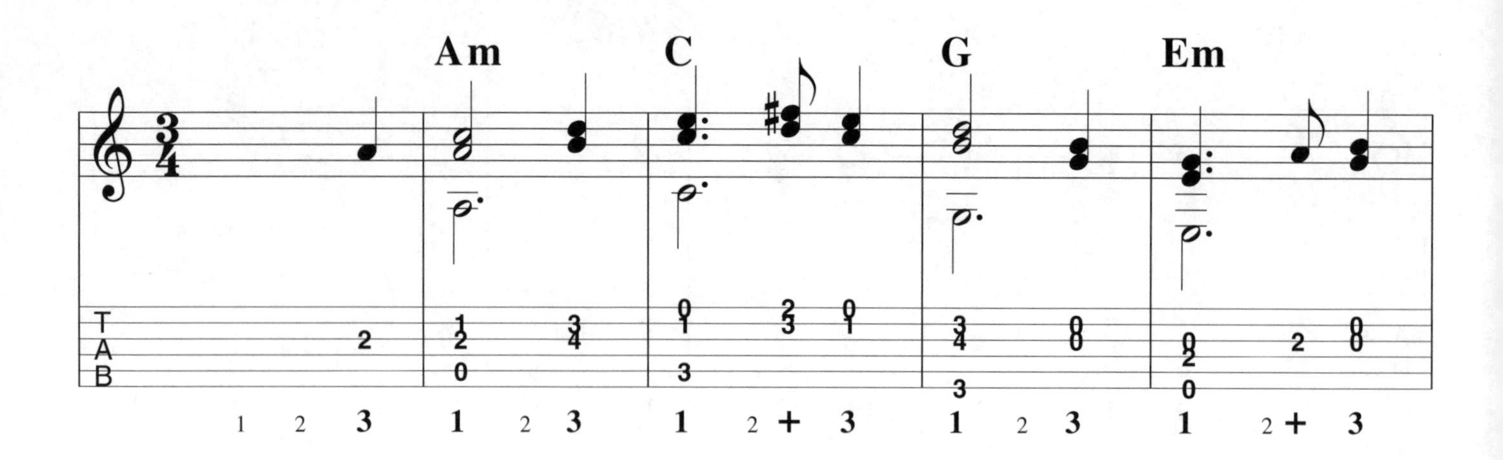
Am
C
G
Em
1 2 3 1 2 3 1 2 + 3 1 2 3 1 2 + 3

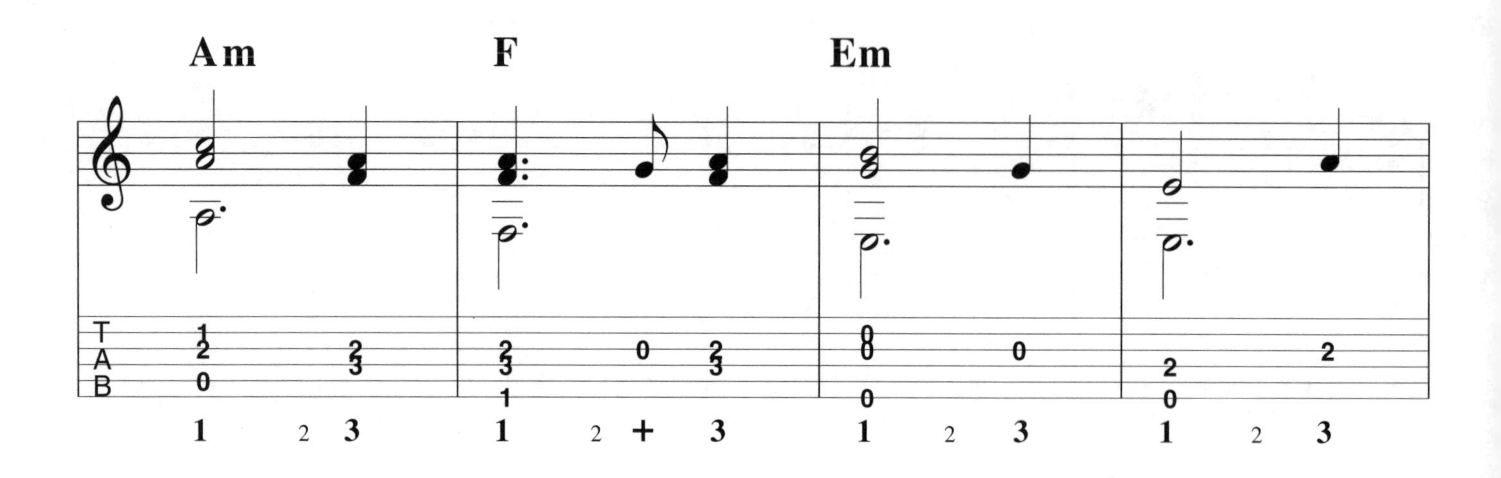
Am
F
Em
1 2 3 1 2 + 3 1 2 3 1 2 3

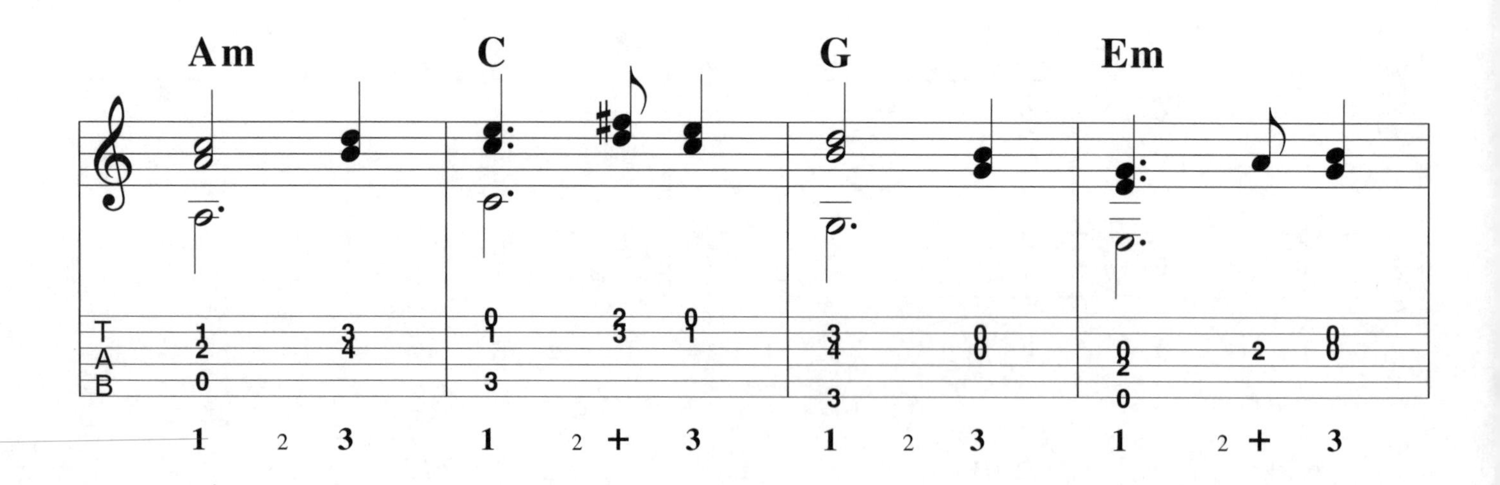
Am
C
G
Em
1 2 3 1 2 + 3 1 2 3 1 2 + 3

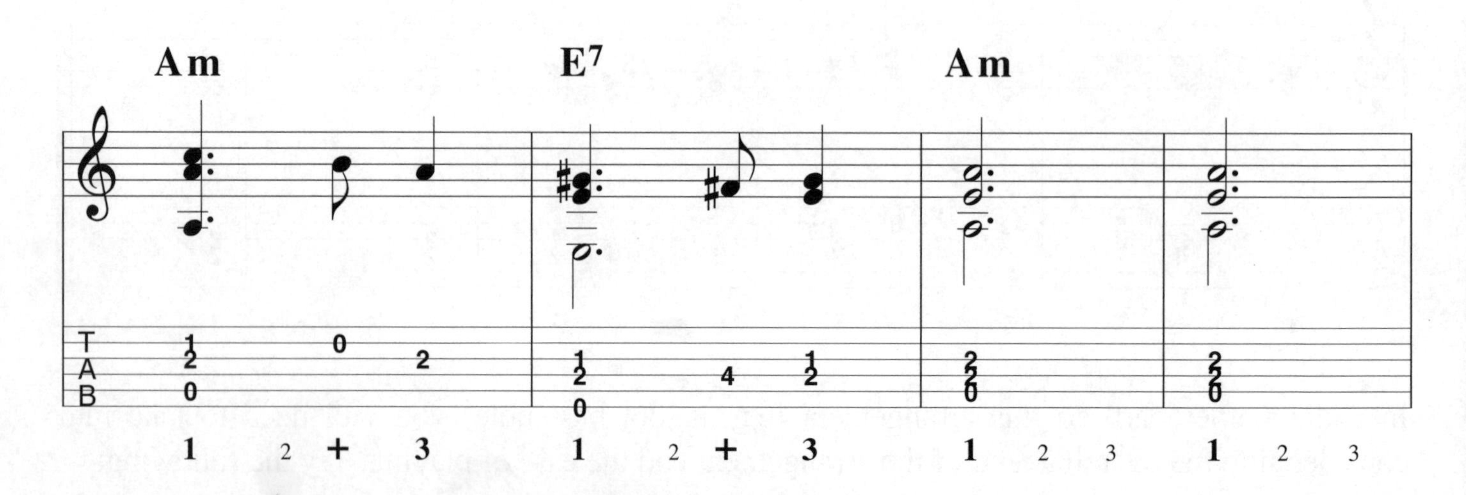
Am
E7
Am
1 2 + 3 1 2 + 3 1 2 3 1 2 3

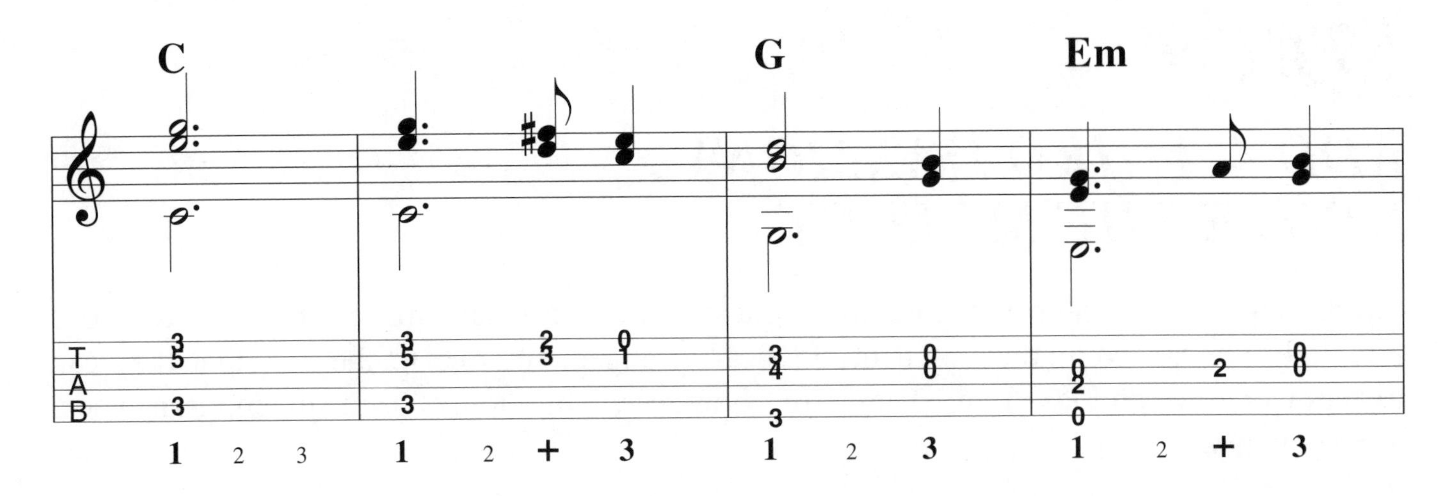
C
G
Em
T
A
B
1 2 3
1 2 + 3
1 2 3
1 2 + 3

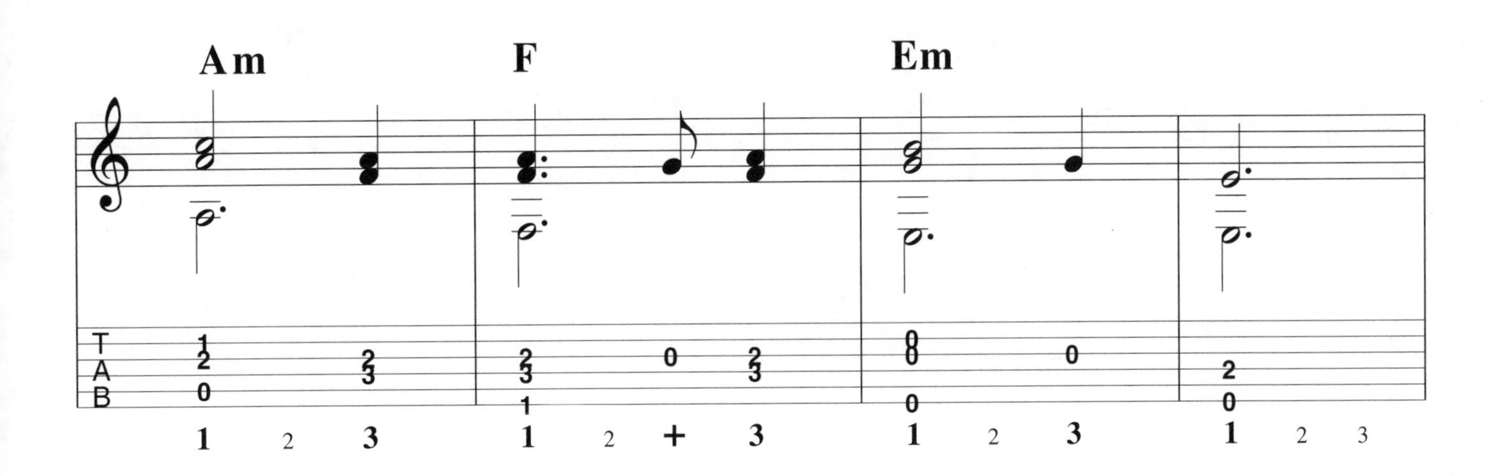
Am
F
Em
T
A
B
1 2 3
1 2 + 3
1 2 3
1 2 3

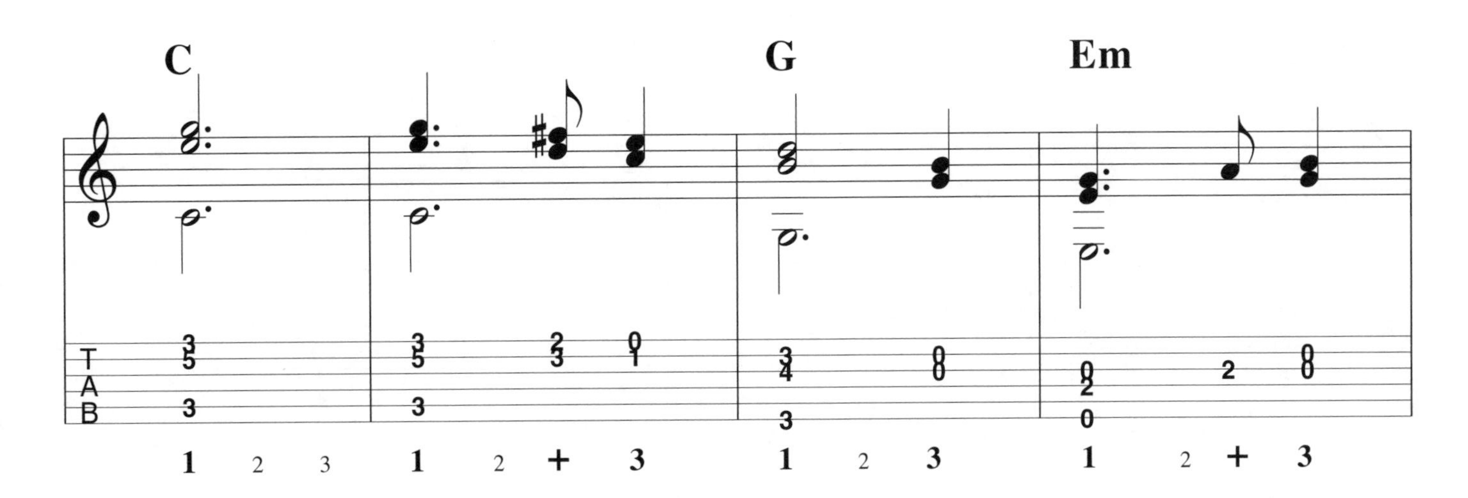
C
G
Em
T
A
B
1 2 3
1 2 + 3
1 2 3
1 2 + 3

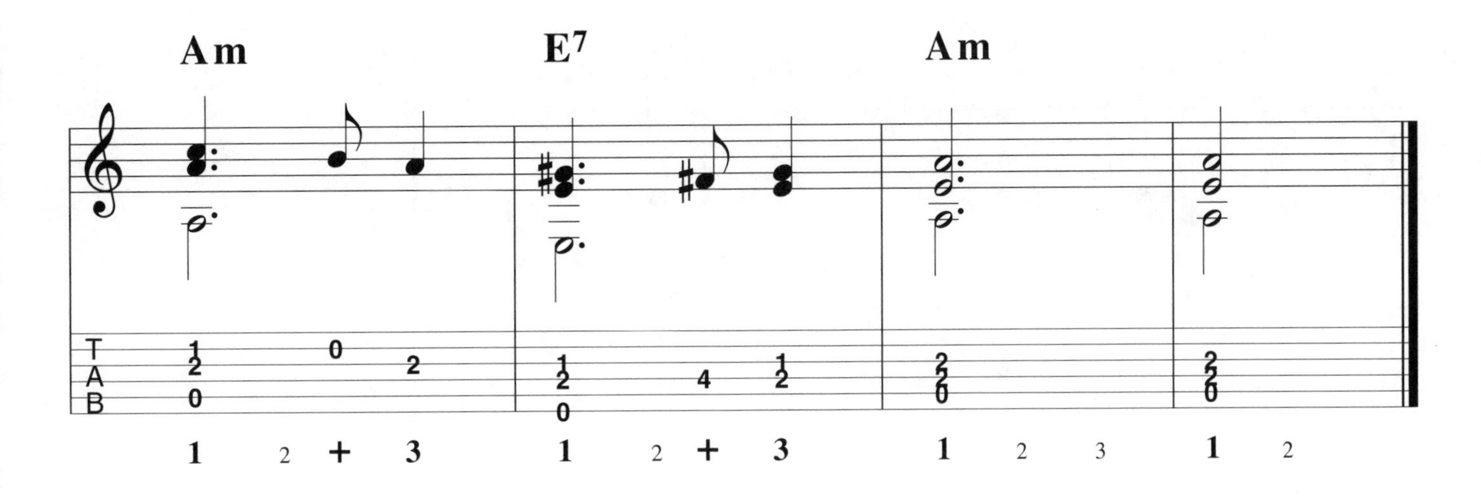
Am
E7
Am
T
A
B
1 2 + 3
1 2 + 3
1 2 3
1 2

STEP 9

ADD A THIRD HARMONY ABOVE THE MELODY

Thirds can be placed above the melody as illustrated in the arrangement below. Thirds above a melody are not commonly used in classical arrangements due to the fact that they can **overpower** the melody line. They are, however, commonly used in modern vocal arrangements.

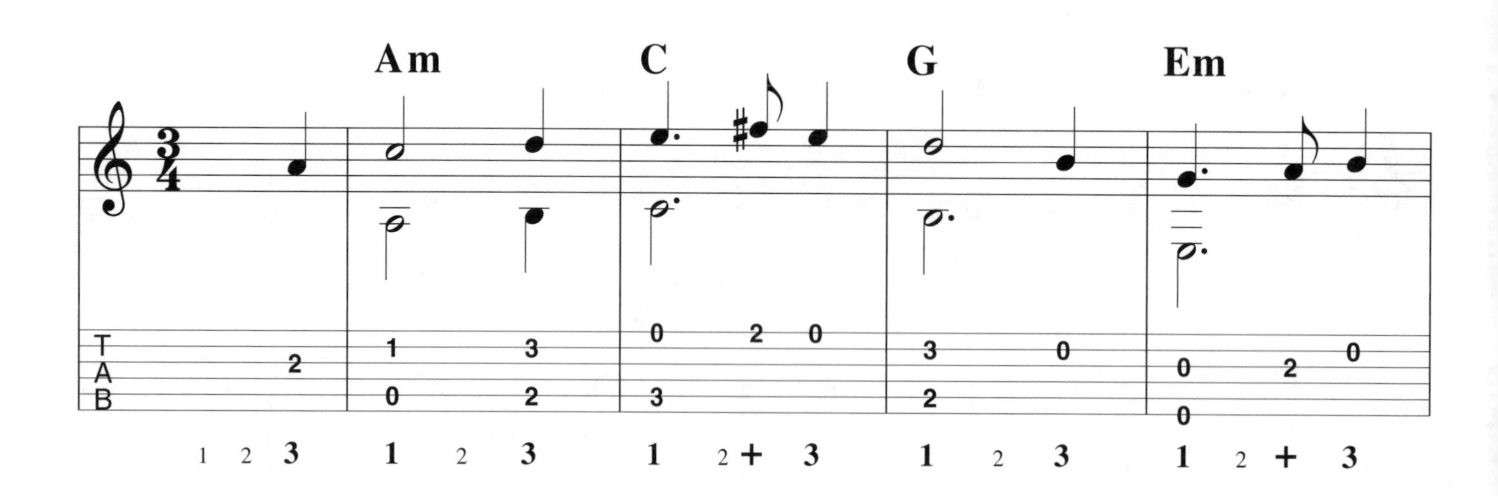

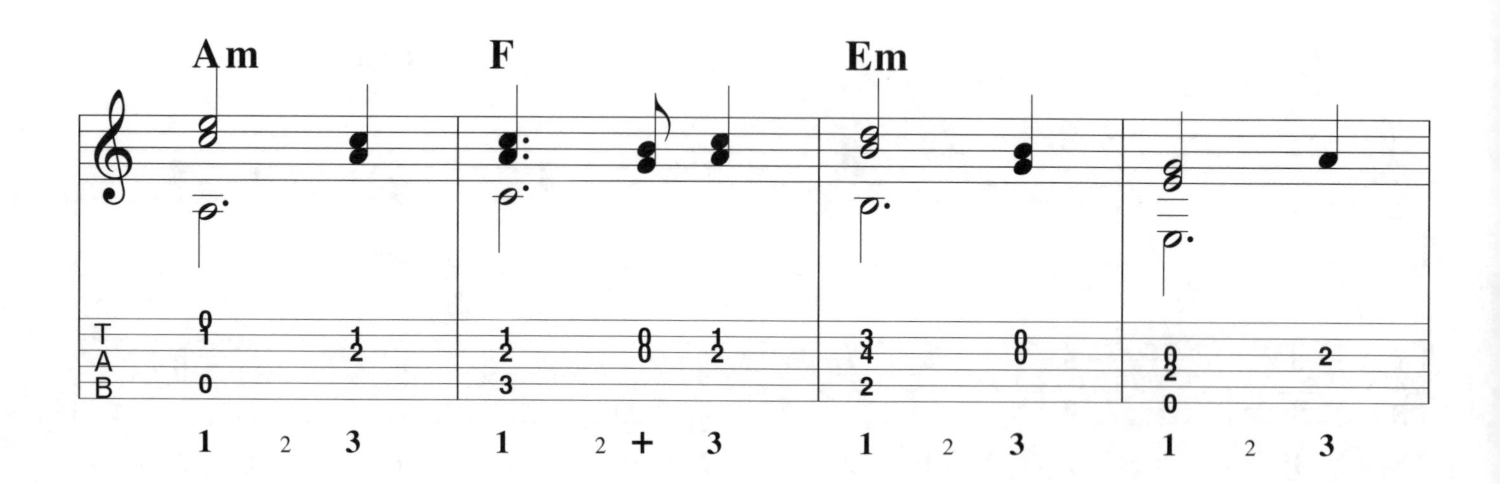

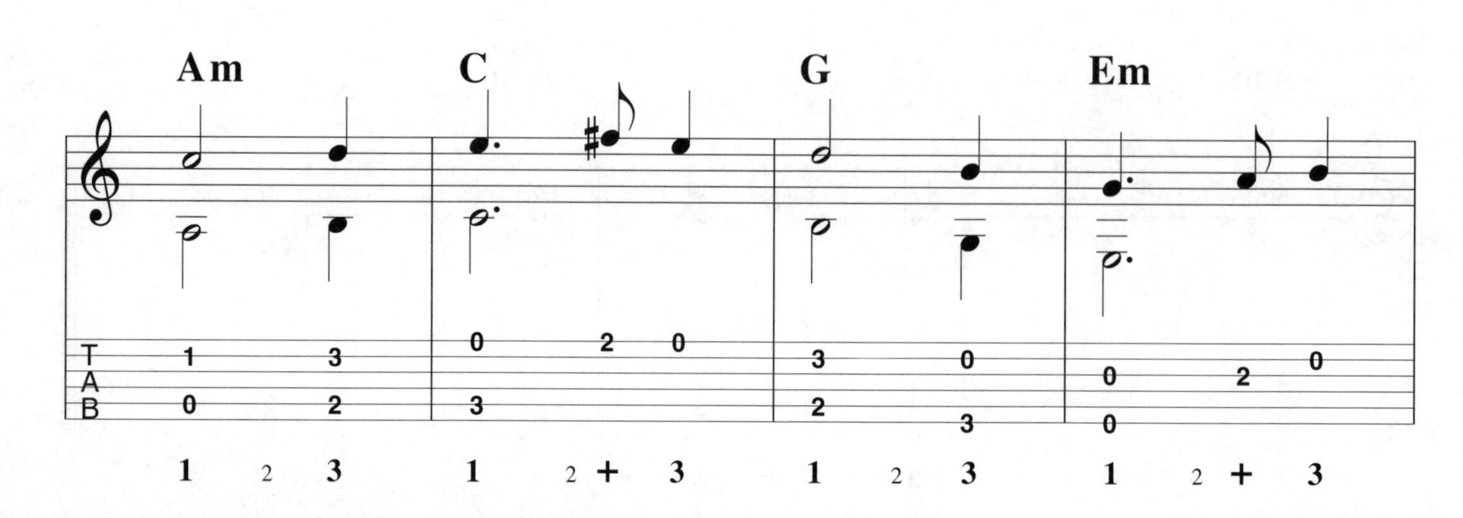

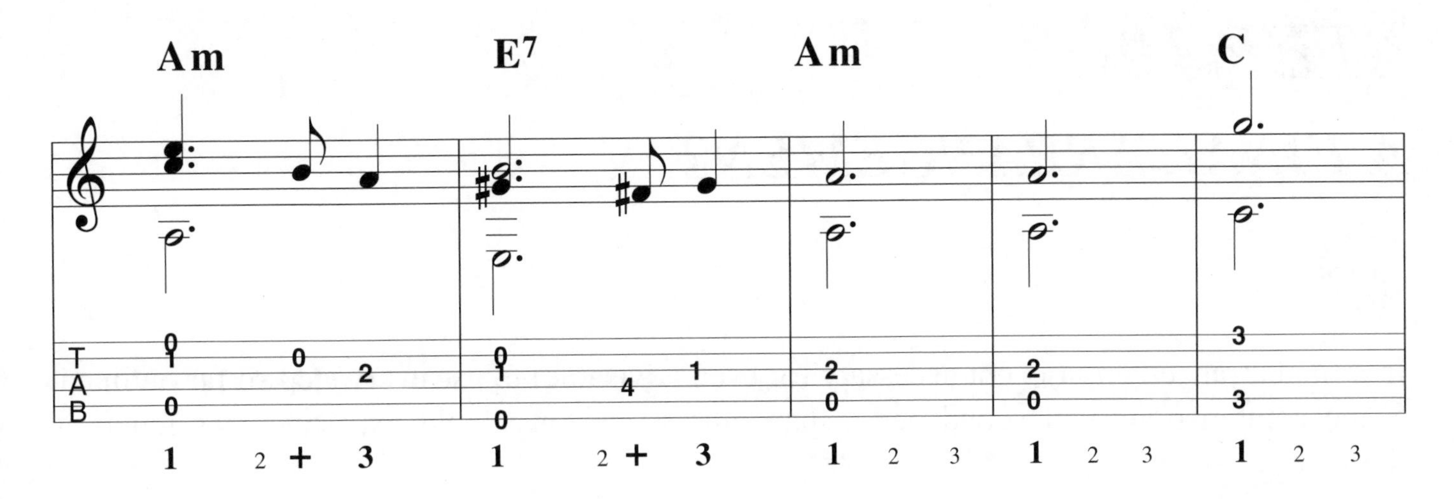
Am E7 Am C
1 2 + 3 1 2 + 3 1 2 3 1 2 3 1 2 3

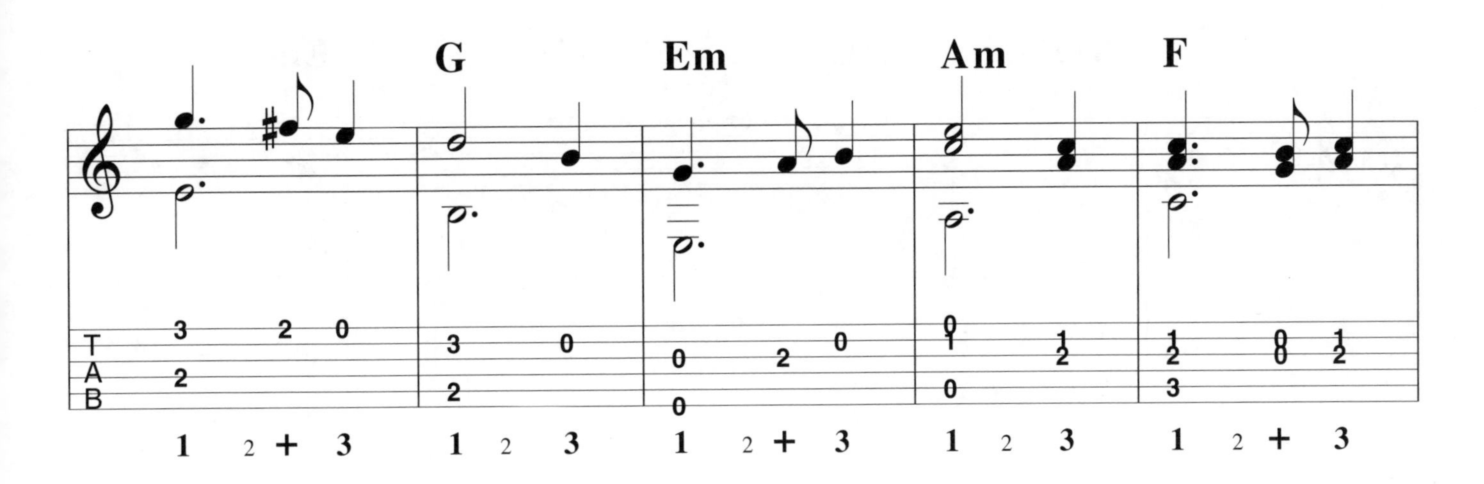
G Em Am F
1 2 + 3 1 2 3 1 2 + 3 1 2 3 1 2 + 3

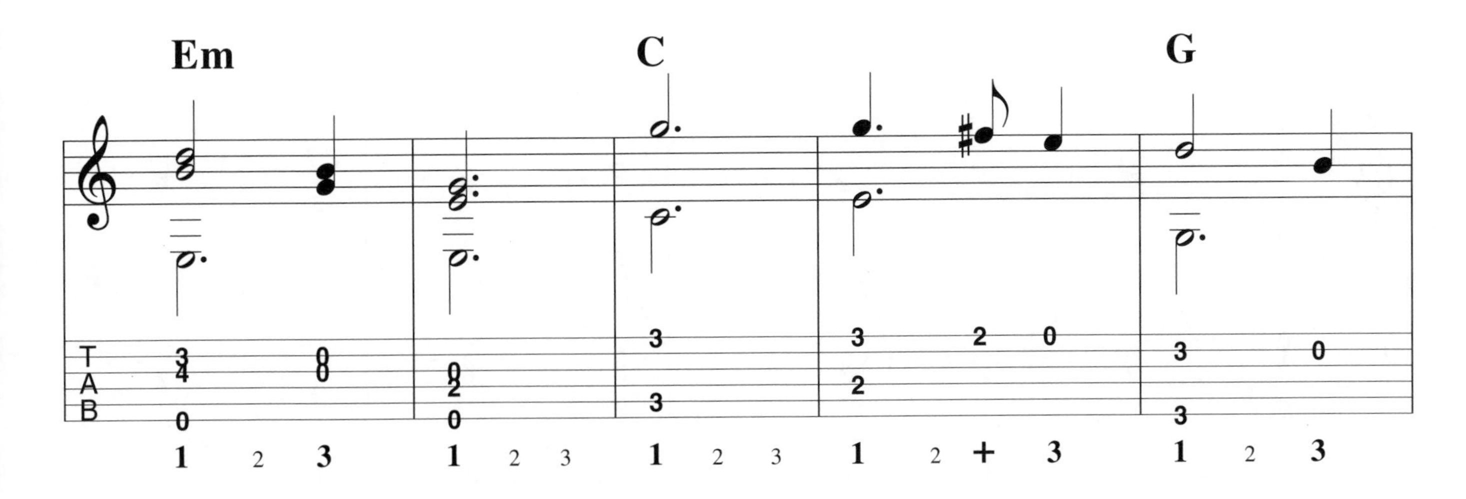
Em C G
1 2 3 1 2 3 1 2 3 1 2 + 3 1 2 3

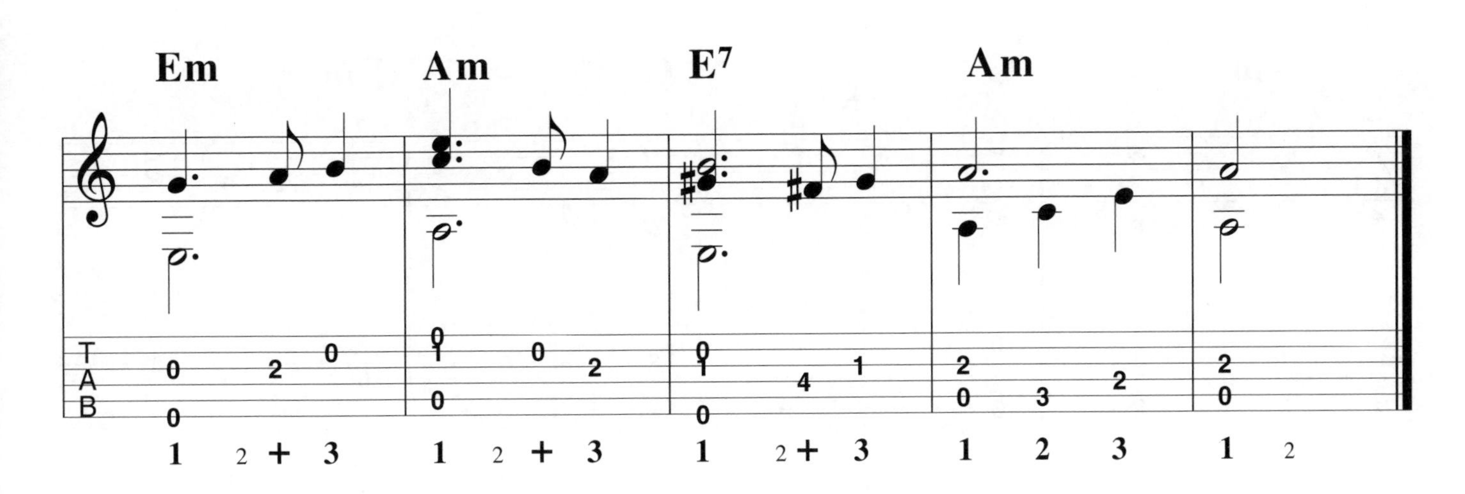
Em Am E7 Am
1 2 + 3 1 2 + 3 1 2 + 3 1 2 3 1 2

STEP 10

A FINAL ARRANGEMENT

In a final arrangement it is not necessary (or even advisable) to use every step so far outlined. Some combinations will sound better than others, so you should experiment as much as possible.

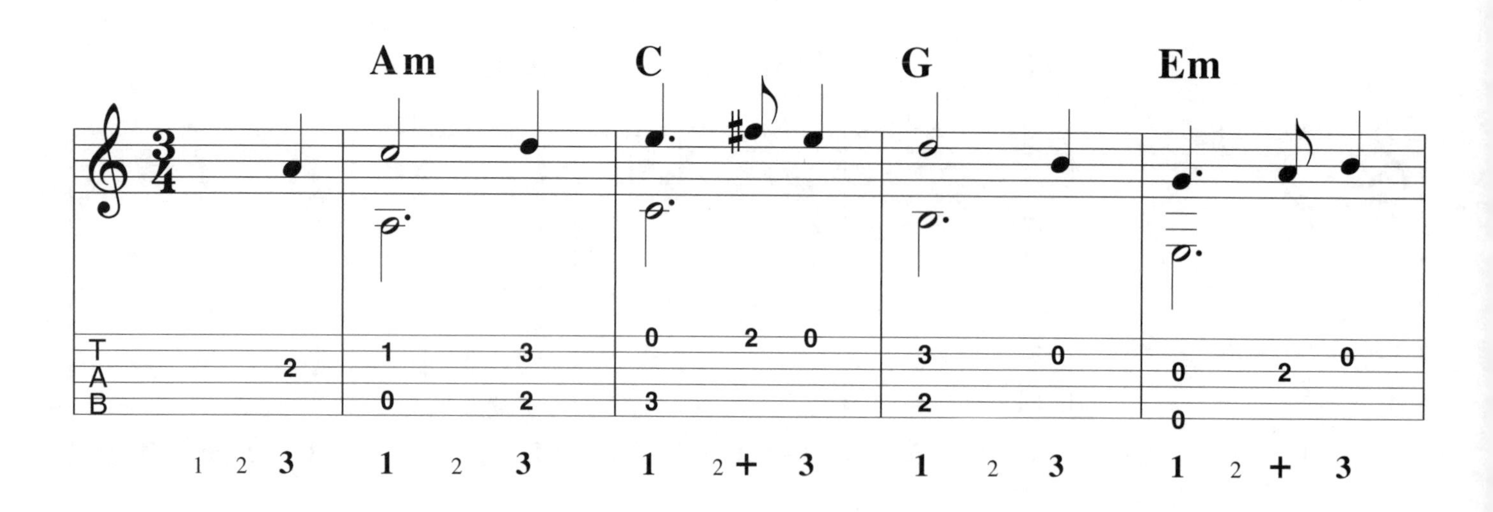

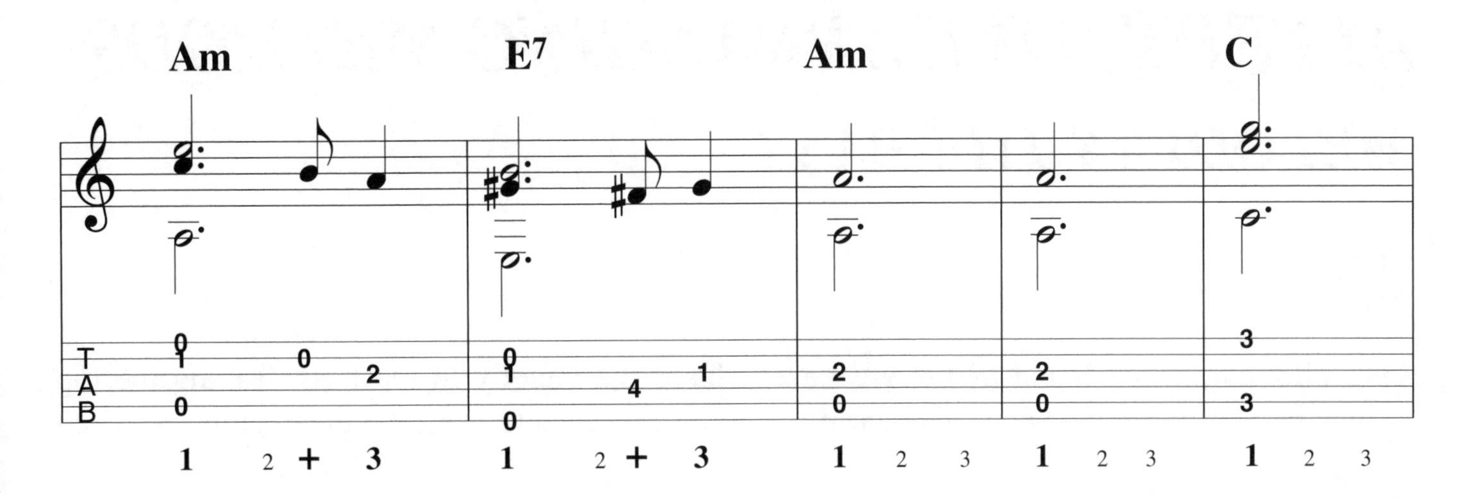
Am
E7
Am
C
T
A
B
1 2 + 3 1 2 + 3 1 2 3 1 2 3 1 2 3

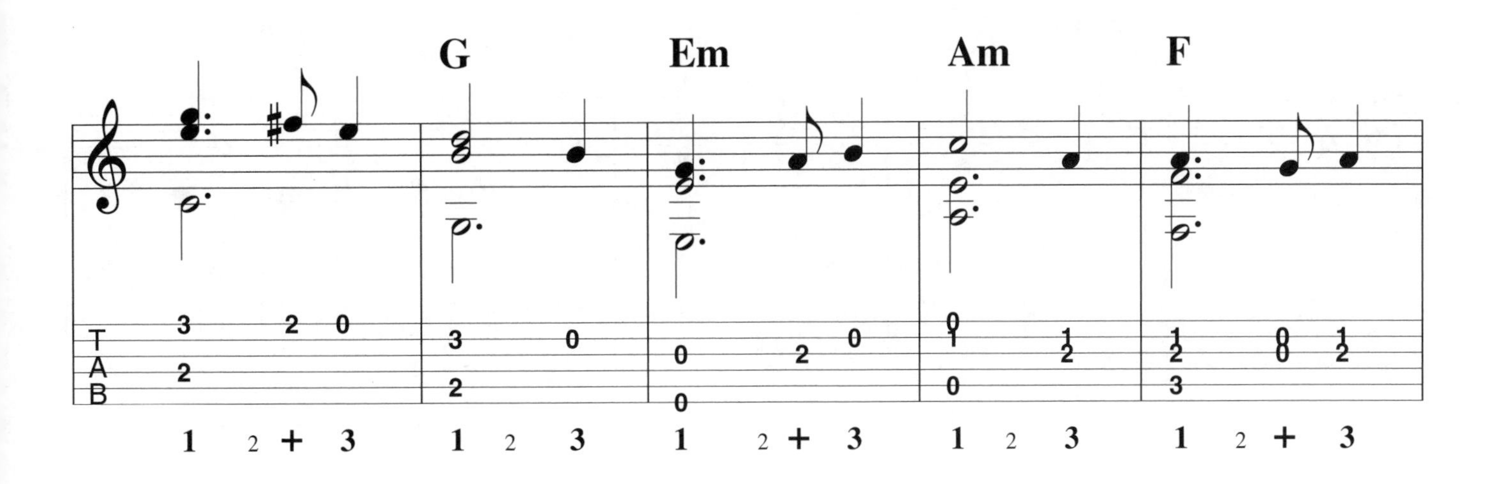
G
Em
Am
F
T
A
B
1 2 + 3 1 2 3 1 2 + 3 1 2 3 1 2 + 3

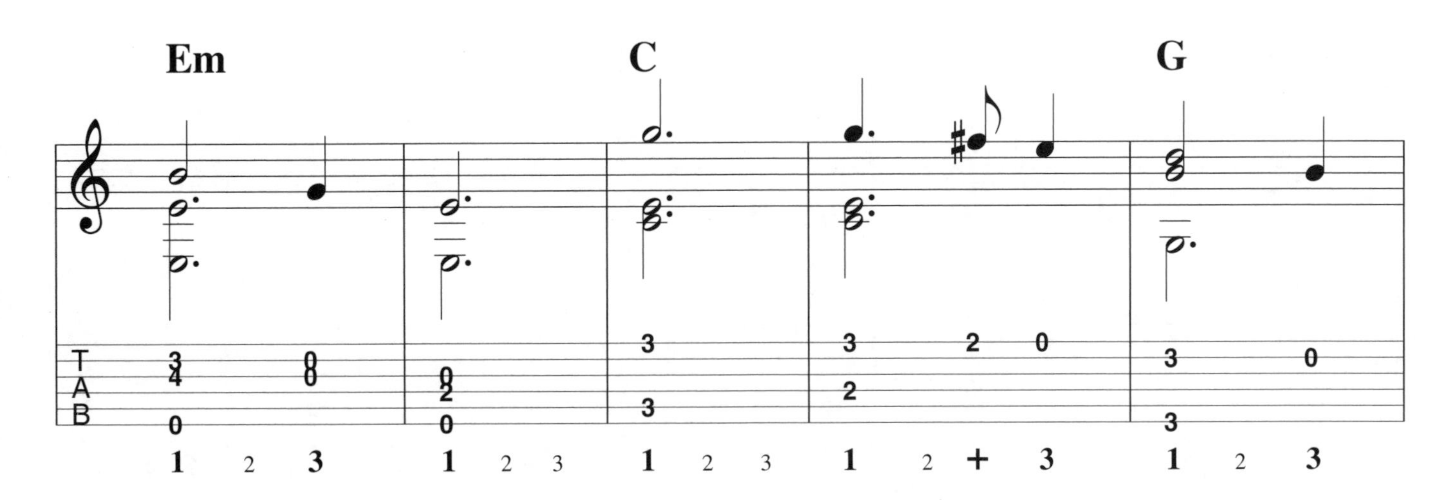
Em
C
G
T
A
B
1 2 3 1 2 3 1 2 3 1 2 + 3 1 2 3

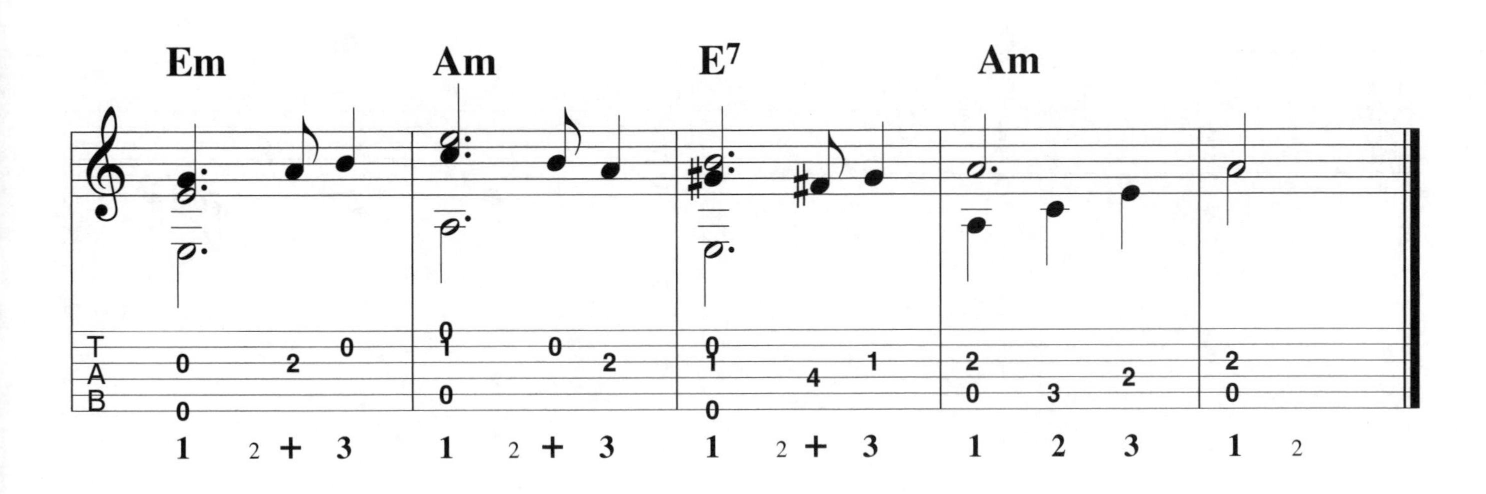
Em
Am
E7
Am
T
A
B
1 2 + 3 1 2 + 3 1 2 + 3 1 2 3 1 2

ALTERNATIVE ARRANGING METHODS

MELODY IN THE BASS

The following arrangement of **Greensleeves** places the melody in the bass, leaving the top strings free for harmony notes. The harmony notes are selected from the given chord for each bar.

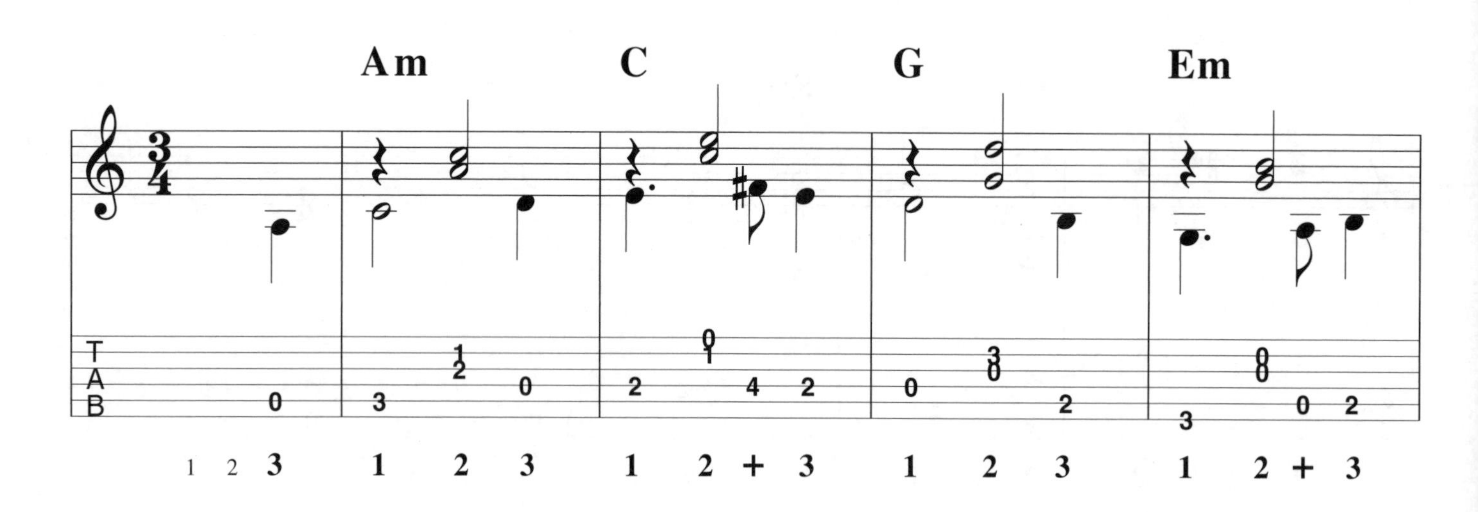

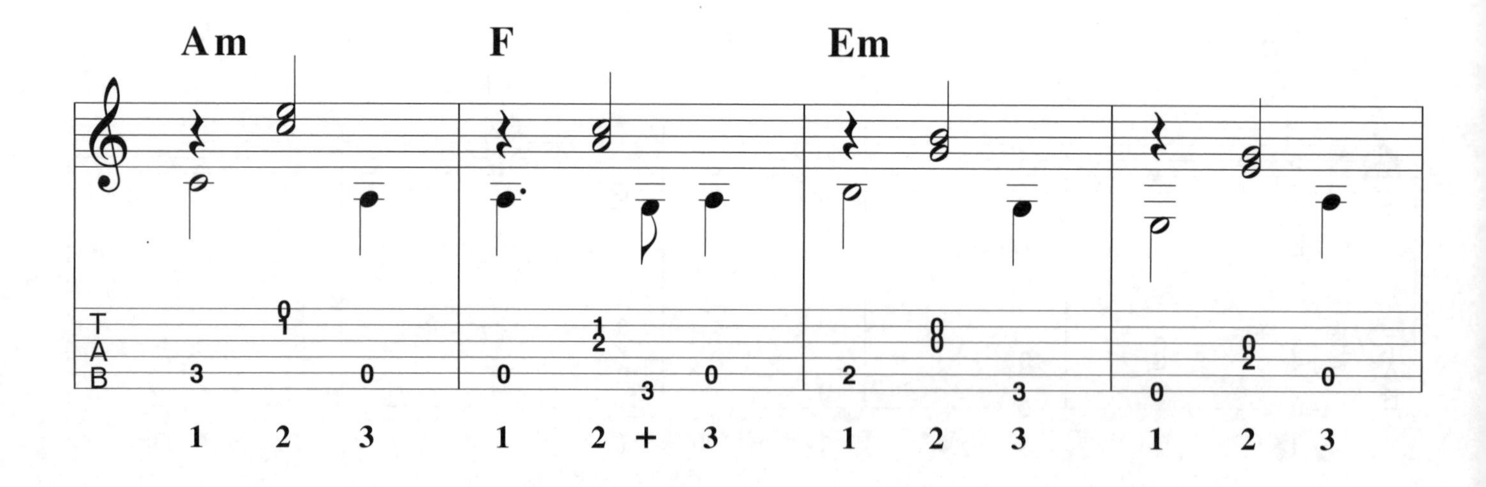

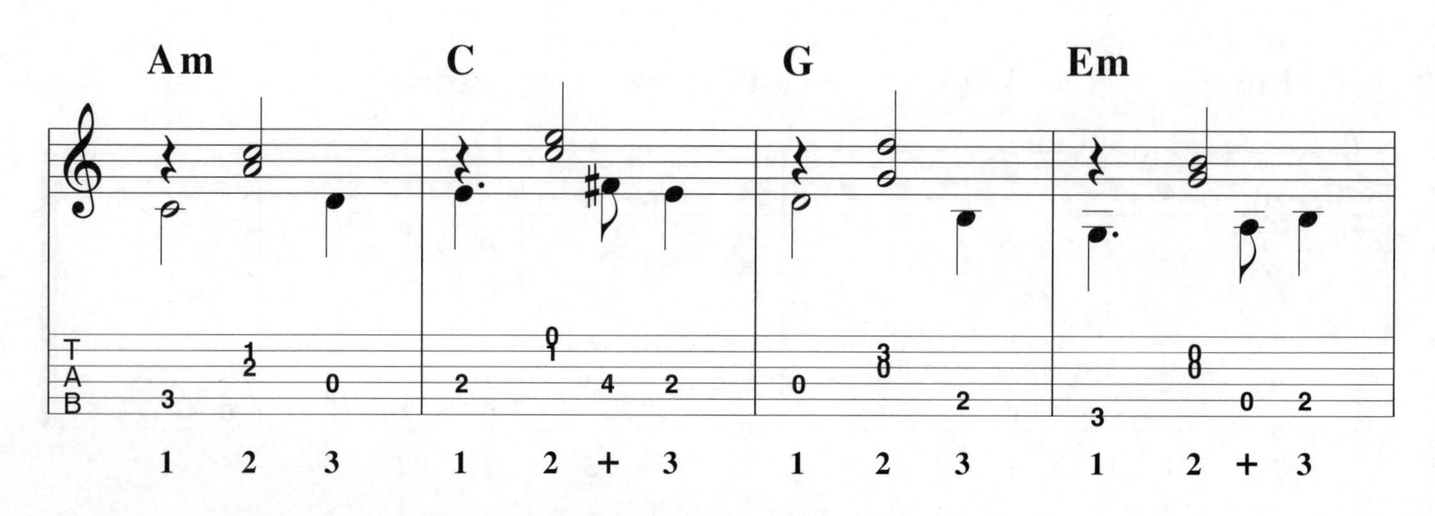

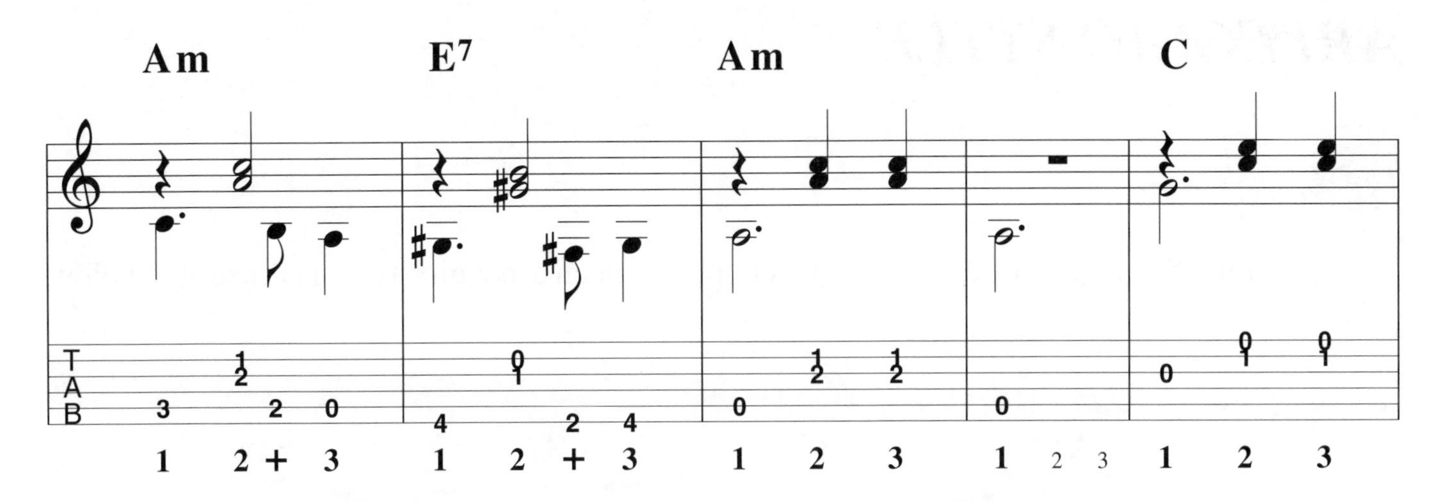
Am
E7
Am
C
1 2 + 3
1 2 + 3
1 2 3
1 2 3
1 2 3

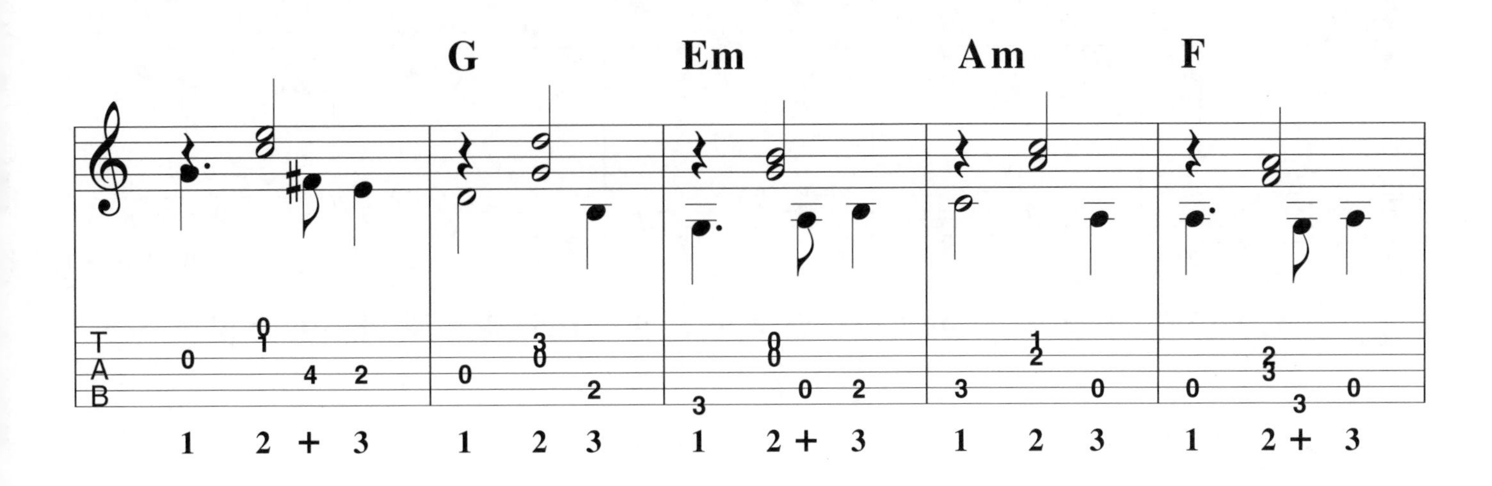
G
Em
Am
F
1 2 + 3
1 2 3
1 2 + 3
1 2 3
1 2 + 3

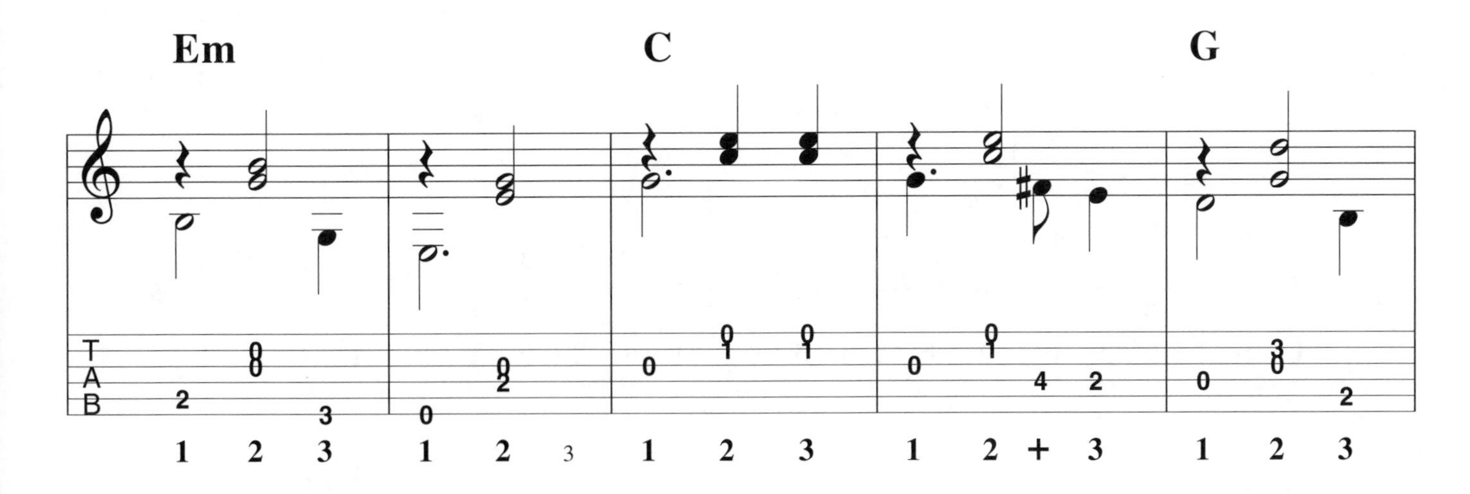
Em
C
G
1 2 3
1 2 3
1 2 3
1 2 + 3
1 2 3

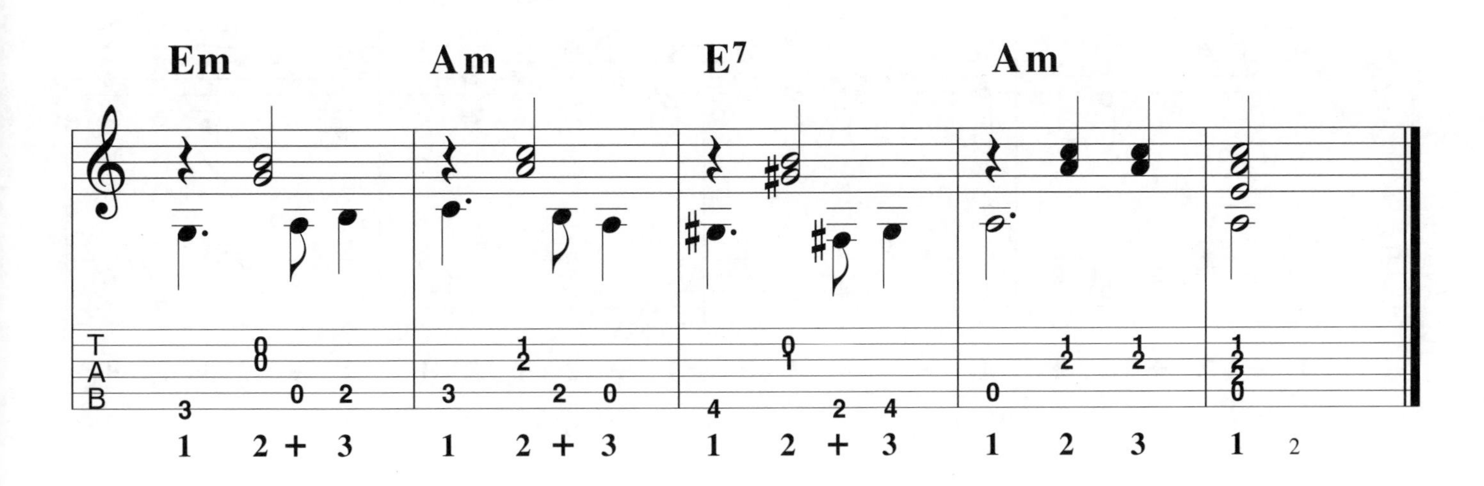
Em
Am
E7
Am
1 2 + 3
1 2 + 3
1 2 + 3
1 2 3
1 2

ARPEGGIO STYLE

An extension of the previous arrangement is to play it in an arpeggio style, as illustrated below.

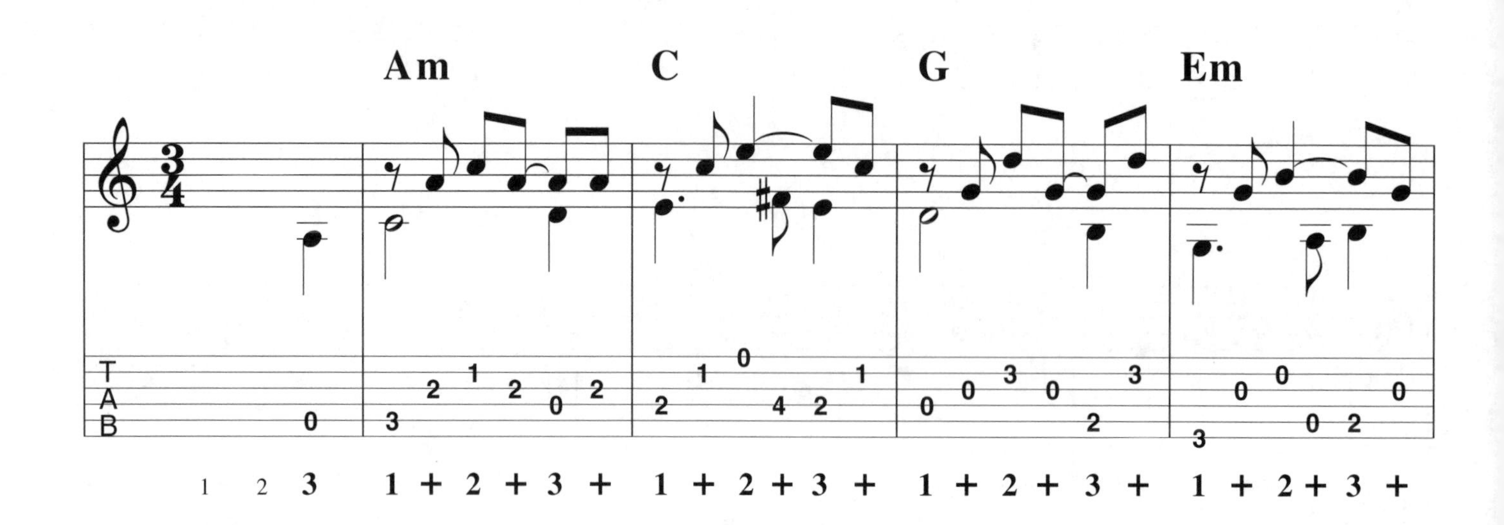

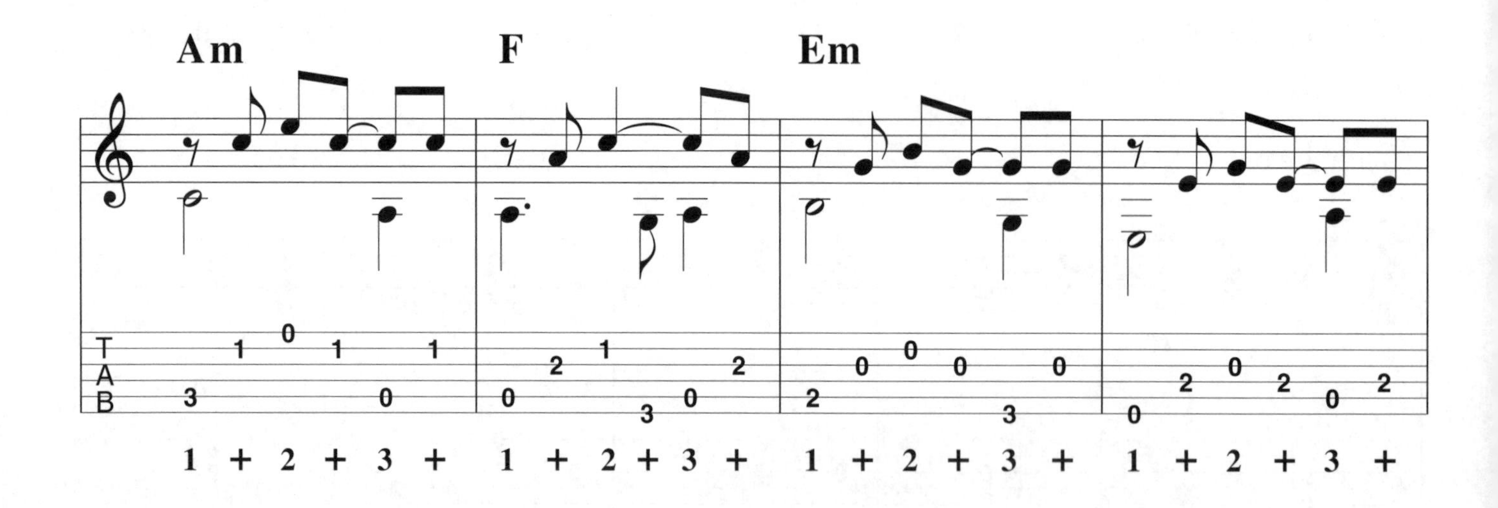

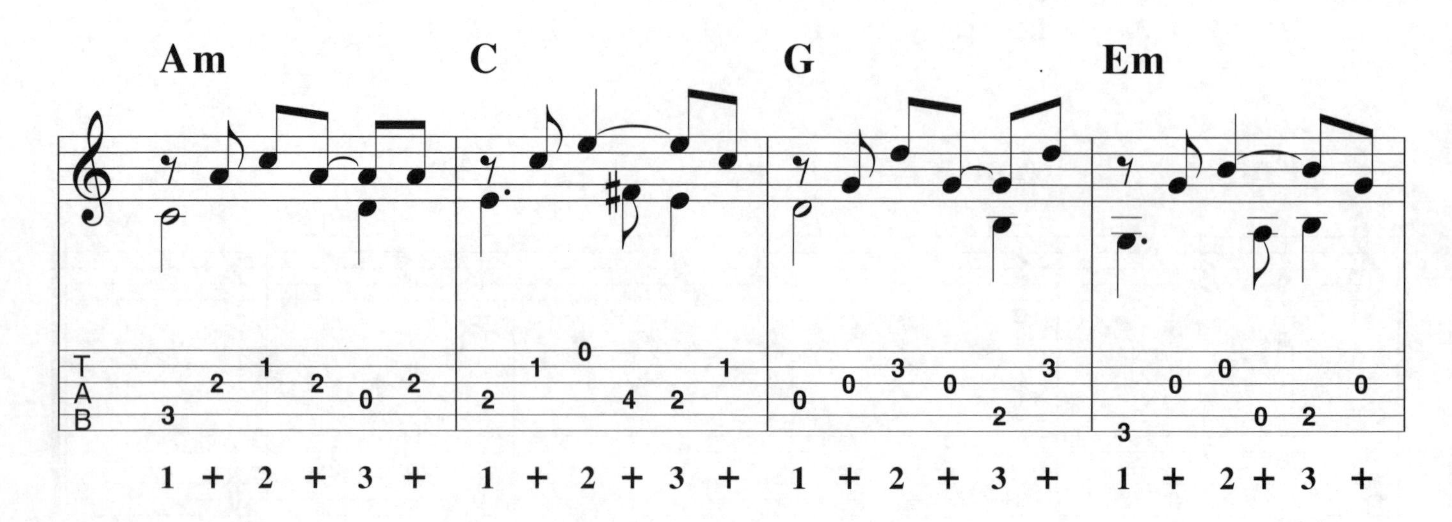

Am E7 Am C
T
A
B
1 + 2 + 3 + 1 + 2 + 3 + 1 + 2 + 3 + 1 2 3 1 + 2 + 3 +

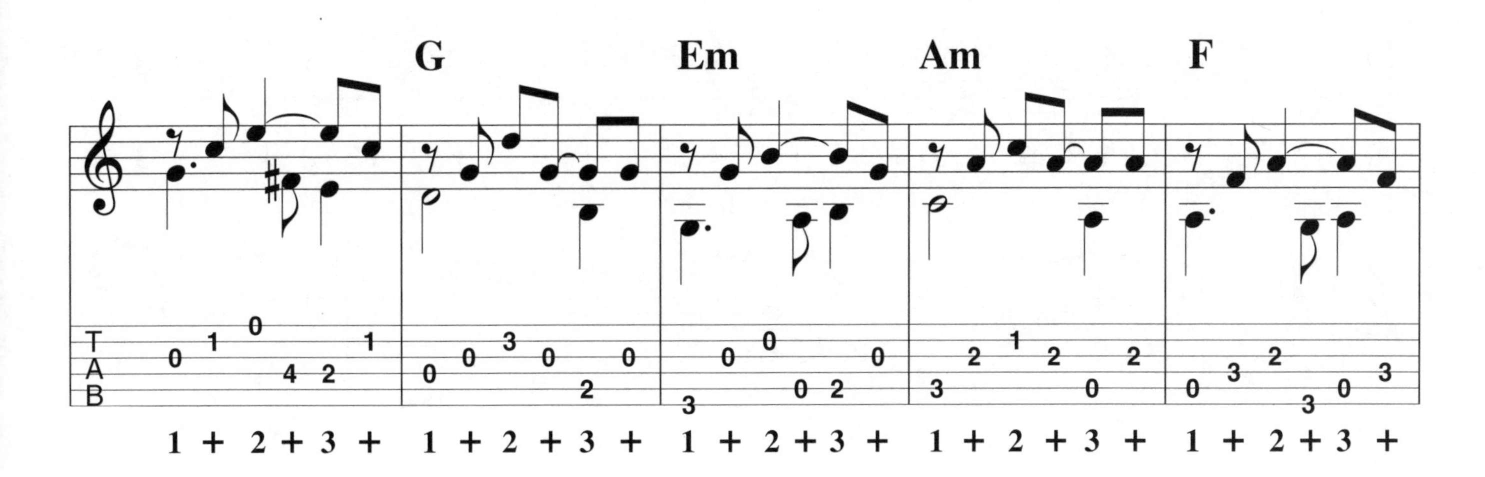
G Em Am F
T
A
B
1 + 2 + 3 + 1 + 2 + 3 + 1 + 2 + 3 + 1 + 2 + 3 + 1 + 2 + 3 +

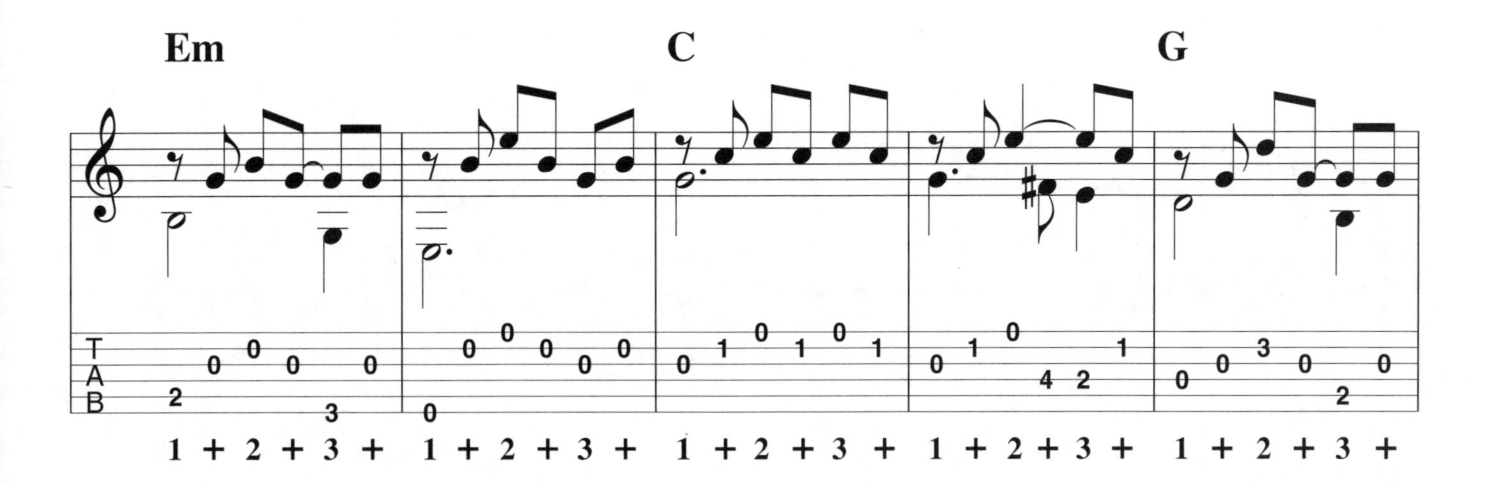
Em C G
T
A
B
1 + 2 + 3 + 1 + 2 + 3 + 1 + 2 + 3 + 1 + 2 + 3 + 1 + 2 + 3 +

Em Am E7 Am
T
A
B
1 + 2 + 3 + 1 + 2 + 3 + 1 + 2 + 3 + 1 + 2 + 3 + 1 2

This arpeggio style can also be applied to arrangements with the melody as the top voice. Try the following arrangement of **Amazing Grace**.

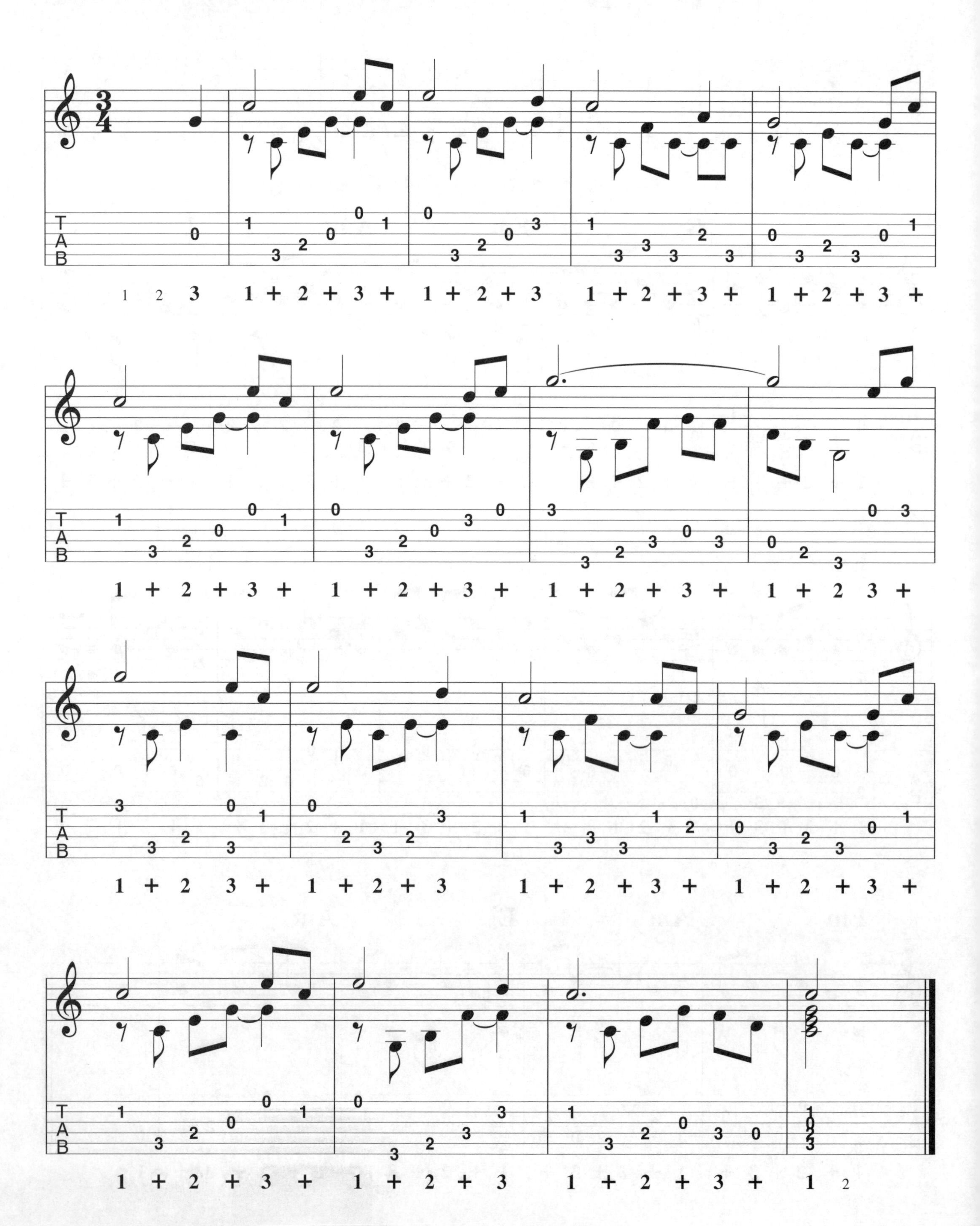

ALTERNATING BASS STYLES ($\frac{4}{4}$ TIME)

The following arrangements of a **turnaround** and a **12 bar blues** illustrate the use of an alternating bass line to accompany a melody. A bass note is played on every beat and alternates between selected chord notes.

This arrangement is a further example of two part writing with the melody notes having stems pointing upwards.

The sixteenth notes, as introduced in **Waltzing Matilda** (page 44) involved the count of '1 e and a'.

NOTE: ♩ = ♫ = ♬

COUNTS: **1** **1 +** **1 e + a**

When a dotted eighth note and sixteenth note are played together the count is as such:

1 e + **a** **1** e + **a**

This count is illustrated in the Tablature below.

TURNAROUND

* See Appendix Four.

12 BAR BLUES

G
1 2 3 + 4 1 2 3 + 4 1 2 3 + 4
C
1 2 3 4 1 2 3 4 e + a 1 2 3 4
G
D
1 2 3 4 e + a 1 2 3 + 4 + 1 2 e + a 3 e + a 4
C
G
1 2 e + a 3 4 1 2 e + a 3 e + a 4 e + a 1 2 3 4

MELODY WITH CLAWHAMMER ACCOMPANIMENT

The following arrangement uses the clawhammer fingerpicking style to accompany a melody.

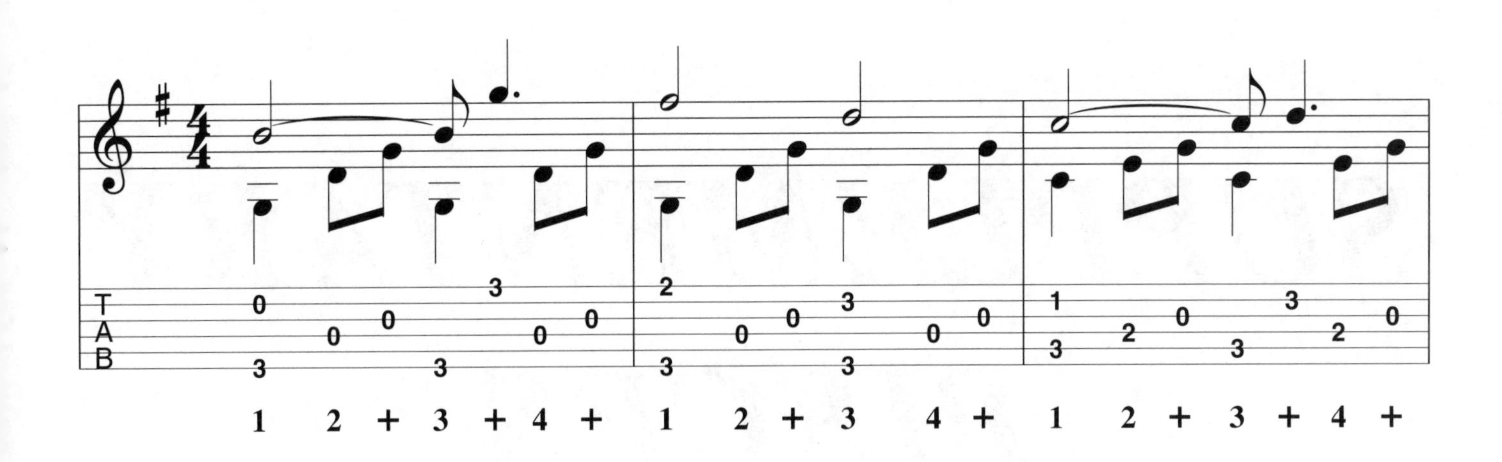

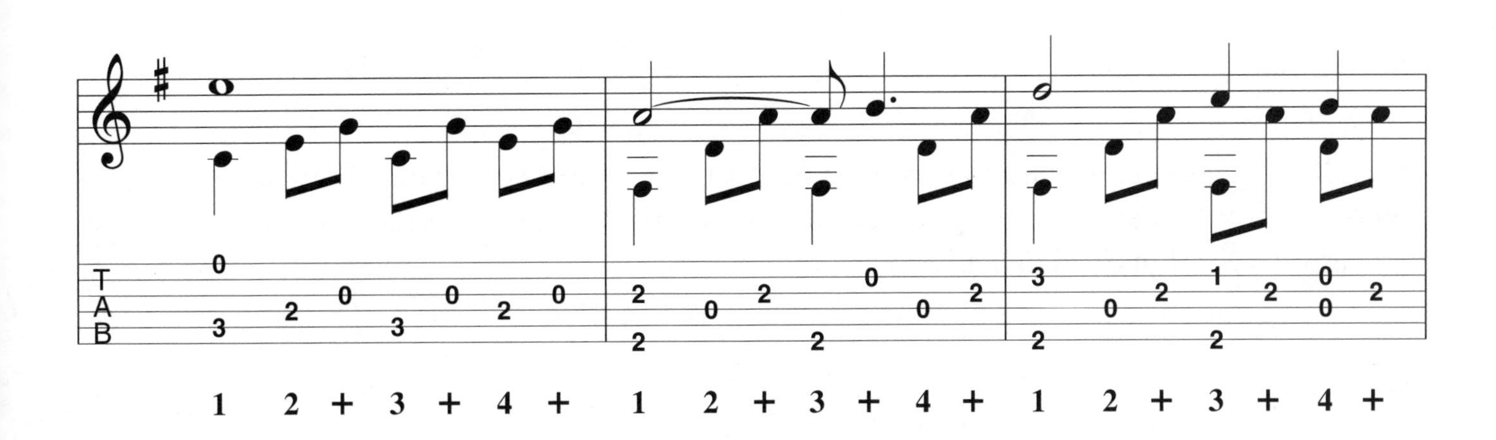

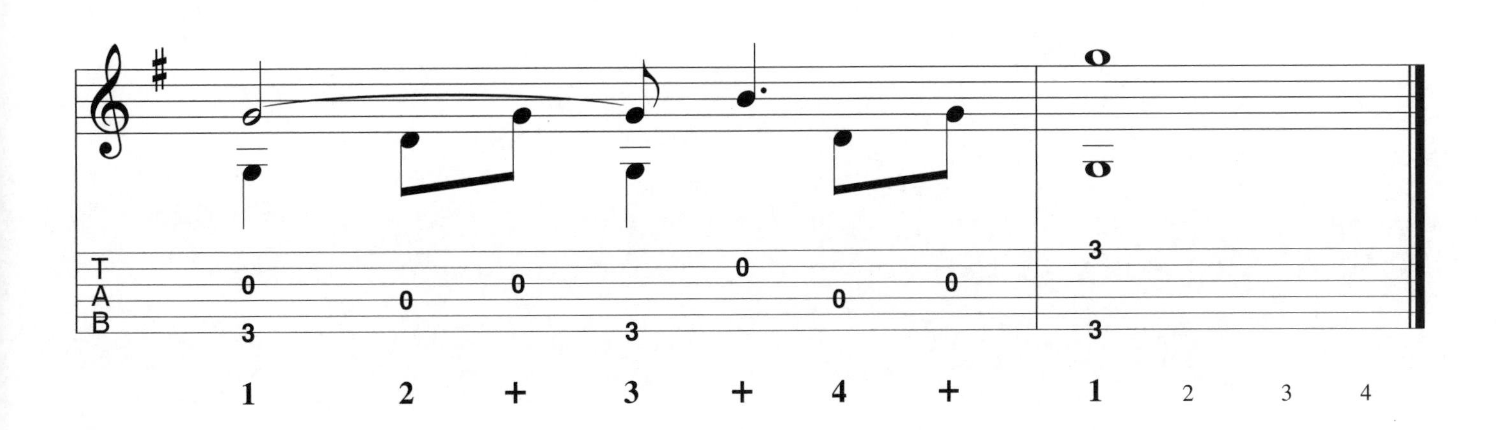

SUPPLEMENTARY PIECES

The following supplementary pieces have been divided into two groups. The first group uses predominantly set pattern picking. In the second group, the music is arranged in two (or more) parts as discussed in Section Three.

GROUP ONE

Estudio

Playing Notes: This piece uses **Pattern 1 (p i m i)**. In bar 3 the first note (**B**) is played on the third string (4th fret) indicated by ③. The fingering for notes is indicated by the uncircled numbers next to the note. **D.C. al Fine** at the end of the piece indicates a repeat from the beginning to the word **Fine**.

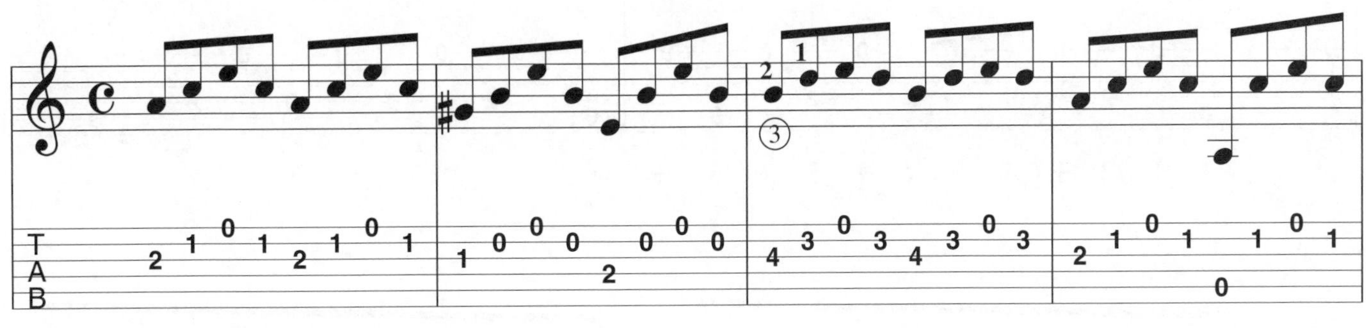

1 + 2 + 3 + 4 + etc.

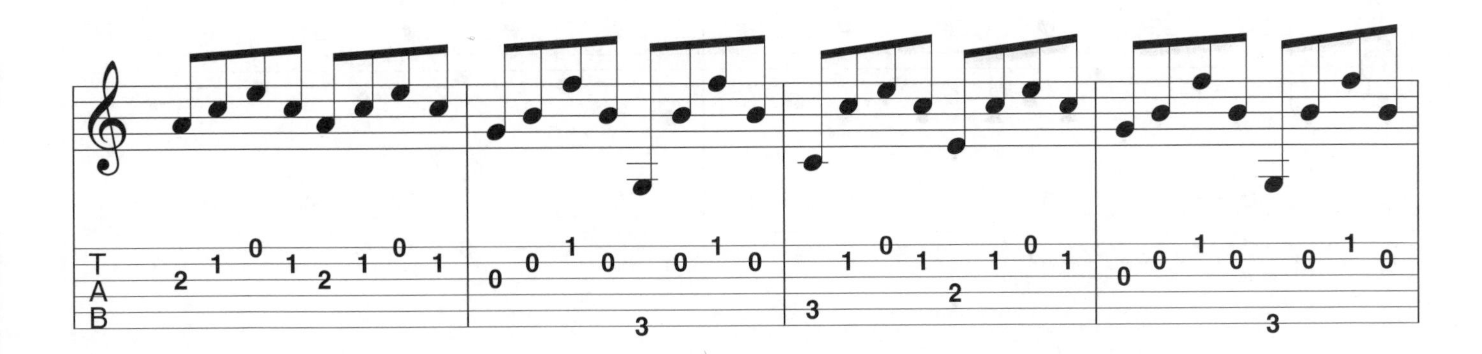

1 + 2 + 3 4

Spanish Study

Playing Notes: The pattern used in this piece is **p m p m**. The time signature 6/4 indicates two dotted half note beats per bar. This is an example of compound time.

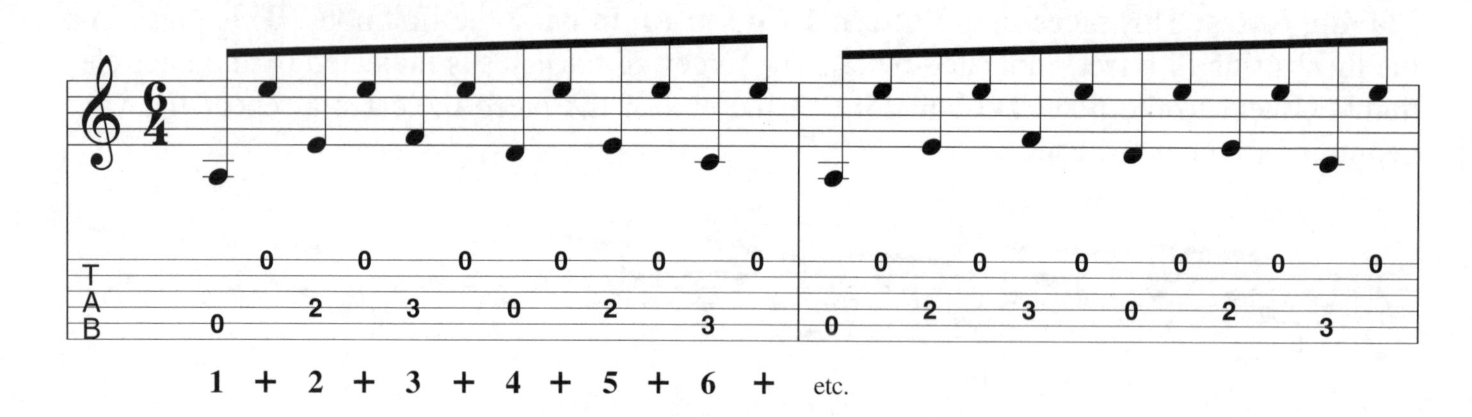

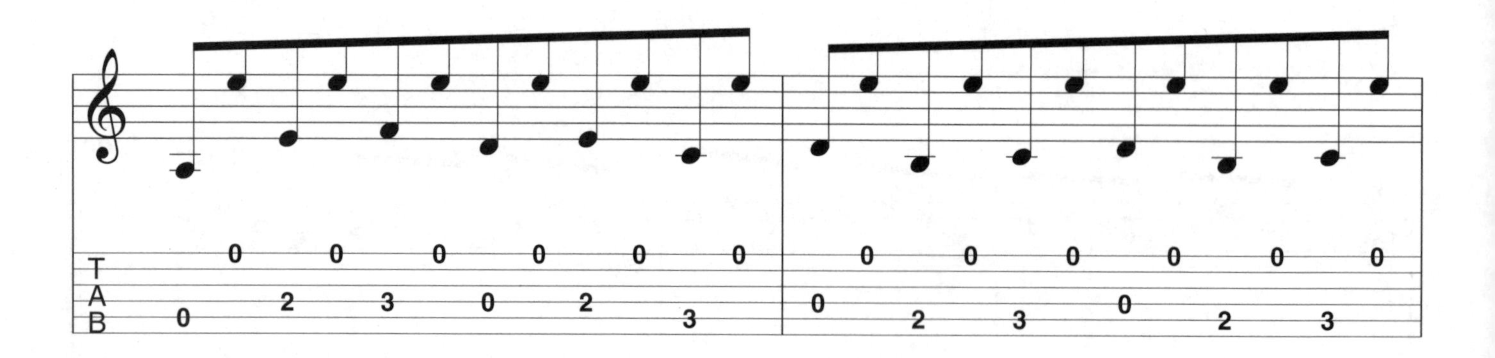

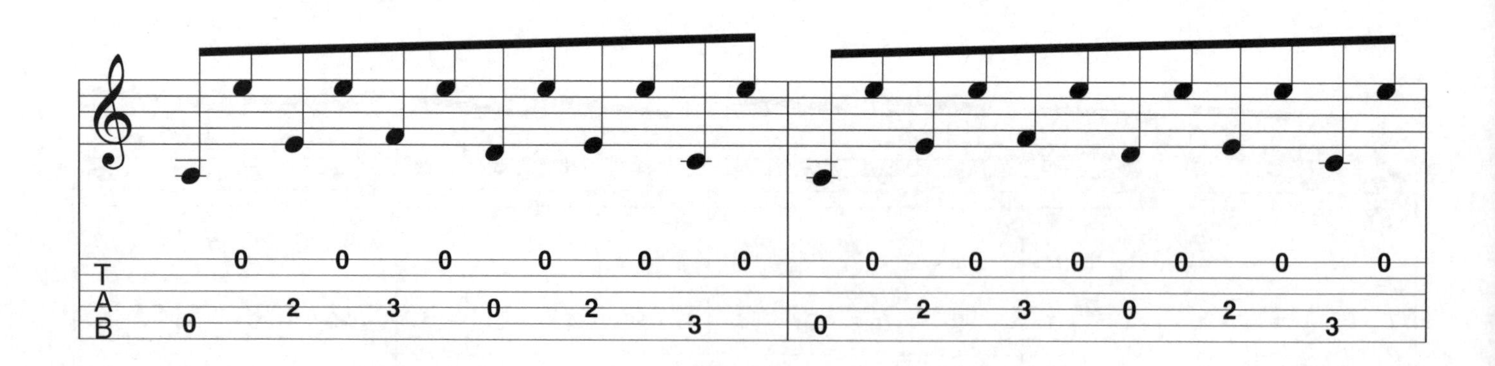

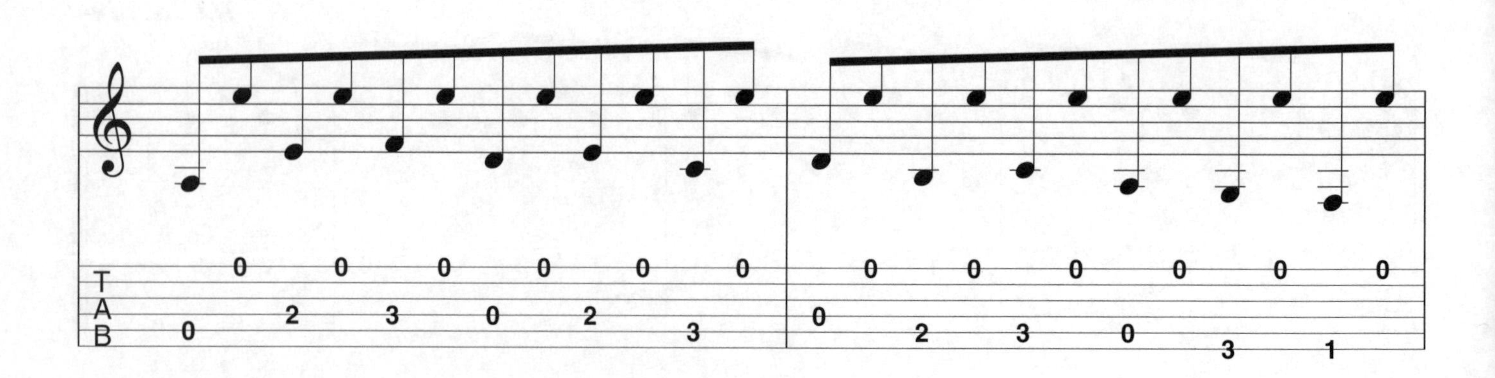

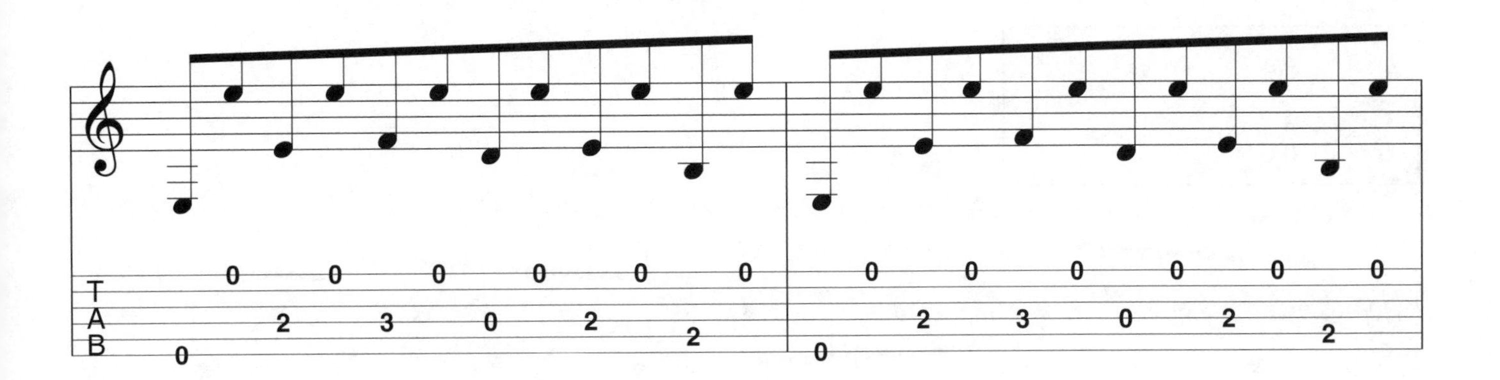

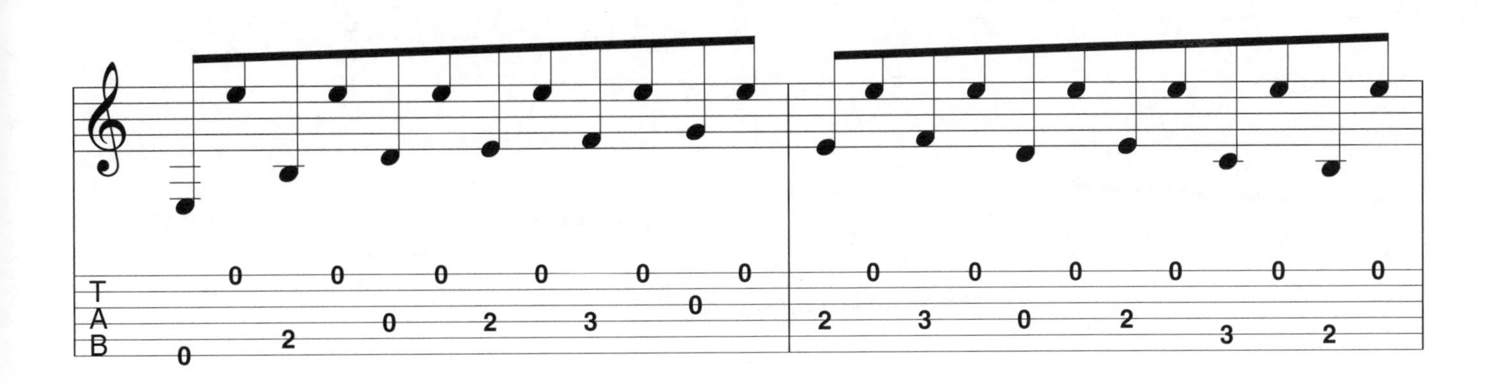

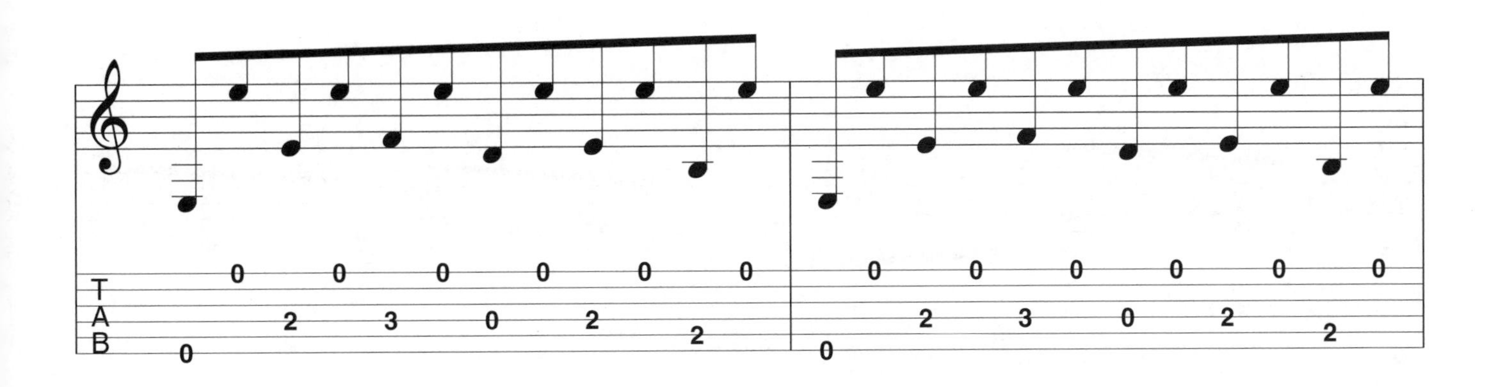

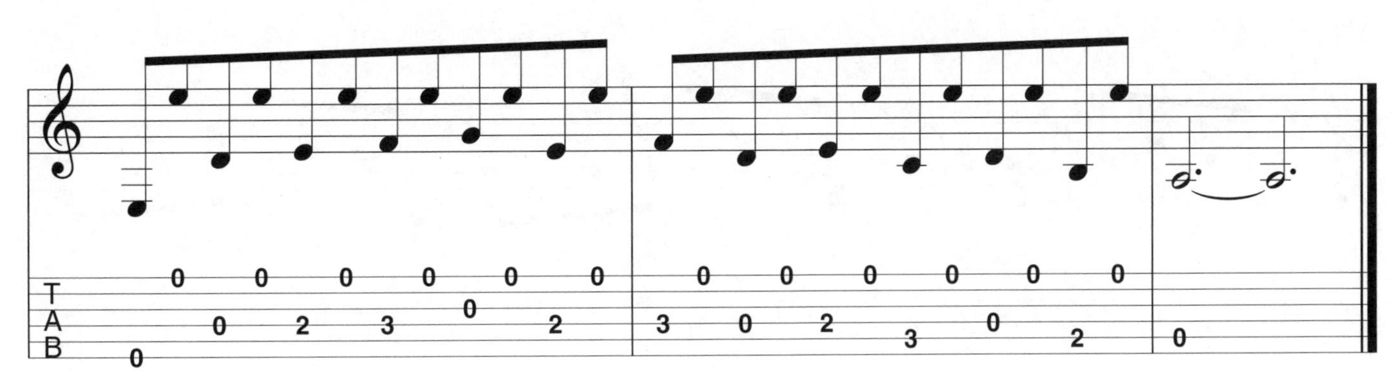

Allegro

Playing Notes: This piece uses three different picking patterns:

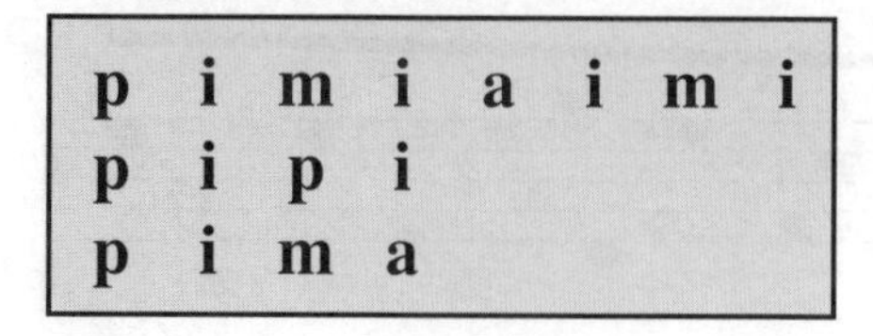

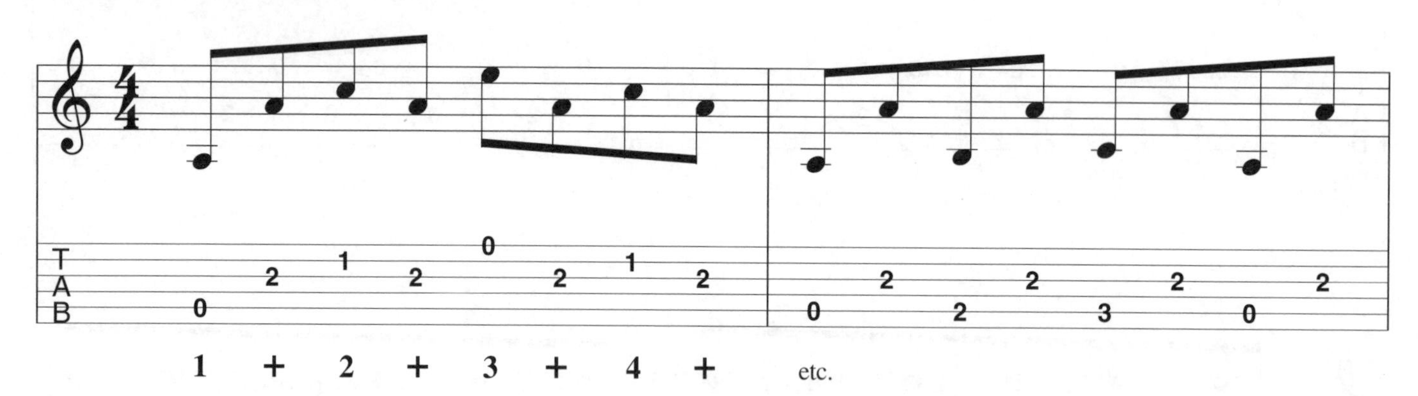

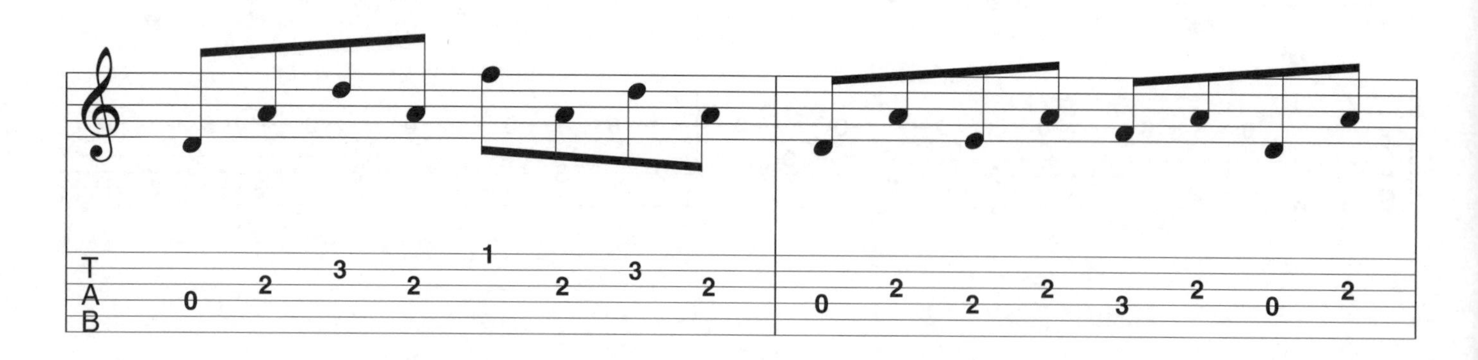

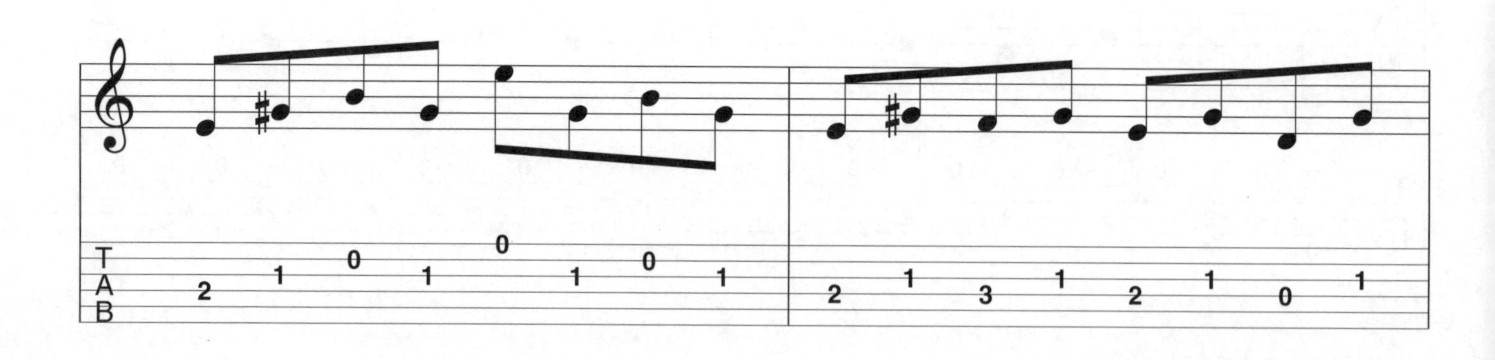

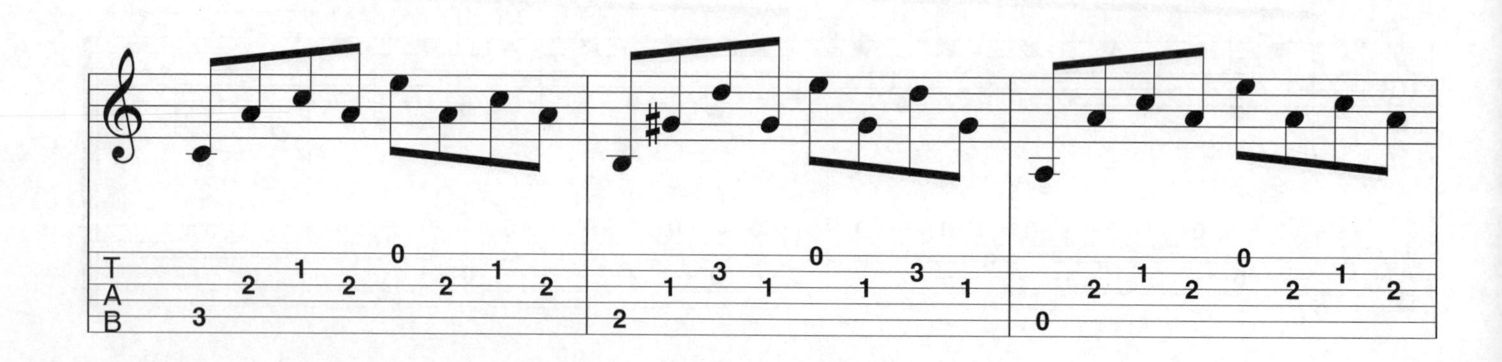

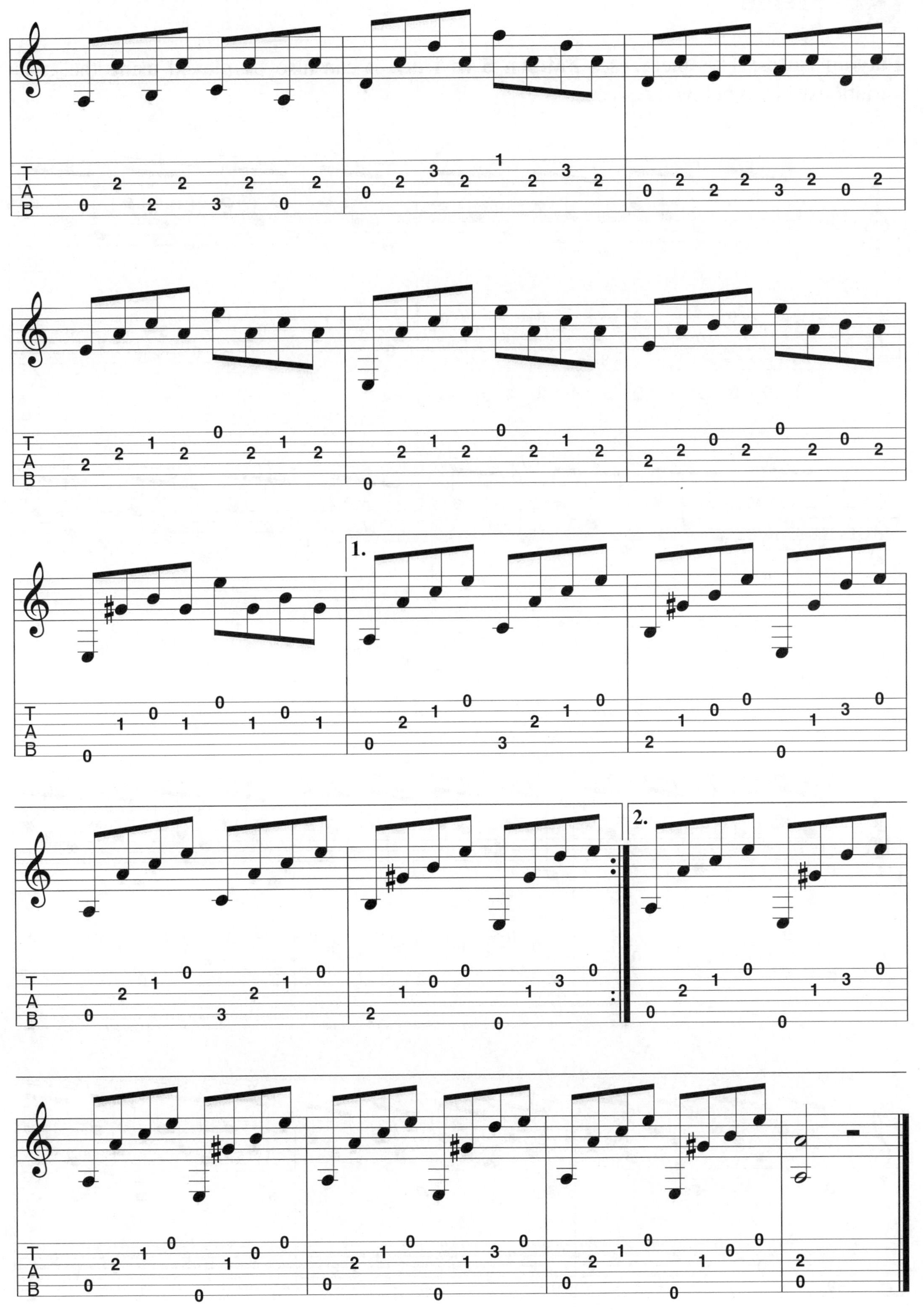
1.
2.

Prelude

Playing Notes: This piece uses **Pattern 5 (p i m)**. It can also be played using the given variations shown below the piece.

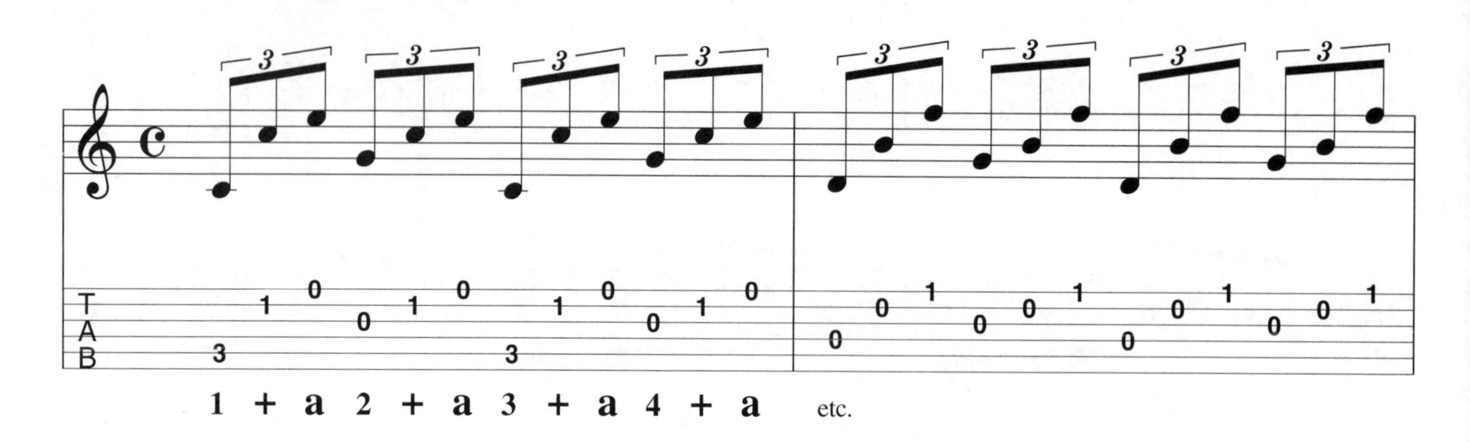

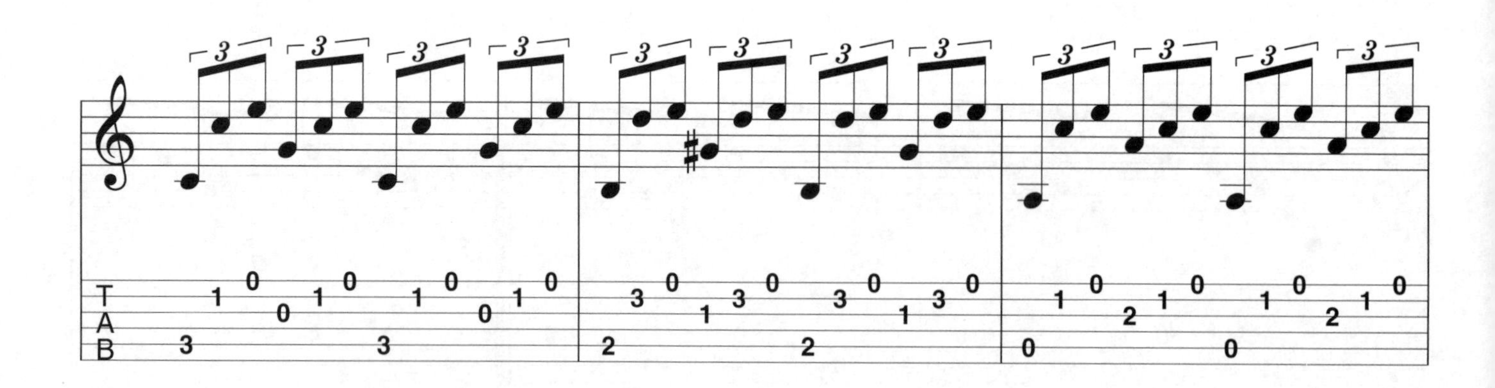

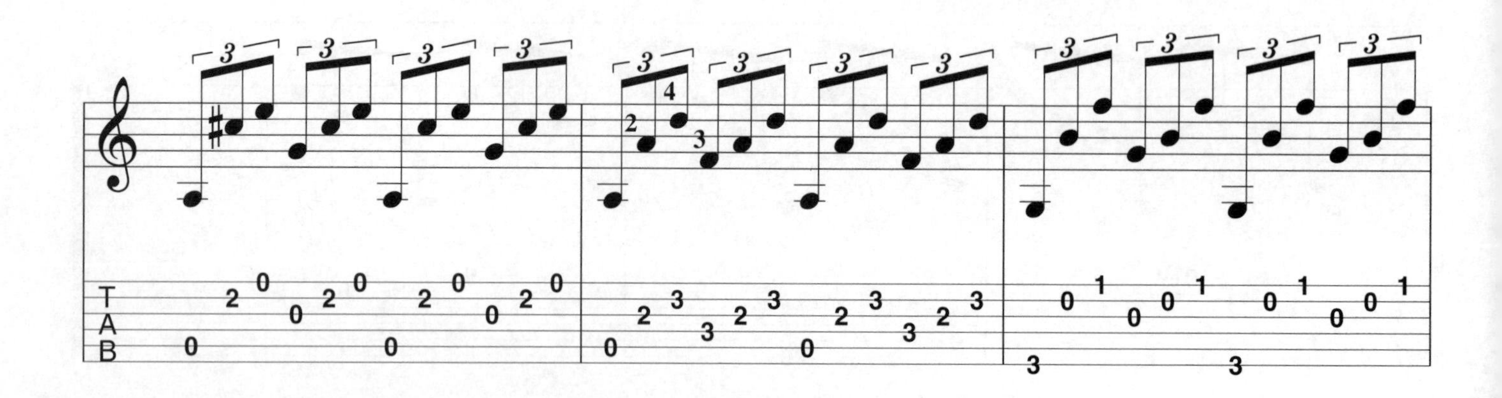

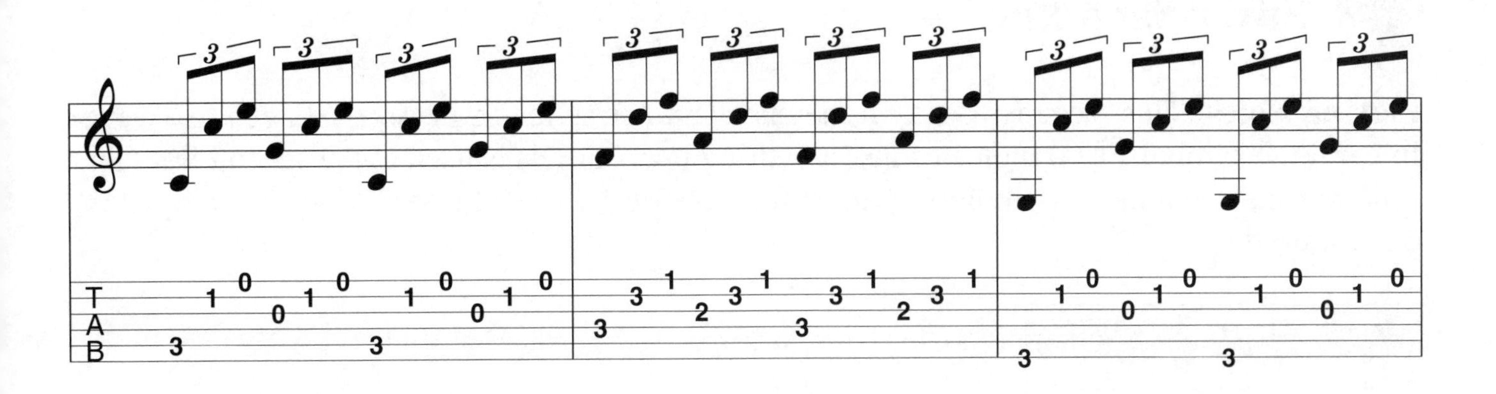

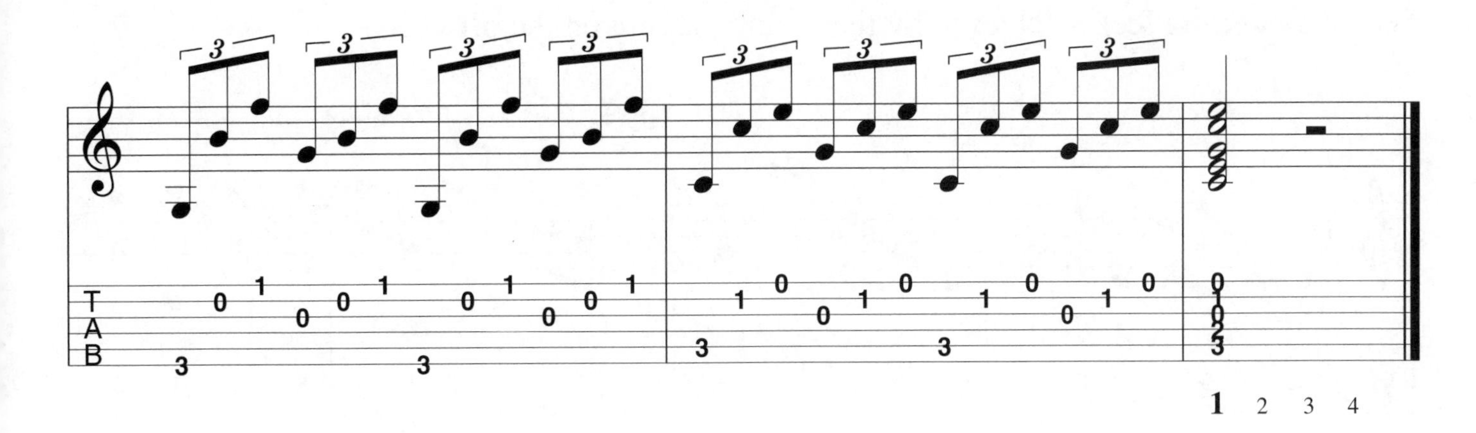

Variation 1

Variation 2

Variation 3

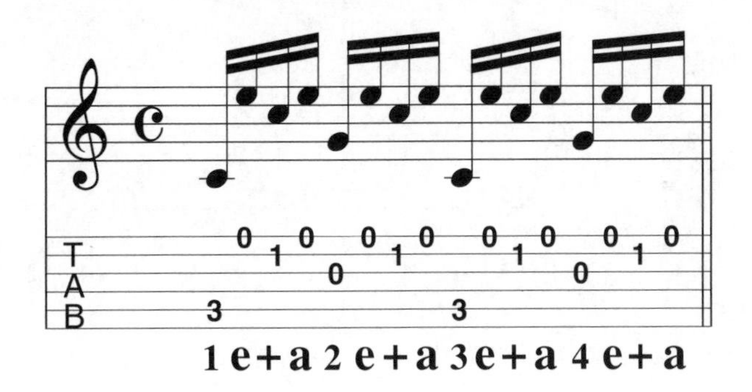

Silver Sand Rag

Playing Notes: This piece is based on the clawhammer styles in Lessons Sixteen to Twenty. In bar 3 the symbol **BII** ④ indicates that a 4-string (④) bar (**B**) is used at the second fret (**BII**). This barring technique is commonly used for ease of playing. In bars 17 to 20 the picking pattern used is:

p	i	m	p	i	m	p
1	+	2	+	3	+	4

Where a **ragtime** feel is achieved by the thumb playing on the **off** beats.

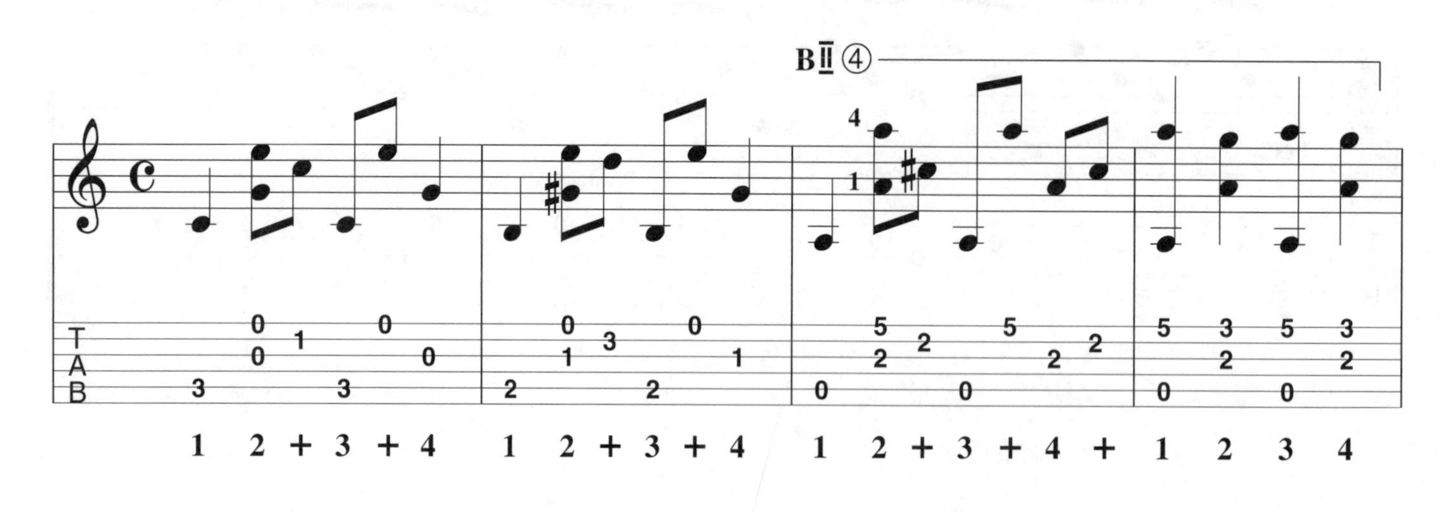

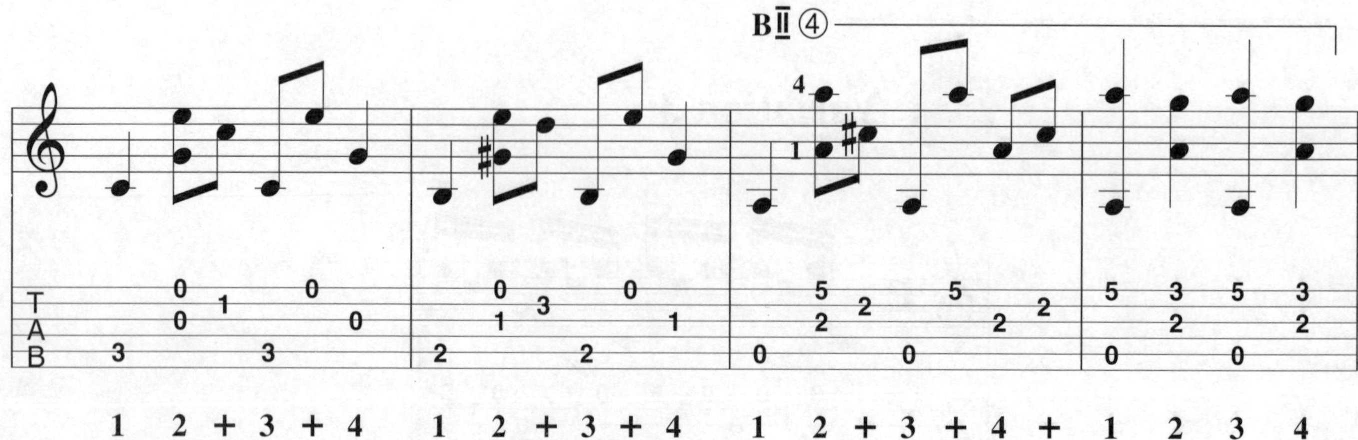

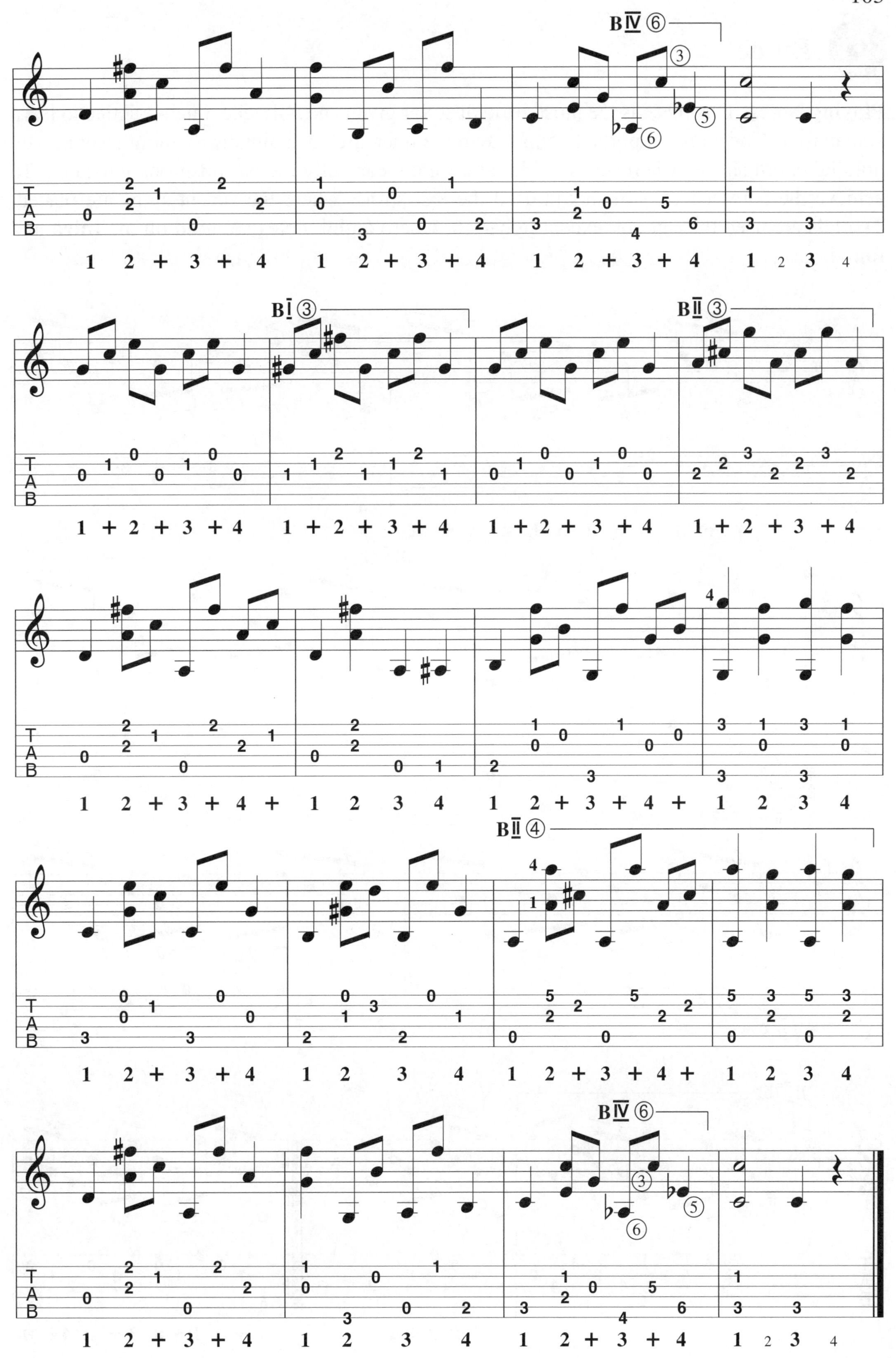
BIV ⑥
BI ③
BII ③
BII ④
BIV ⑥

Etude

Playing Notes: This piece is the most difficult so far given and will take much practice to learn and master. The most important things to remember are to maintain a smooth sound (by holding chord shapes wherever possible) and follow carefully the bar positions indicated. To achieve the correct feel, you should used the rest stroke where the accent signs are placed. **Triplets** are used throughout, except in bar 16, where eighth notes are used on the **third** and **fourth** beats.

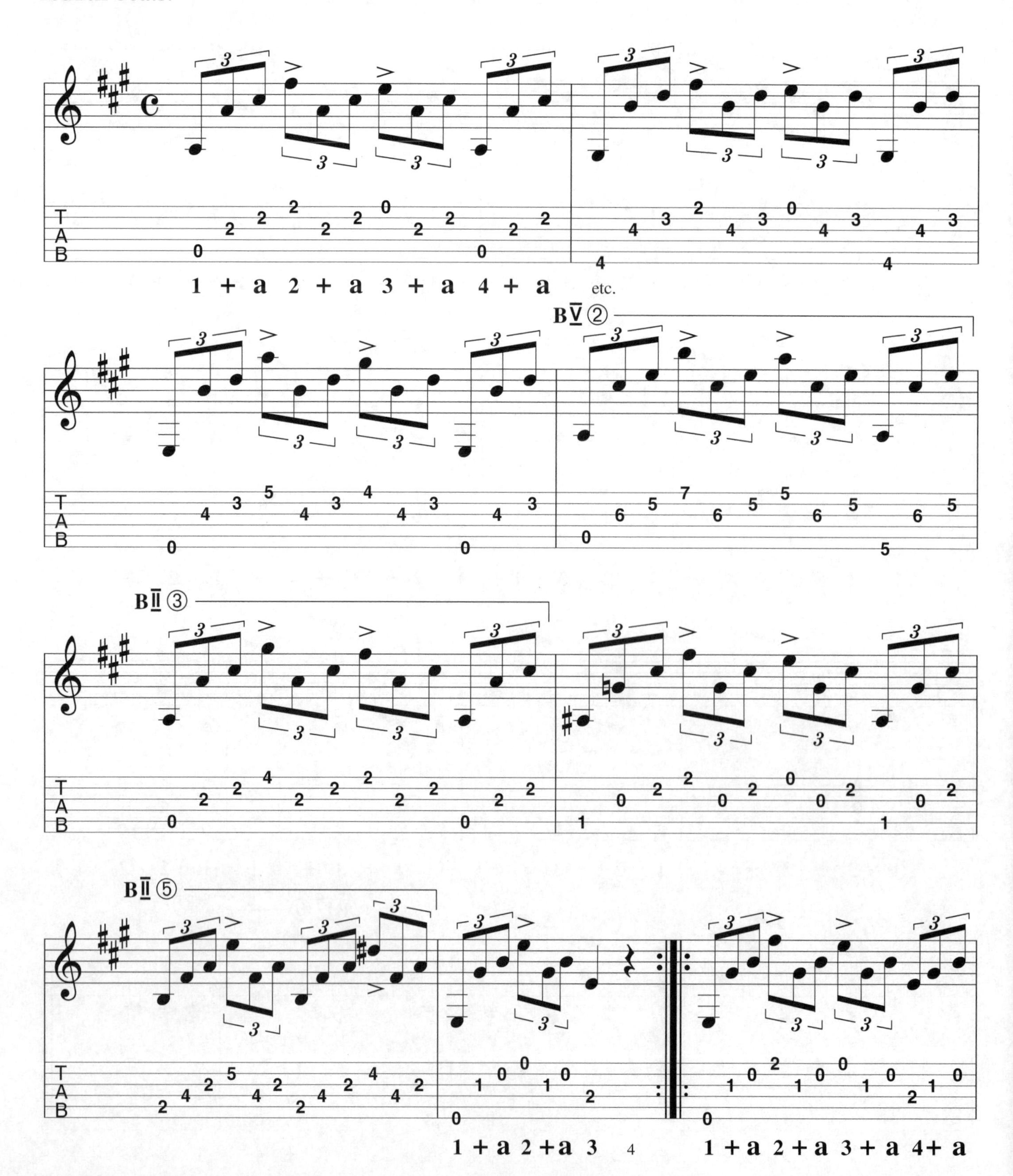

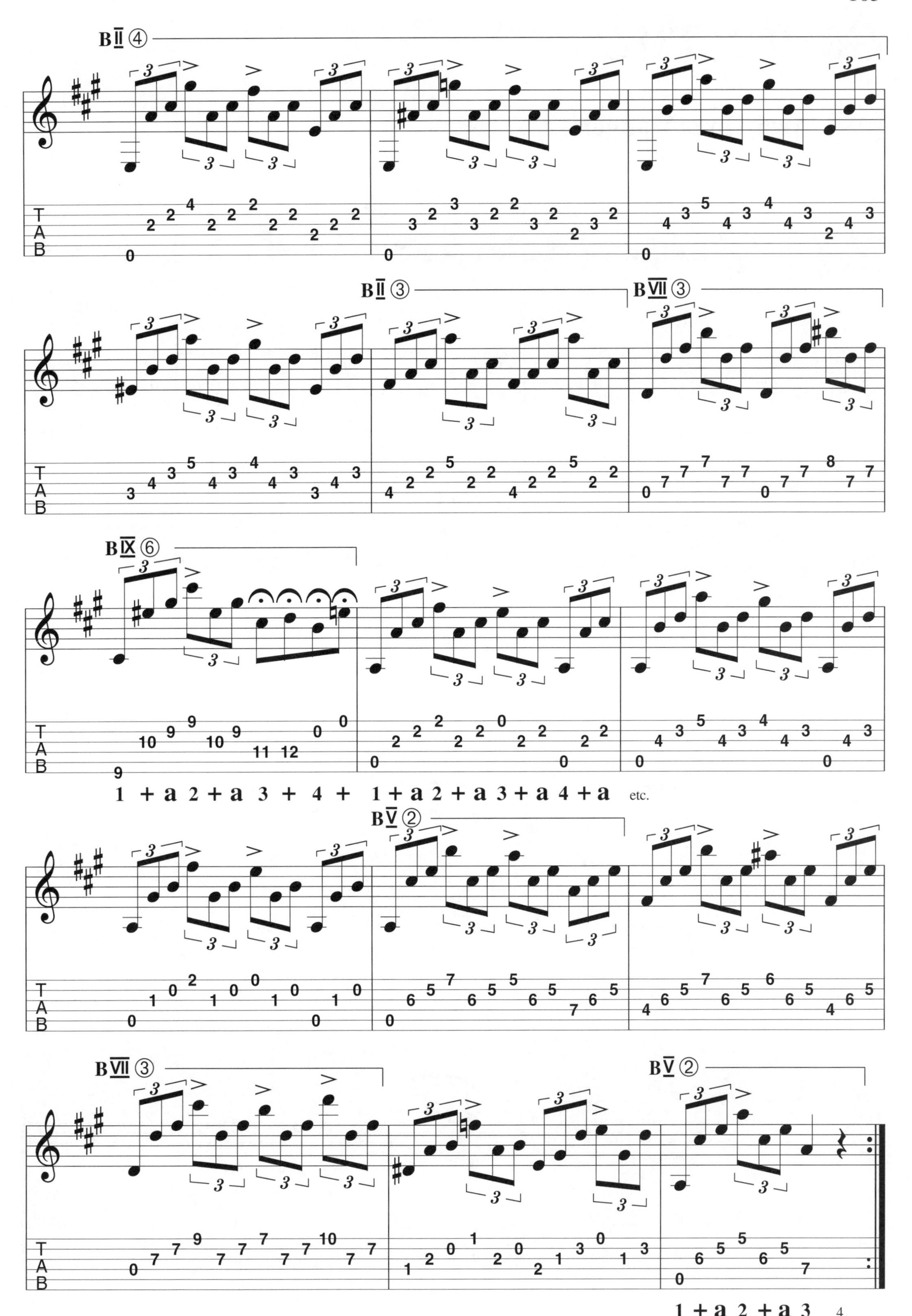
BII ④
BII ③
BVII ③
BIX ⑥
1 + a 2 + a 3 + 4 + 1 + a 2 + a 3 + a 4 + a etc.
BV ②
BVII ③
BV ②
1 + a 2 + a 3 4

GROUP TWO

Away in a Manger

The First Noel

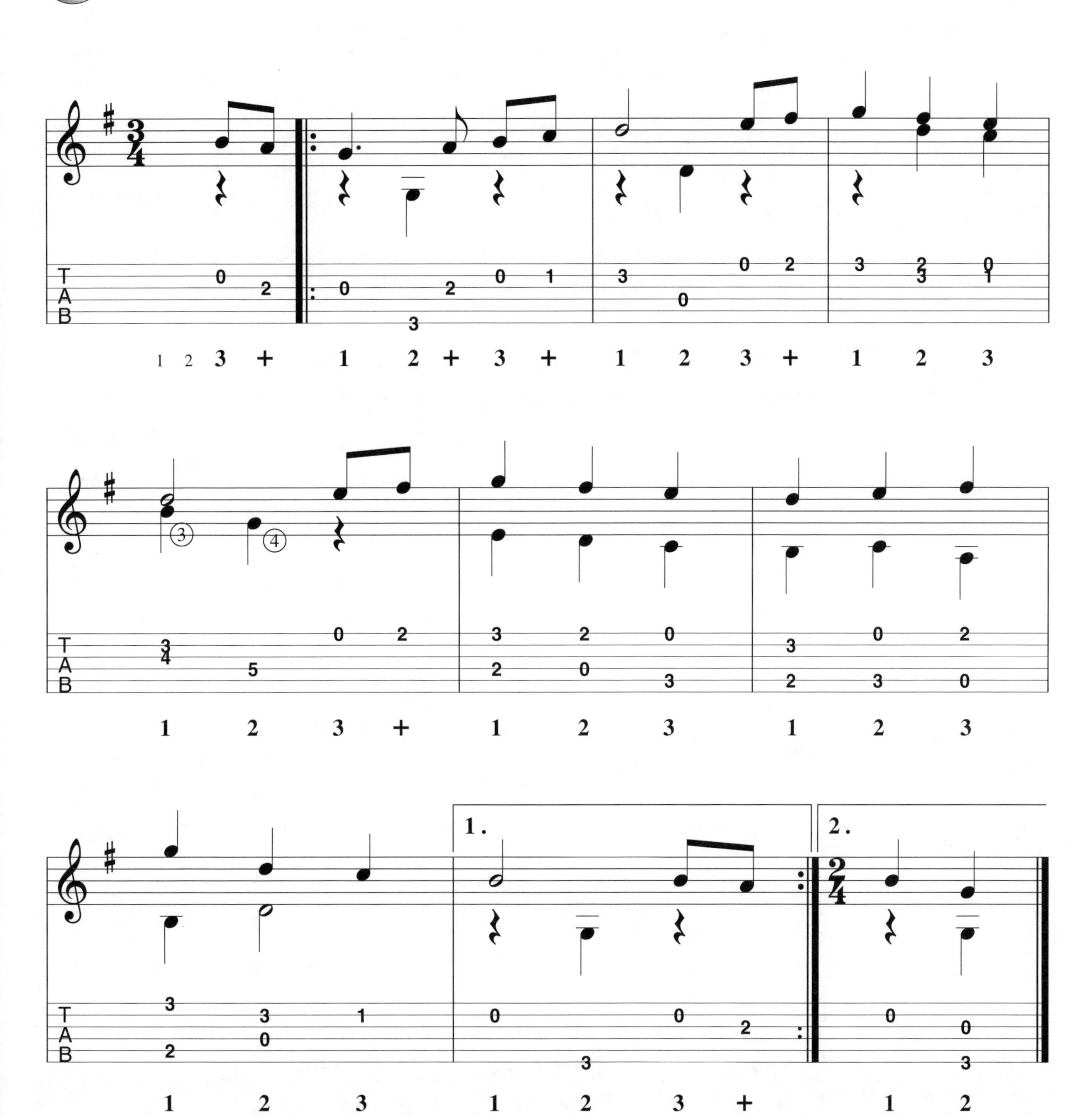

Minuet

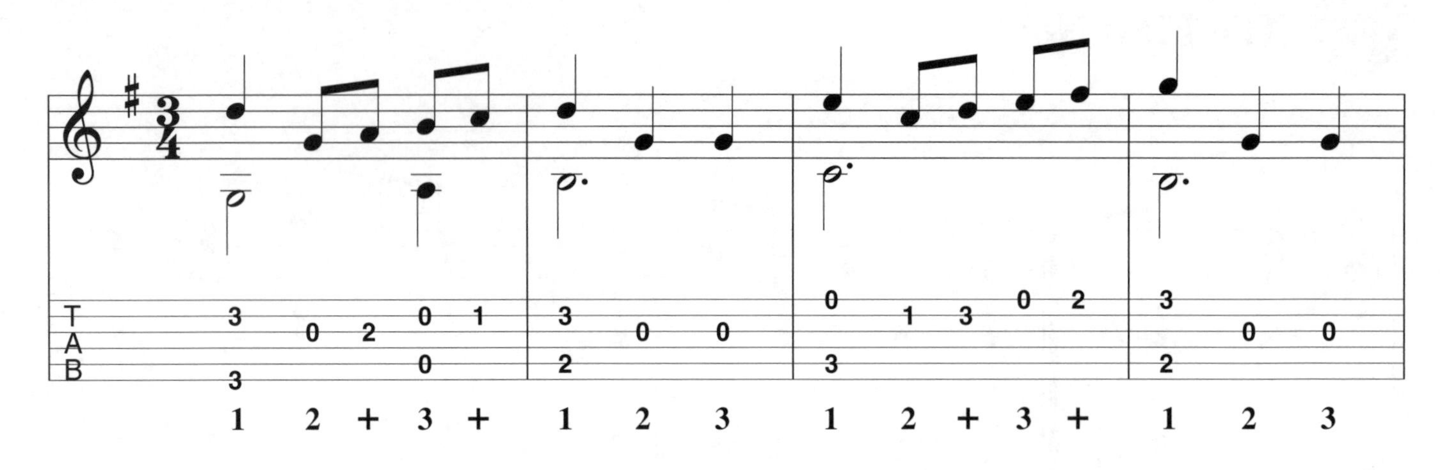

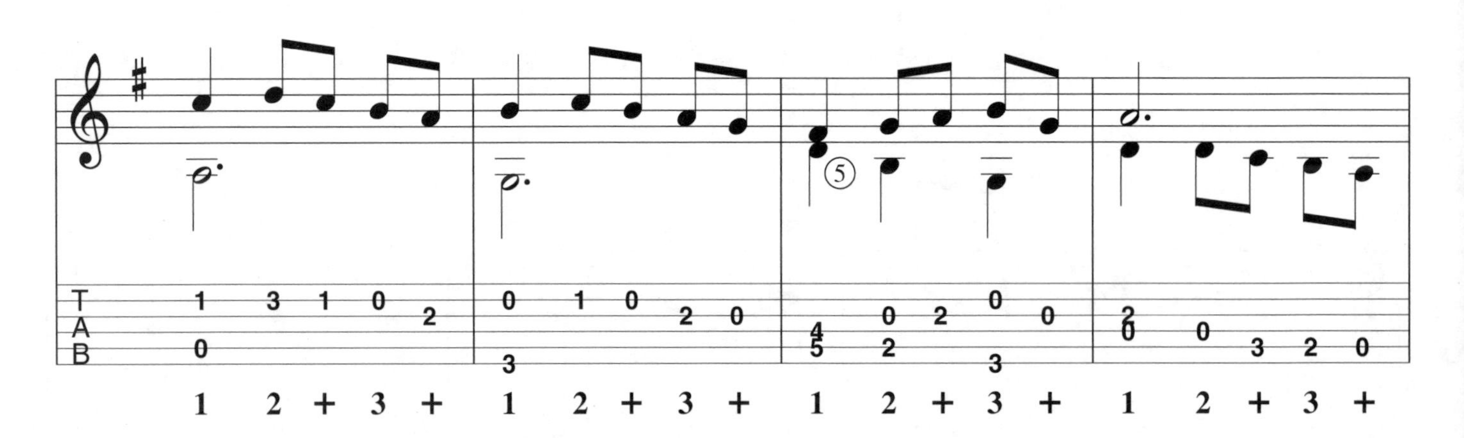

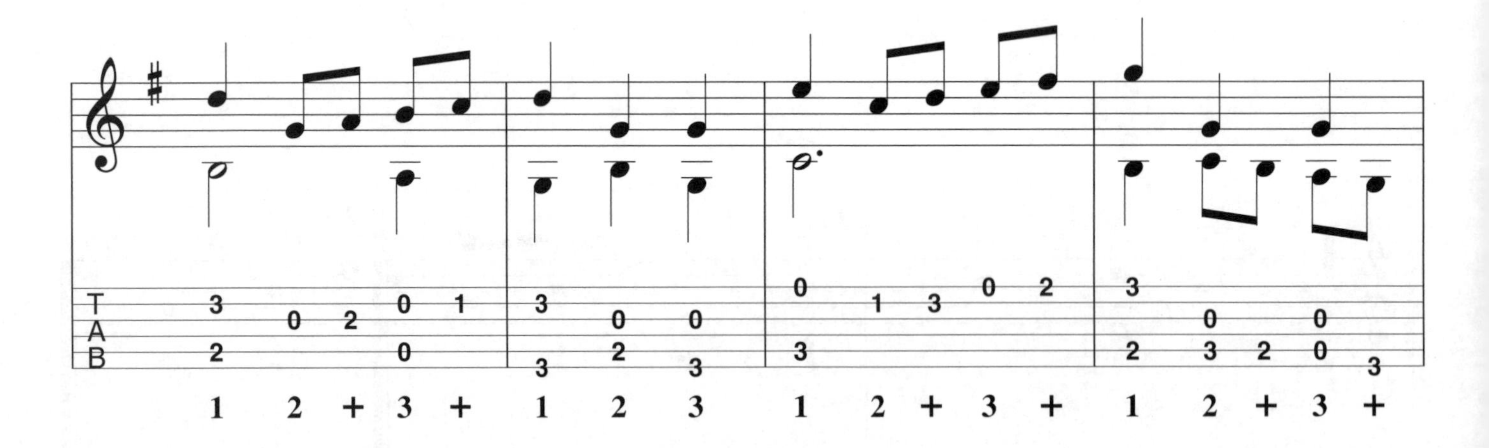

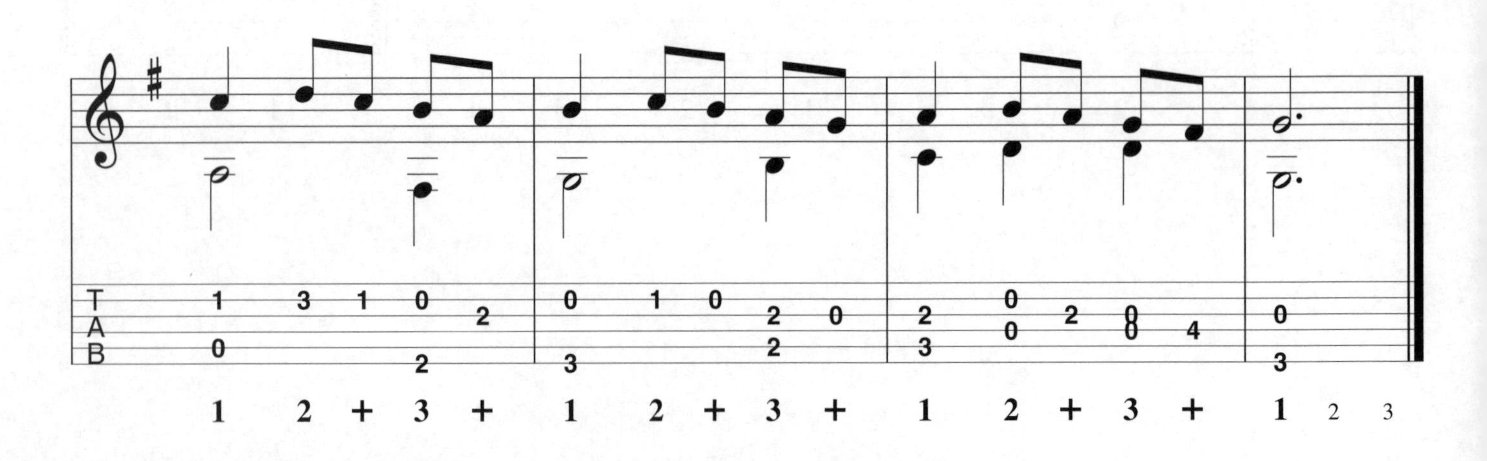

Silent Night

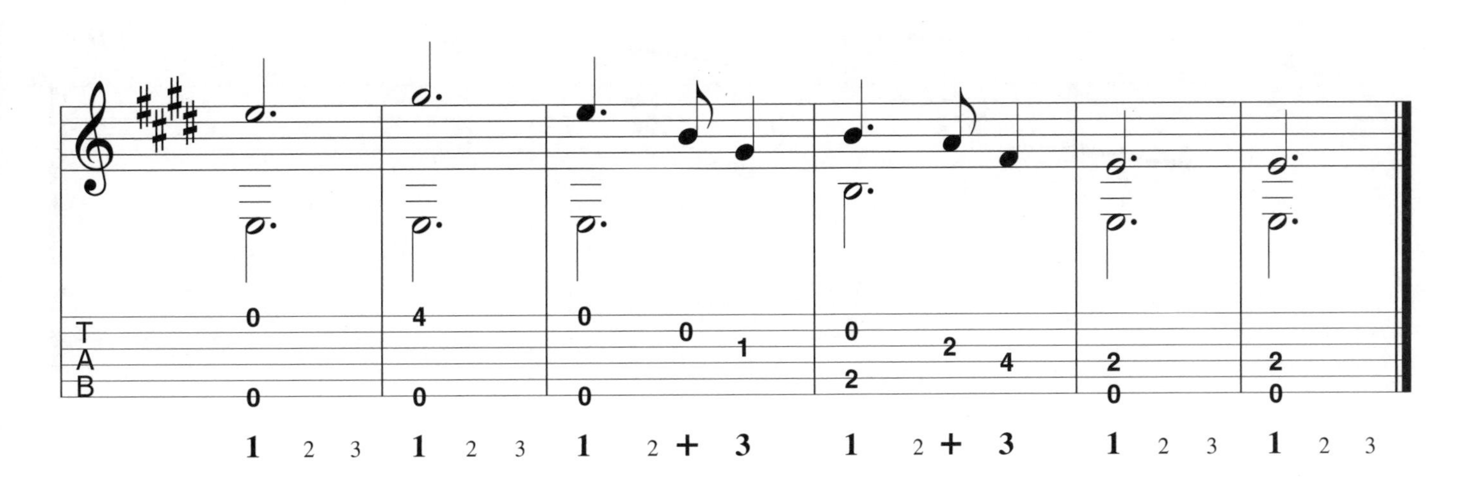

Lagrima

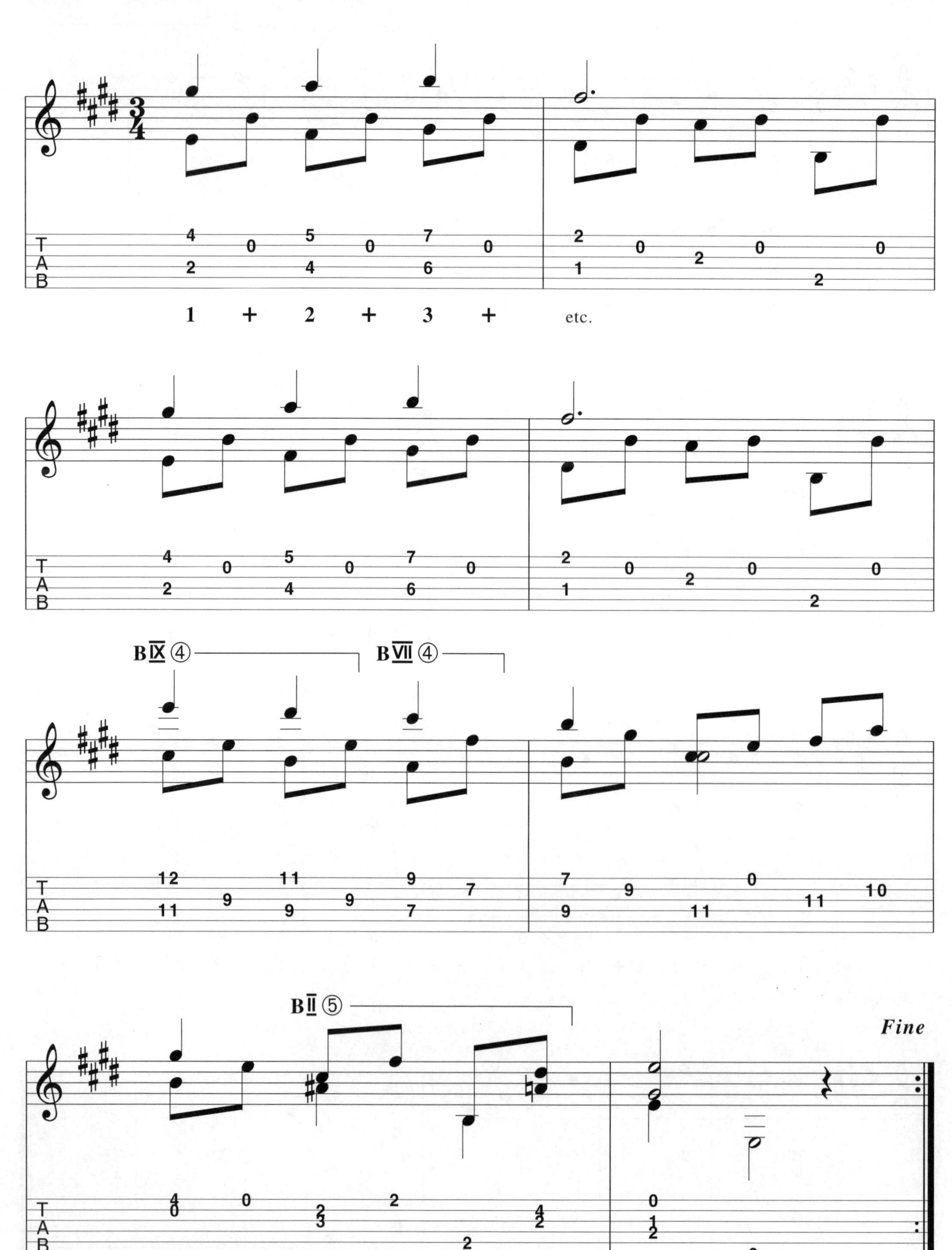

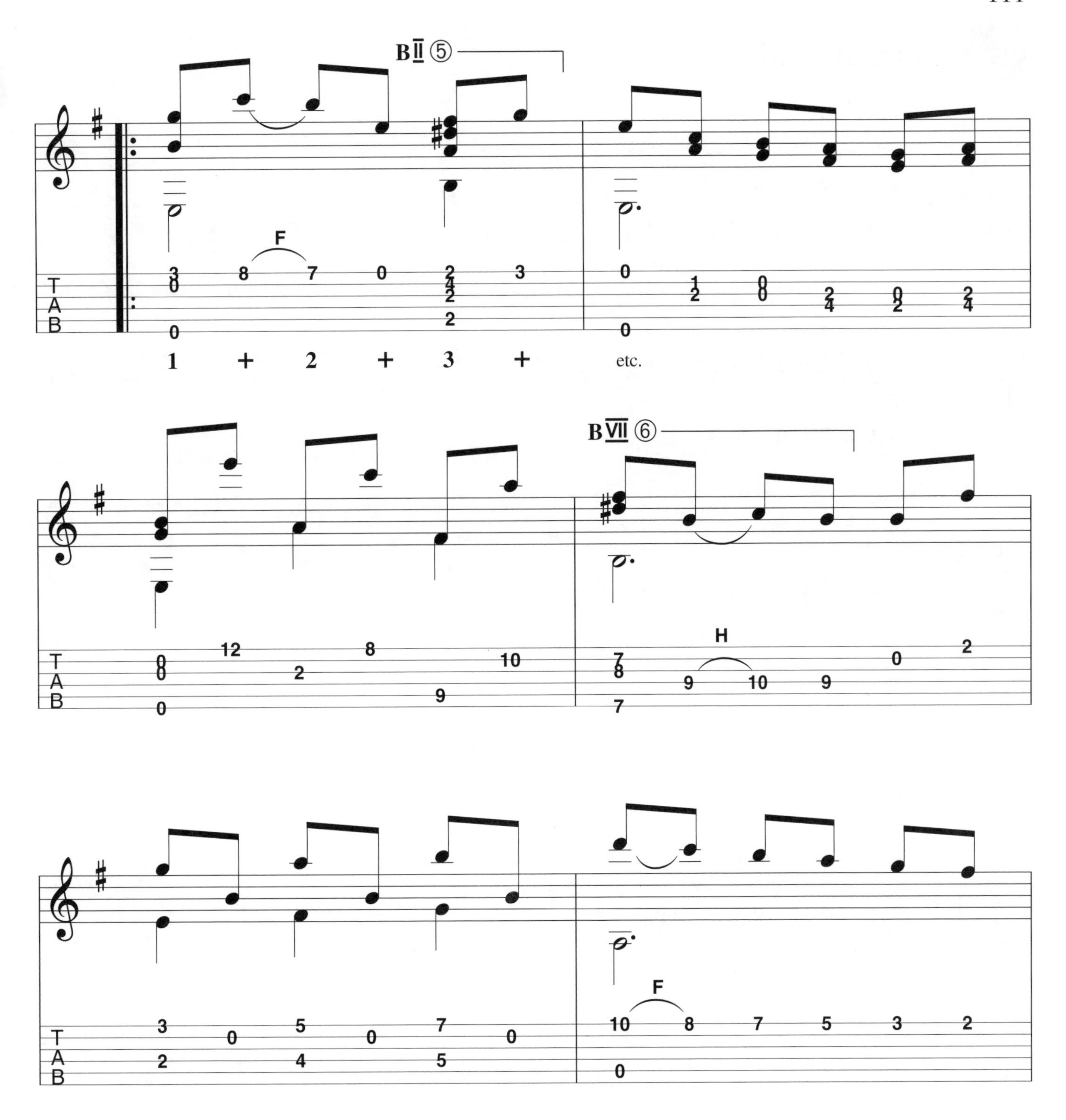
B II ⑤
F
1 + 2 + 3 +
etc.
B VII ⑥
H
F

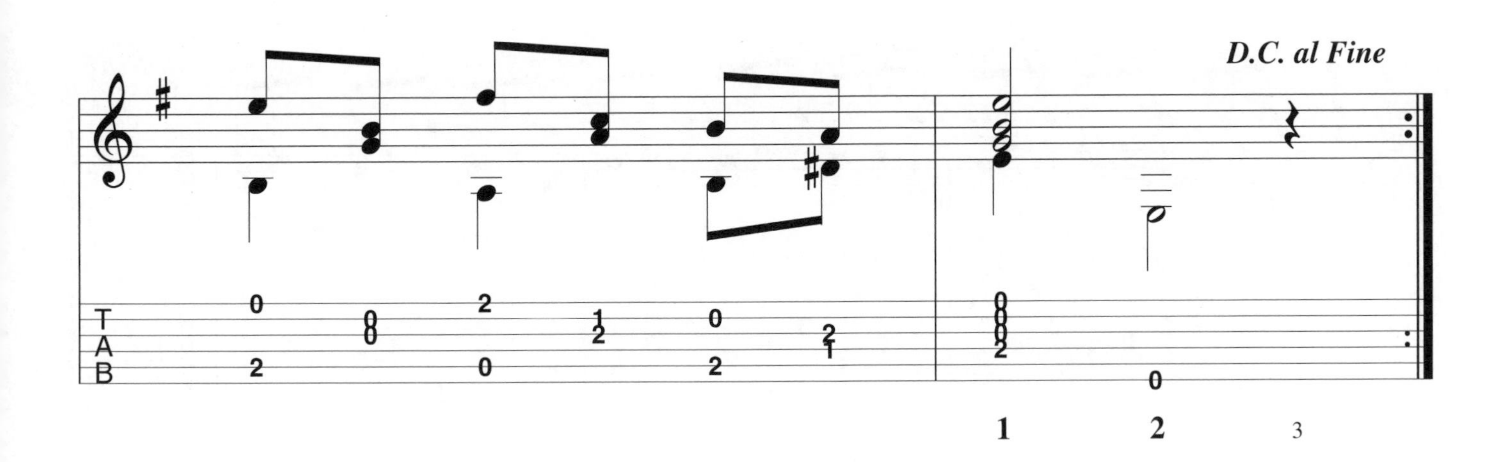
D.C. al Fine
1 2 3

Spanish Ballad

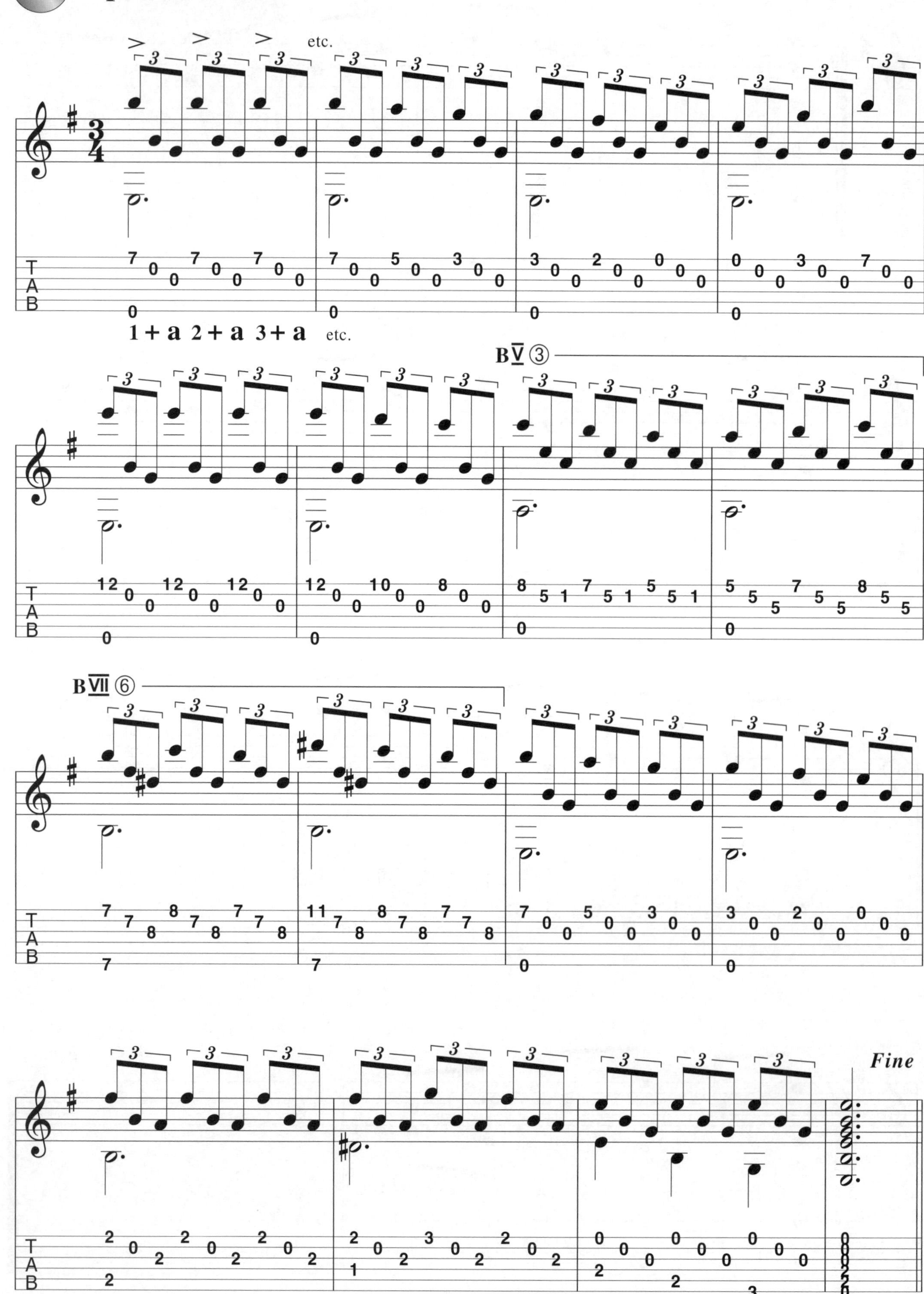

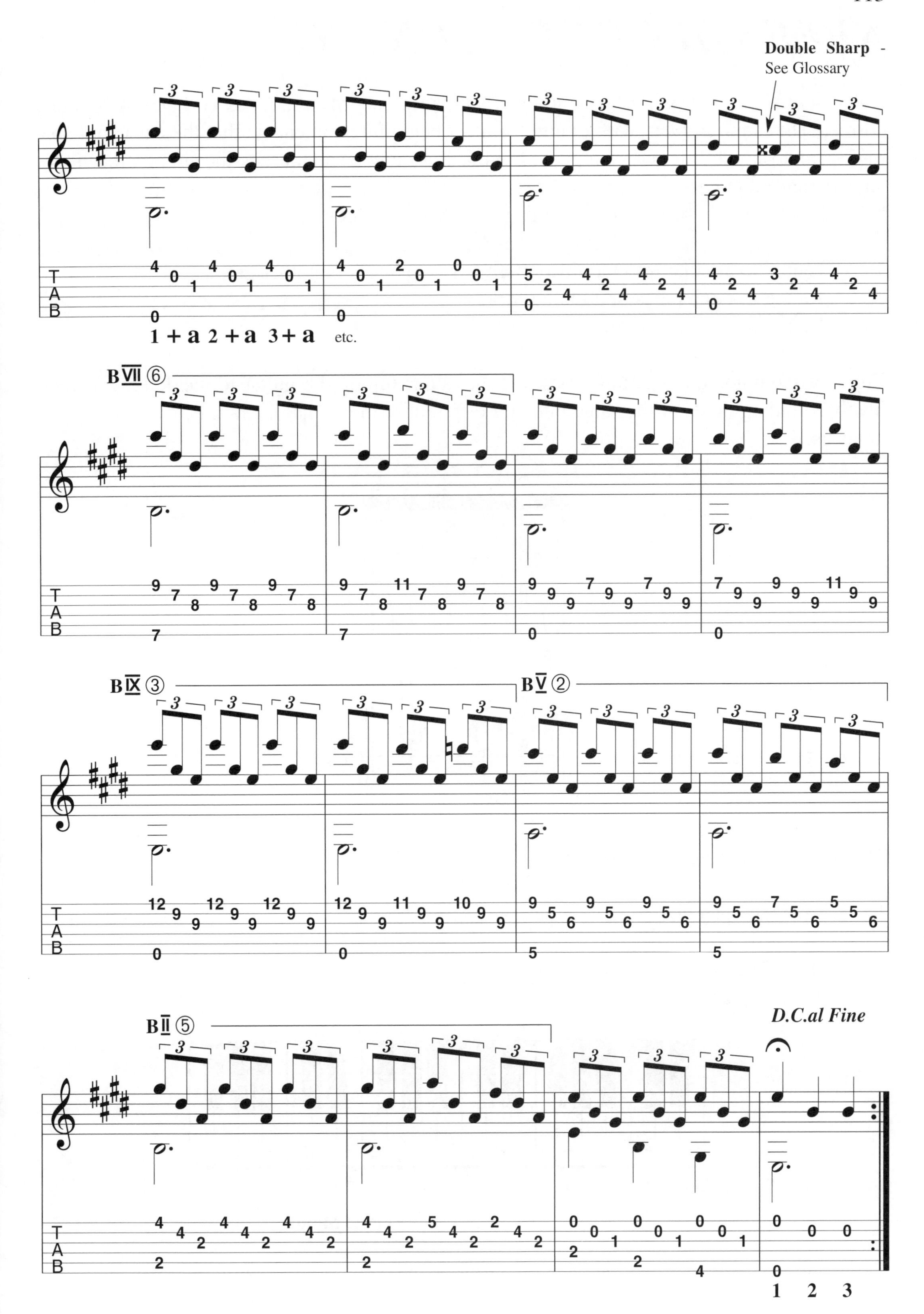

Double Sharp - See Glossary
1 + a 2 + a 3 + a etc.
BVII ⑥
BIX ③
BV ②
BII ⑤
D.C.al Fine
1 2 3

APPENDIX ONE - TUNING

It is essential for your guitar to be in tune, so that the chords and notes you play will sound correct. The main problem with tuning for most beginning students is that the ear is not able to determine slight differences in pitch. For this reason you should seek the aid of a teacher or an experienced guitarist.
Several methods can be used to tune the guitar. These include:

1. Tuning to another musical instrument (e.g. a piano, or another guitar).
2. Tuning to pitch pipes or a tuning fork.
3. Tuning the guitar to itself.

The most common and useful of theses is the latter; tuning the guitar to itself. This method involves finding notes of the same pitch on different strings. The diagram below outlines the notes used:

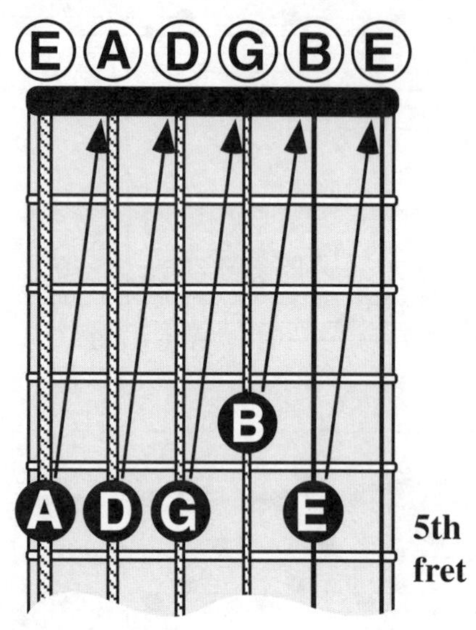

The method of tuning is as follows:

1. Tune the open 6th string to either:

    (a) The open 6th string of another guitar.
    (b) A piano.

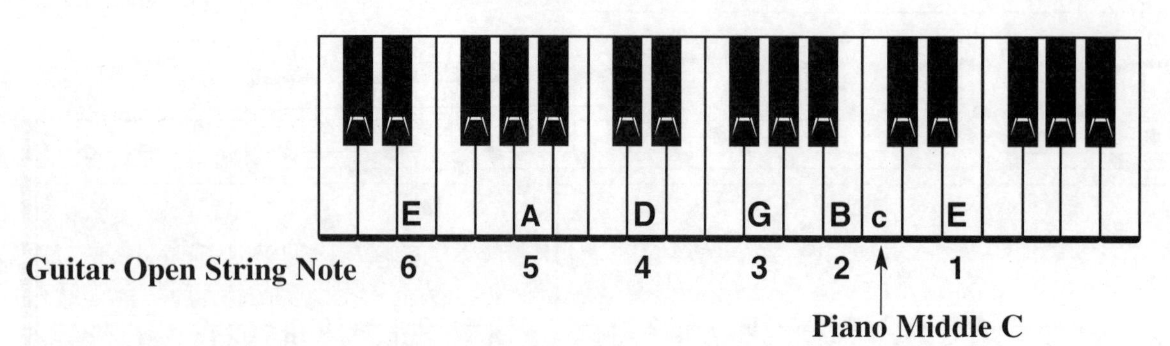

The piano note equivalent to the open 6th string is indicated on the diagram.

(c) Pitch pipes, which produce notes that correspond with each of the 6 open strings.

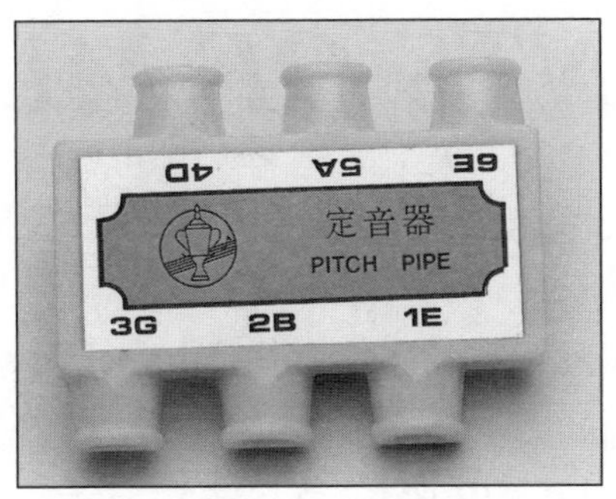

(d) A tuning fork. Most tuning forks give the note A.

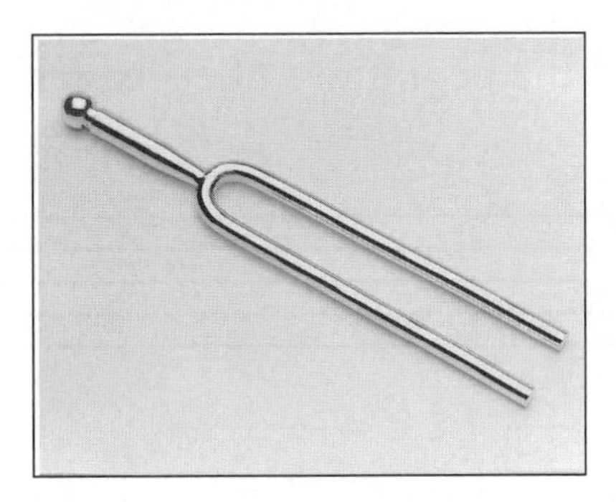

To produce sound from the tuning fork, hold it by the stem and tap one of the prongs against something hard. This will set up a vibration, which can be heard clearly when the bass of the stem is then placed on a solid surface, e.g. a guitar body.

2. Place a finger on the 6th string at the 5th fret. Now play the open a (5th string). If the guitar is to be in tune, then these two notes must have the same pitch (i.e. sound the same). If they do not sound the same, the 5th string must be adjusted to match the note produced on the 6th string. Thus the 5th string is tuned in relation to the 6th string.

3. Tune the open 4th string to the note on the 5th fret of the 5th string, using the method outlined above.

4. Tune all other strings using g the same procedure, remembering that the open B string (2nd) is tuned to the 4th fret (check diagram) while all other strings are tuned to the 5th fret.

5. Strum an open E major chord, to check if your guitar is tuned correctly. At first you may have some difficulty deciding whether or not the chord sound is correct, but as your ear improves you will become more familiar with the correct sound of the chord.

Tuning may take you many months to master, and you should practice it constantly. The guidance of as teacher will be an invaluable aid in the early stages of guitar tuning.

APPENDIX TWO - THE RUDIMENTS OF MUSIC

The musical alphabet consists of 7 letters: **A B C D E F G**

Music is written on a **staff**, which consists of 5 parallel lines between which there are 4 spaces.

MUSIC STAFF

The treble or 'G' clef is placed at the beginning of each staff line.

Treble or 'G' Clef →

This clef indicates the position of the note G. (It is an old fashioned method of writing the letter G, with the centre of the clef being written on the second staff line.)

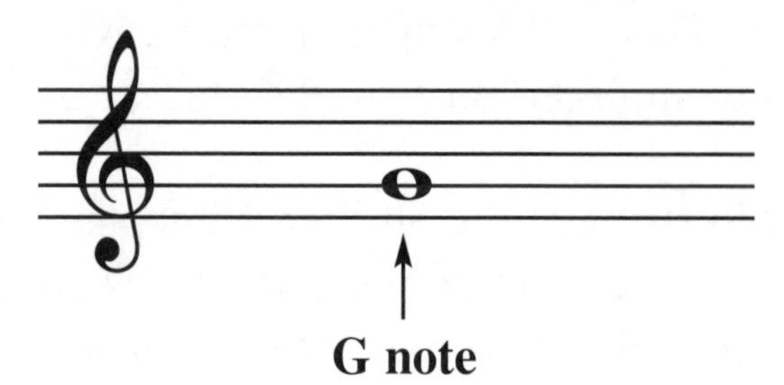

G note

The other lines and spaces on the staff are named as such:

Extra notes can be added by the use of short lines, called **leger lines**.

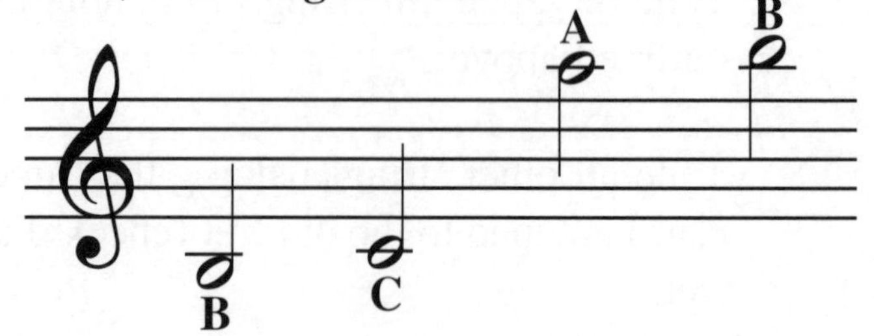

When a note is placed on the staff its head indicates its position, e.g.:

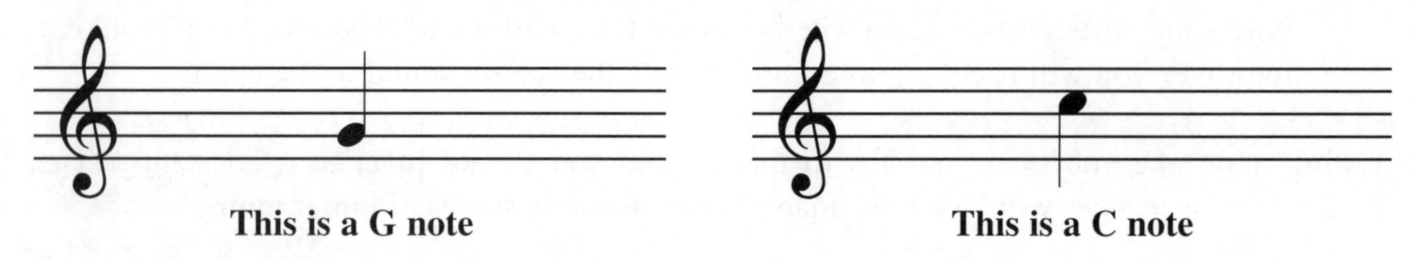

This is a G note **This is a C note**

When the note head is below the middle staff line the stem points upward and when the head is above the middle line the stem points downward. A note placed on the middle line (**B**) can have its stem pointing either up or down.

Bar lines are drawn across the staff, which divides the music into sections called **bars** or **measures**. A **double bar line** signifies either the end of the music, or the end of an important section of it.

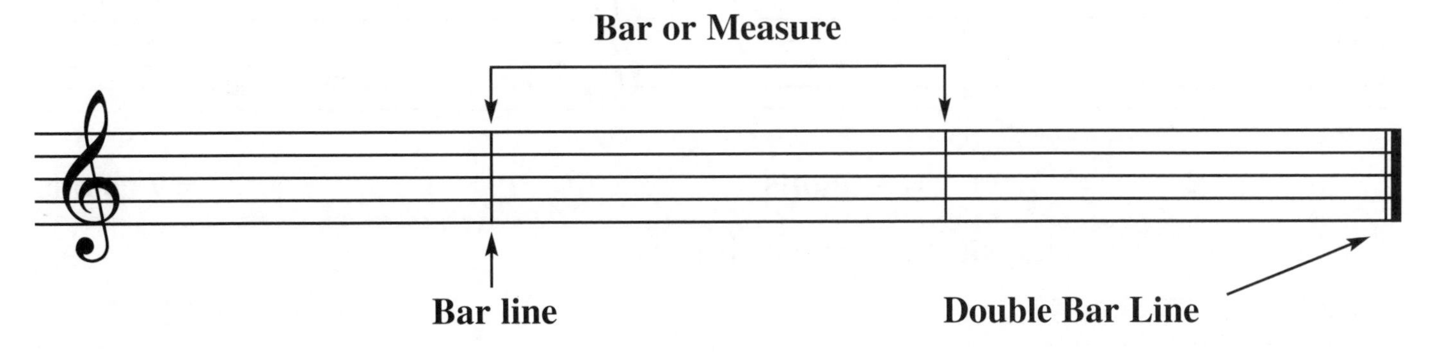

NOTE VALUES

The table below sets out the most common notes used in music and their respective time values (i.e. length of time held). For each note value there is an equivalent rest, which indicates a period of silence.

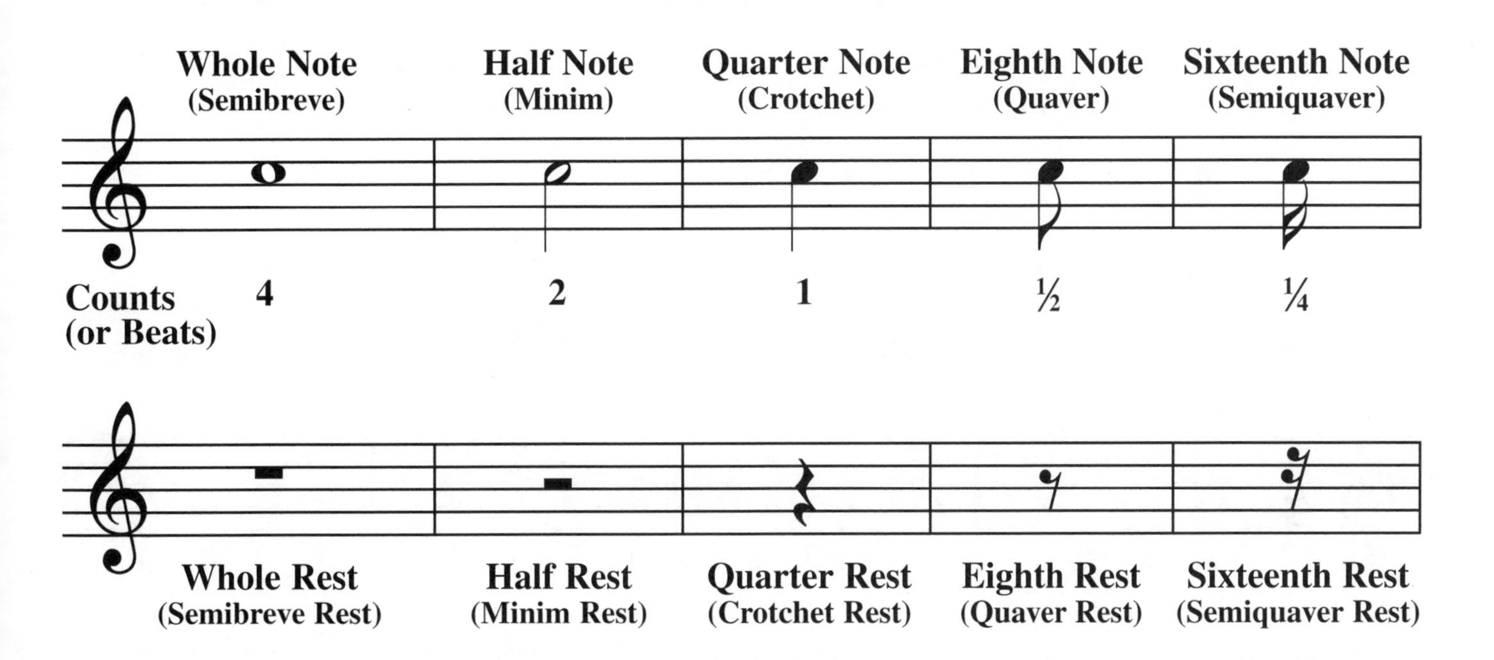

If a **dot** is placed after a note it increases the value of that note by half, e.g.

Dotted half note 𝅗𝅥. **(2 + 1) = 3 counts**

Dotted quarter note ♩. **(1 + ½) = 1½ counts**

Dotted whole note 𝅝. **(4 + 2) = 6 counts**

A **tie** is a curved line joining two or more notes of the same pitch, where the second note(s) **is not played** but its time value is added to that of the first note. Here are two examples:

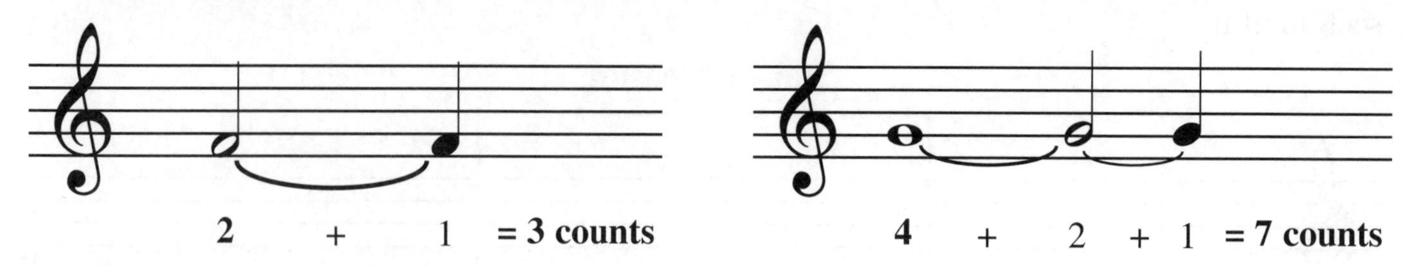

In both of these examples only the first note is played.

TIME SIGNATURES

At the beginning of each piece of music, after the treble clef, is the **time signature**.

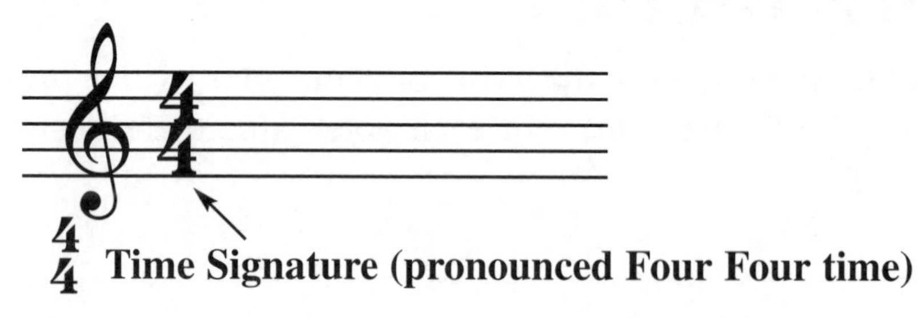

$\frac{4}{4}$ Time Signature (pronounced Four Four time)

The time signature indicates the number of beats per bar (the top number) and the type of note receiving one beat (the bottom number). For example:

4 – this indicates 4 beats per bar.
4 – this indicates that each beat is worth a quarter note (crotchet).

Thus in $\frac{4}{4}$ time there must be the equivalent of 4 quarter note beats per bar, e.g.

$\frac{4}{4}$ is the most common time signature and is sometimes represented by this symbol called **common time**.

Common Time

Other time signatures used in this book are $\frac{3}{4}$ and $\frac{6}{8}$ time. $\frac{3}{4}$ indicates 3 quarter note beats per bar, e.g.

$\frac{6}{8}$ time indicates 2 dotted quarter note beats per bar, which can be divided into 2 groups of eighth notes as such:

$\frac{6}{8}$ is an example of compound time because the beat is a dotted note. $\frac{4}{4}$ and $\frac{3}{4}$ are examples of simple time because the beat is an undotted note.

NOTES IN THE OPEN POSITION

The open position on the guitar contains the notes of the open strings and the first three frets. Outlined below are the position of these notes on the staff and on the fretboard.

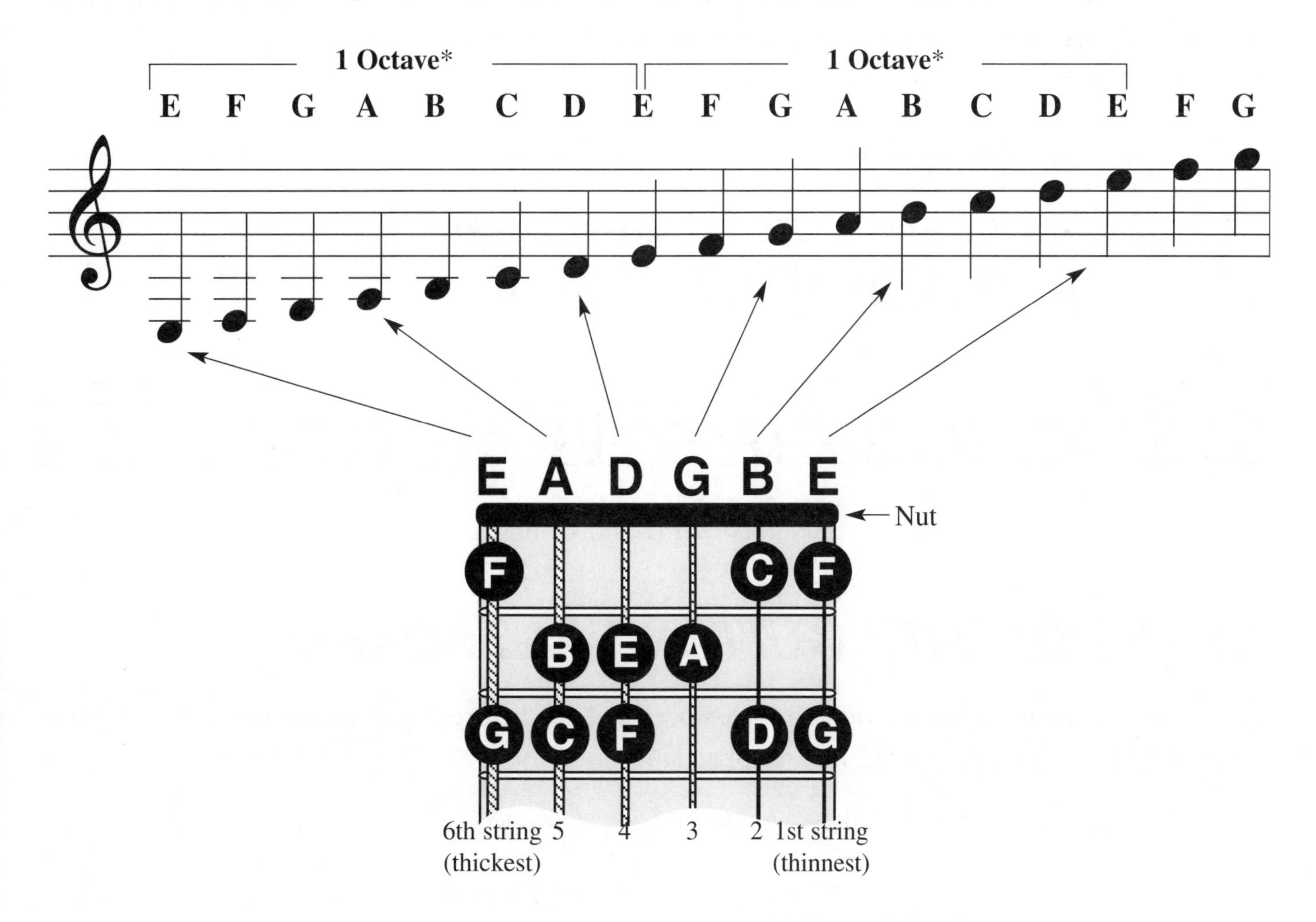

* An octave is the distance between two notes that have the same letter name and are 8 consecutive notes apart. The example above uses E notes, showing 2 octaves.

CHROMATIC NOTES

A sharp (♯) raises the pitch of a note by one semi-tone (1 fret).
A flat (♭) lowers the pitch of a note by one semi-tone.
In music notation the ♯ and ♭ sings (called accidentals) are always placed before the note.

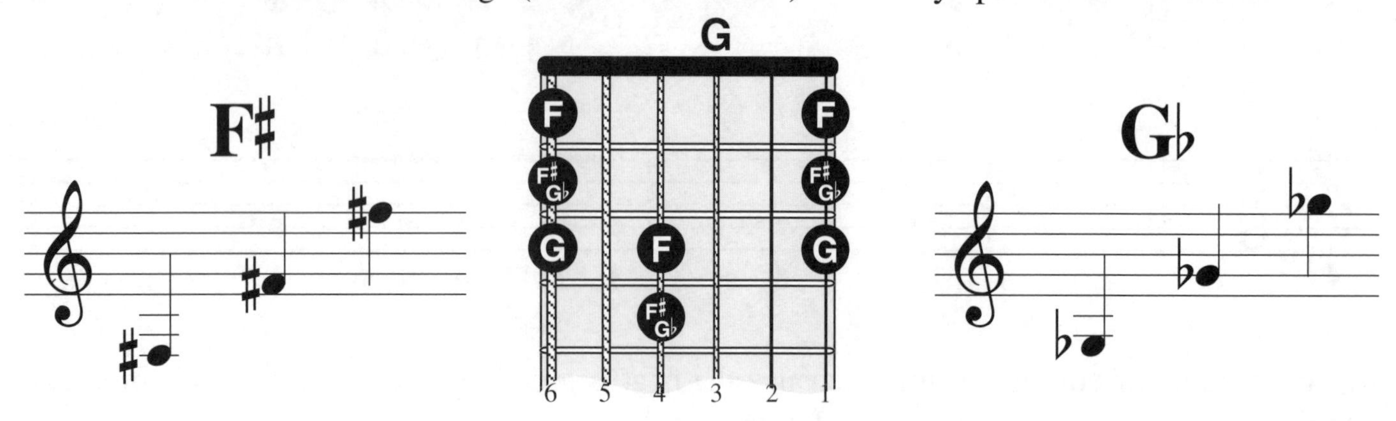

This example illustrates that the same note has two different names (i.e. F♯ and G♭ have the same position on the fretboard).

A natural (♮) cancels the effect of a sharp or flat.

A sharp or flat, when placed before a note, affects the same note if it re-occurs in the remainder of that bar. It does not, however, affect notes in the next bar, e.g.:

With the inclusion of sharps and flats, there are 12 different notes with one octave, e.g.:

A A♯/B♭ BC C♯/D♭ D D♯/E♭ EF F♯/G♭ G G♯/A♭ A

Note that there are no sharps of flats between B and C, and E and F.

NOTES ON THE GUITAR FRETBOARD

On the guitar many notes of the same pitch repeat in different positions. For example, the following G note can be played in four places.

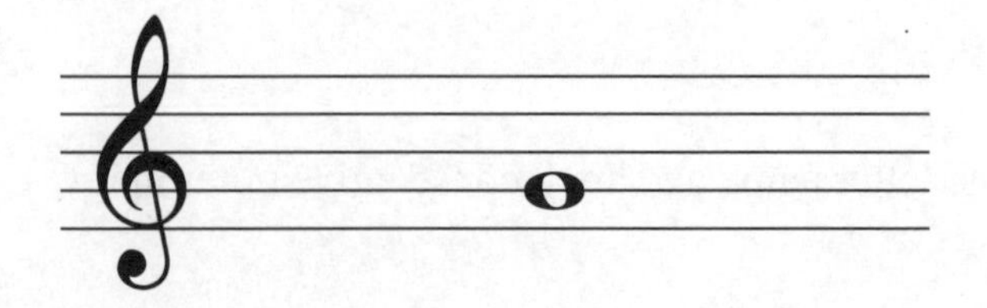

3rd string, open
4th string, 5th fret
5th string, 10th fret
6th string, 15th fret

The music notation below illustrates the complete range of notes on the guitar, using the open position and the first string up to the 19th fret as examples. The diagram, however, illustrates all the possible positions of these notes, covering the entire fretboard.

TABLATURE

Tablature is a method of indicating the position of notes on the fretboard. There are six **tab** lines each representing one of the six strings of the guitar. Study the following diagram.

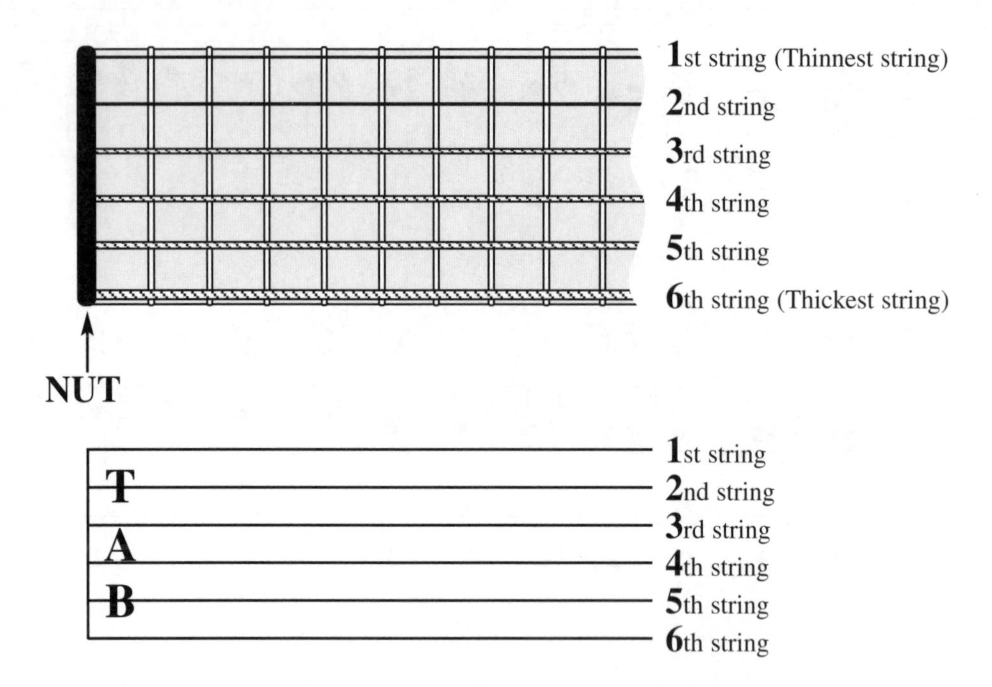

When a number is placed on one of the lines, it indicates the fret location of a note e.g.

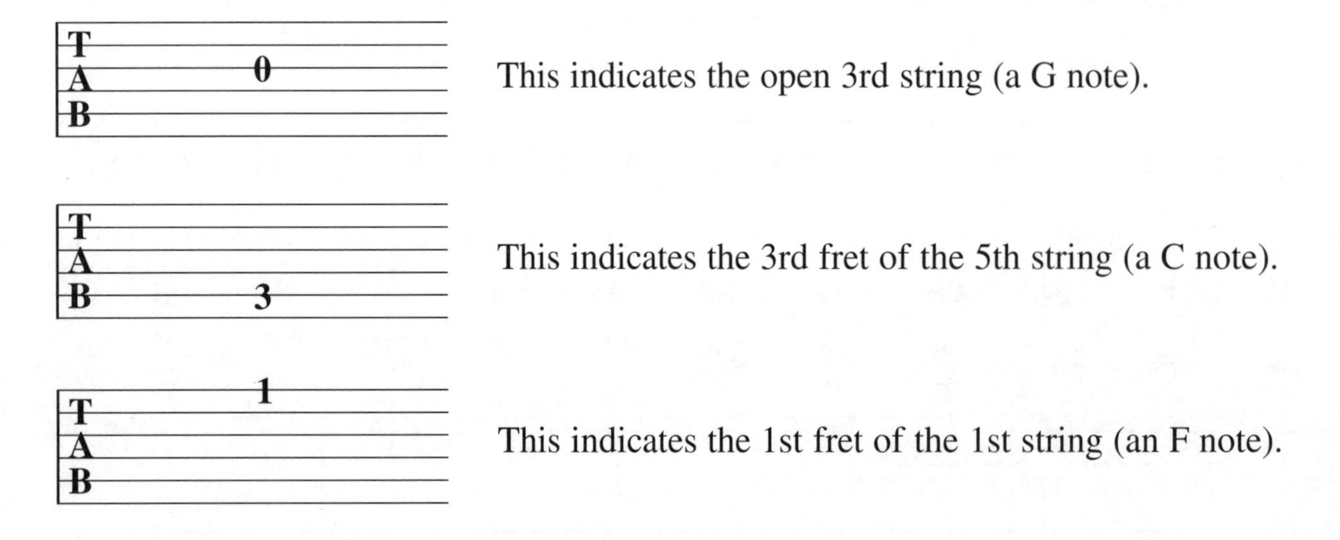

This indicates the open 3rd string (a G note).

This indicates the 3rd fret of the 5th string (a C note).

This indicates the 1st fret of the 1st string (an F note).

The tablature, as used in this book, does not indicate the time values of the notes, only their position on the fretboard. You can read the time values by following the count written beneath the tablature. e.g.

T A B 5 5 5 4

count 1 2 + 3 4

In this example the 1st note is worth 1 count, the 2nd and 3rd notes are worth half a count each and the 4th note is worth 2 counts.

APPENDIX THREE - TRANSPOSING

The term **Transposing** is used to describe the process whereby a progression (or song) is changed from one key to another. This is done for two main reasons:

1. Singing - to sing the whole song at a lower or higher pitch (depending on the singer's vocal range).
2. Ease of playing - because of the musical structure of the guitar, some keys are easier to play in than others (e.g. Beginning students may not be able to play a song in the key of say E♭, but could perhaps play it in the key of C).

Consider the following turnaround in the key of **C**:

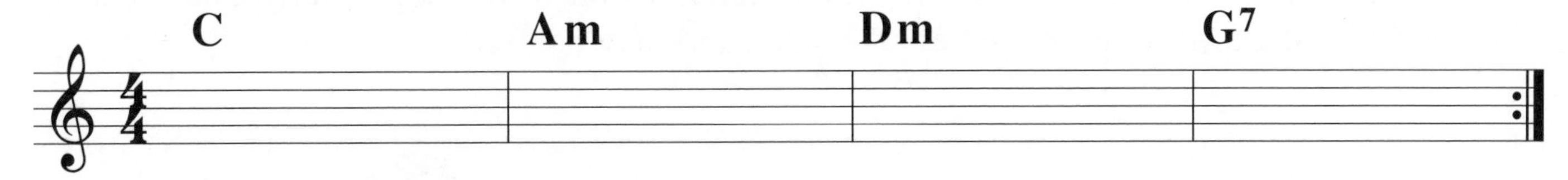

If you needed to transpose this progression into the key of G, the following method may be used:

1. Write out the C chromatic* scale.
2. Write out the G chromatic scale, with each note directly below its counterpart in the C chromatic scale, as such:

C chromatic	C	C♯	D	D♯	E	F	F♯	G	G♯	A	A♯	B	C
	1↓		3↓					4↓		2↓			
G chromatic	G	G♯	A	A♯	B	C	C♯	D	D♯	E	F	F♯	G

3. When the given progression is transposed to the key of G, the first chord, C major, will become G major. This can be seen by relating the two chromatic scales via arrow one.
4. The second chord of the progression, Am, will become Em (arrow two). Although the chord name will change when transposing, its type (i.e. major, minor seventh etc.) will remain the same.
5. The complete transposition will be:

Key of C:

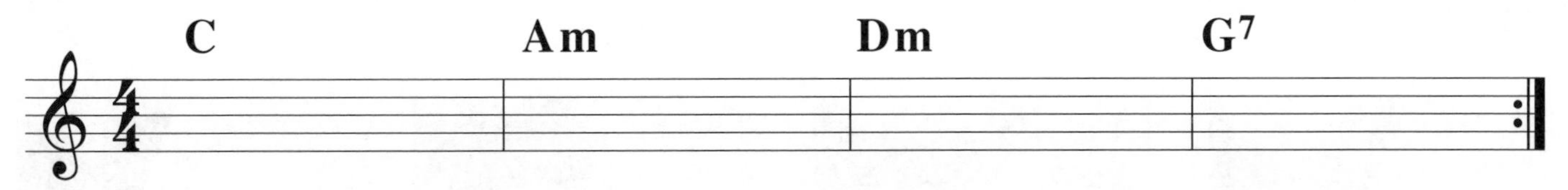

Key of G:

G   Em   Am   D7

Play both progressions and notice the similarity in sound.

* See Glossary

In the early stages you will mainly transpose for ease of playing, and thus the easiest keys for a song to be transposed into are C, G and D (for major keys) and Am, Em and Bm (for minor keys). Remember to write the second chromatic scale directly under the first, note for note, in order to transpose correctly, Try transposing the previous progression into the key of D major.

THE CAPO

The **capo** is a device which is placed across the neck of the guitar (acting as a moveable nut). It has 2 uses:

1. To enable the use of easier chord shapes, without changing the key of a song.
2. To change the key of a song, without changing the chord shapes.

Expanding upon point 1, if a song is in a key which is within your singing range, but involves playing difficult chords (e.g. in the key of E♭), a capo may be used.

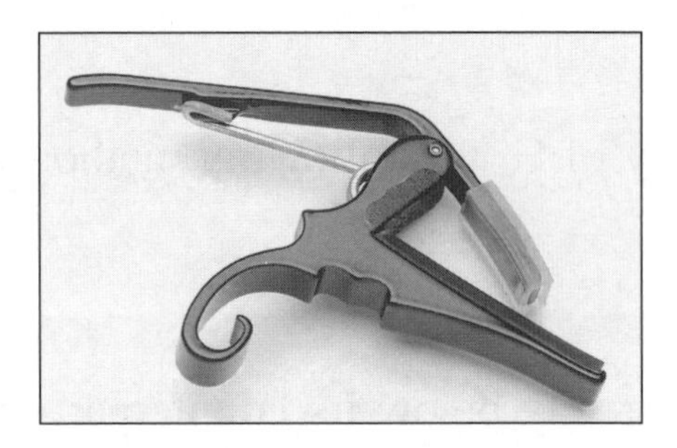

Capos come in various shapes and sizes.

The capo allows you to play the song in the same key, yet at the same time use easier (open) chords. Consider a turnaround in E♭:

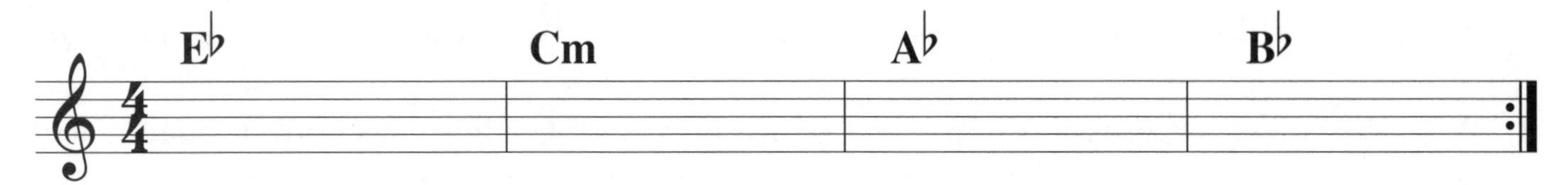

If you place the capo on the third fret, the following chords can be played without changing the song's key.

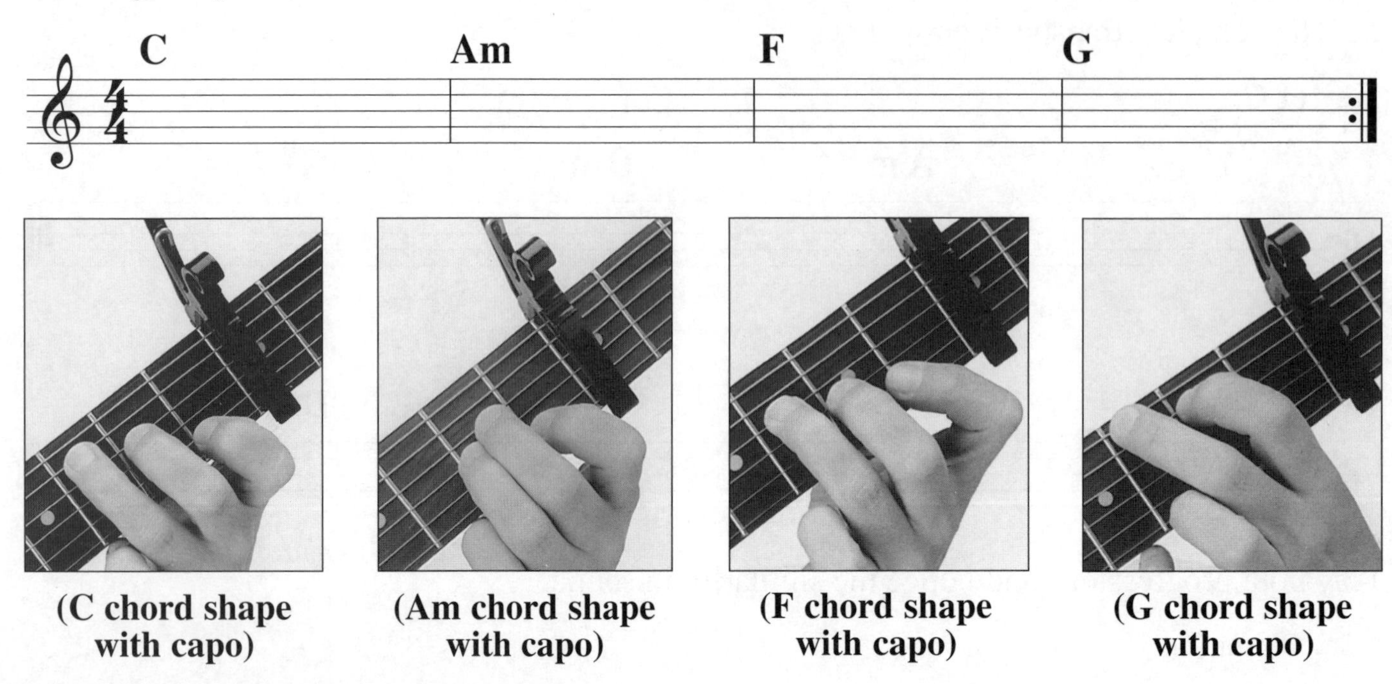

(C chord shape with capo)

(Am chord shape with capo)

(F chord shape with capo)

(G chord shape with capo)

If you have studied bar chords, you will notice that the capo is acting as a bar.

To work out which fret the capo must be placed on, simply count the number of semitones between the **capo** key you have selected to change to* (e.g. D, as used in the above example) and the original key (i.e. E♭ as above). Hence C to E♭ = 3 semitones, and therefore the capo must be placed on the third fret.

Expanding upon point 2, consider a song in the key of C, using the turnaround progression:

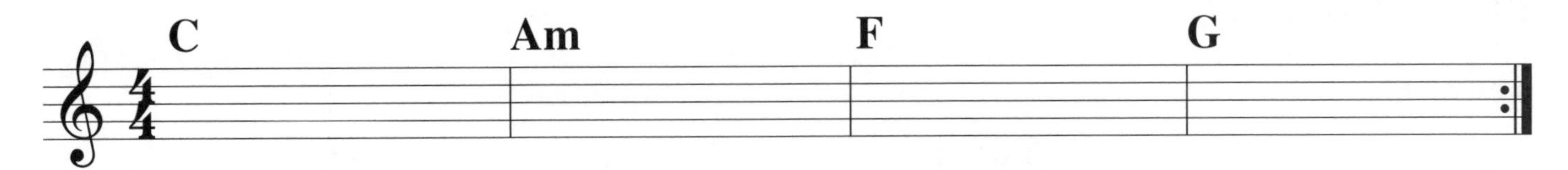

A singer may decide that this key is unsuitable for his or her voice range and may wish to use the key of, say, E♭. The progression, transposed to E♭, will become:

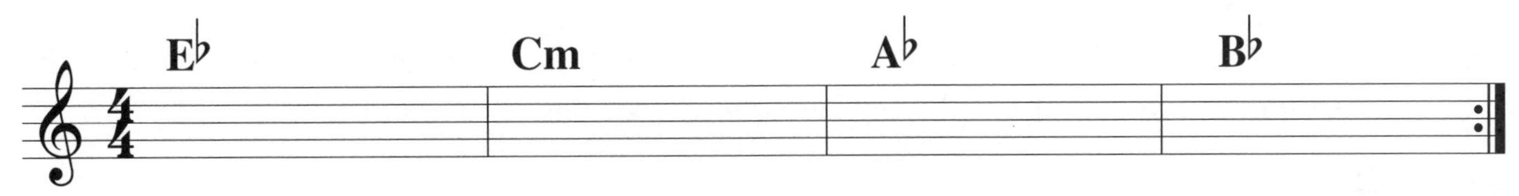

Instead of changing to these new chord shapes (i.e. having to use bar chords), the guitarist may still play the **C**, **Am**, **F** and **G** chords, but **must place the capo at the 3rd fret** to do so.

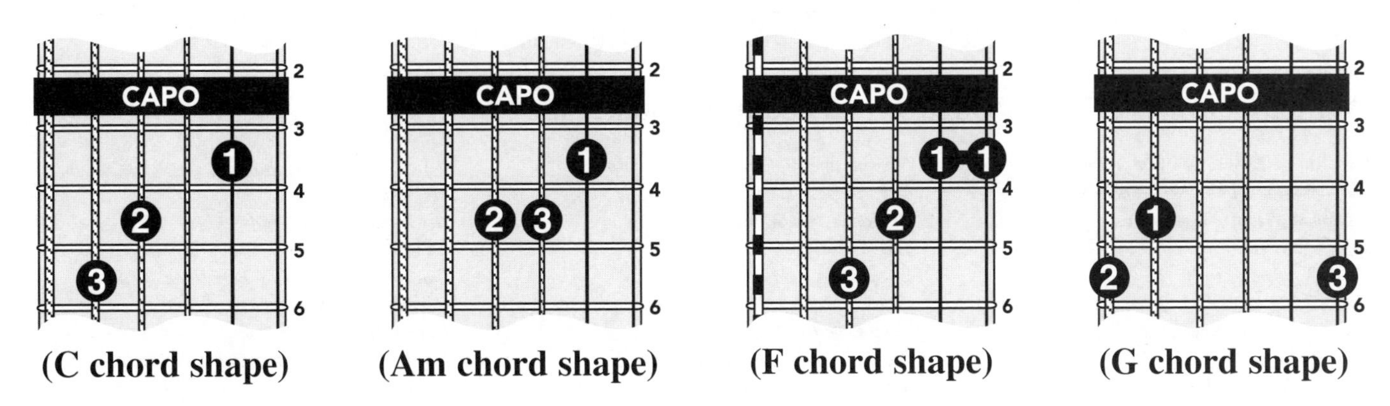

(C chord shape) **(Am chord shape)** **(F chord shape)** **(G chord shape)**

ORIGINAL KEY (C)

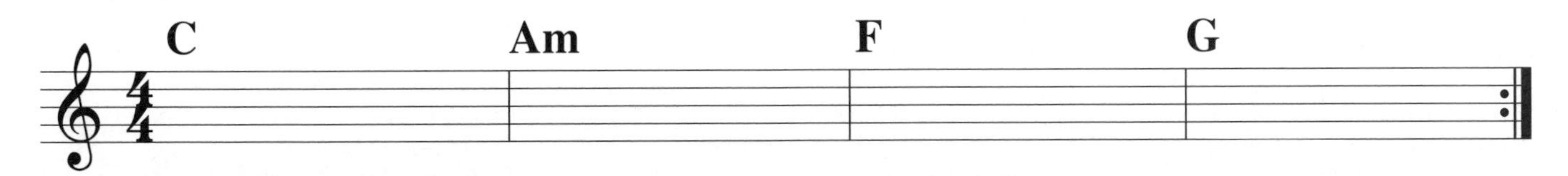

ORIGINAL KEY (E♭)

* Remember you are not actually changing key but merely changing the chord shapes, for ease of playing.

APPENDIX FOUR - SONG LIST

In modern music there are several standard chord progressions that are the basis of many songs. The most common of these progressions are **Turnarounds** and **Twelve Bar Blues**.

TURNAROUNDS

There are two main turnarounds, which are labelled **Turnaround One** and **Turnaround Two**.

TURNAROUND ONE

Key of C

C | Am | F | G^7

This turnaround can be played in any key by transposing (see Appendix Three). Here is the same turnaround in the key of G, playing two chords per bar.

Key of G

G Em | C D^7

Written below is a list of songs which use turnaround one.*

I Will Always Love You – Whitney Houston
The Night Has a 1000 Eyes – Bobby Vee
It's Raining Again – Supertramp
More – Various Artists
Ti Amo – Umberto Tozzi
Crocodile Rock (chorus) – Elton John
One Last Kiss – Various Artists
Stand By Me – John Lennon
Dream – Everly Brothers
Return to Sender – Elvis Presley
Telstar – Tornadoes
Always Look on the Bright Side of Life – Monty Python
Why do Fools Fall in Love – Frankie Lyman/Diana Ross
Sarah – Fleetwood Mac
Take Good Care of my Baby – Bobby Vee/Smokey
Where have all the Flowers Gone – Various Artists
Runaround Sue – Dion & the Belmonts
Tell Me Why – The Beatles
Let's Twist Again – Chubby Checker
Stay (Just a Little Bit Longer) – The Four Seasons/Jackson Browne
Cool for Cats – U.K. Squeeze
Y.M.C.A – The Village People
Tired of Toein' the Line – Rocky Burnett
You Drive Me Crazy – Shakin' Stevens
Should I do it – Pointer Sisters
Poor Little Fool – Rick Nelson
You Don't Have to Say You Love Me – Dusty Springfield/Elvis Presley
Breaking up is Hard to do – Neil Sedaka/Partridge Family
Oh Carol – Neil Sedaka
Two Faces Have I – Lou Christie
Every Day – Buddy Holly
Poetry in Motion – Johnny Tillotson
Sweet Little 16 – Neil Sedaka
Big Girls Don't Cry – Four Seasons
Sherry – Four Seasons
How Do You Do It – Jerry & The Pacemakers
Shout, Shout – Rocky Sharp & The Replays
Aces With You – Moon Martin
Houses of the Holy – Led Zeppelin
Uptown Girl – Billy Joel
Build Me Up Buttercup – The Foundations
'Happy Days' – Theme
Joane – Michael Nesmith
Goodnight Sweetheart – Various Artists
Looking For An Echo – Ol'55
Summer Holiday – Cliff Richard
Be My Baby – The Ronettes/Rachel Sweet
Everlasting Love – Rachel Sweet/Love Affair
I Go To Pieces (verse) – Peter & Gordon
Love Hurts – Everly Brothers/Jim Capaldi/Nazareth
Gee Baby – Peter Shelley
Classic – Adrian Gurvitz
Teenage Dream – T-Rex
Blue Moon – Various Artists
The Tide is High – Blondie
Dennis – Blondie
It Ain't Easy – Normie Rowe
My World – Bee Gees
Hey Paula – Various Artists
It's Only Make Believe – Glen Campbell
Can't Smile Without You – Barry Manilow
Crossfire – Bellamy Brothers
Bobby's Girl – Marcie Blane
Do That To Me One More Time – Captain & Tenile
Please Mr Postman – Carpenters/ The Beatles
Sharin' The Night Together – Dr Hook
9 to 5 (Morning Train) – Sheena Easton
Diana – Paul Anka
Enola Gay – Orchestral Manoeuvres in the Dark
Some Guys Have All the Luck – Robert Palmer
So Lonely – Get Wet
Hungry Heart – Bruce Springsteen
Land of Make Believe (chorus) – Buck Fizz
Daddys Home – Cliff Richard
The Wonder of You – Elvis Presley
So You Win Again – Hot Chocolate
Hang Five – Rolling Stones
Paper Tiger – Sue Thompson
Venus – Frankie Avalon
Costafine Town – Splinter
If You Leave – OMD
True Blue – Madonna

* Some of the songs listed under **Turnarounds** vary from the basic structure of this progression. For example, the turnaround progression may be used in the verses, but not in the chorus.

TURNAROUND TWO

Turnaround Two uses a different minor chord in the second bar.

Key of C

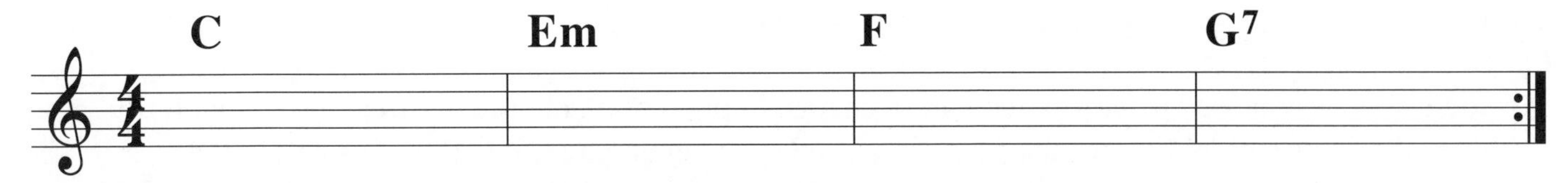

Crocodile Rock (verse) – Elton John
I started a Joke – The Bee Gees
Different Drum – Linda Ronstadt
Key Largo – Bertie Giggins
Black Berry Way – The Move
Georgy Girl – Seekers
Where Do You Go To My Lovely – Peter Sarsted
Mrs Brown, You've Got a Lovely Daughter – Hermans Hermits
Toast and Marmalade for Tea – Tin Tin
Movie Star – Harpo
It's A Heatache – Bonnie Tyler
I Don't Like Mondays – The Boomtown Rats
My Angel Baby – Toby Beau
Land Of Make Believe (verse) – Bucks Fizz
I'm In the Mood for Dancing – The Nolans
What's in a Kiss – Gilbert O'Sullivan
My Baby Loves Love – Joe Jeffries
Dreamin' – Johnny Burnett
Cruel To Be Kind – Nick Lowe
Where Did Our Love Go – Diana Ross & The Supremes
Hurdy Gurdy Man – Donovan
I Go To Pieces (chorus) – Peter & Gordon
Get It Over With – Angie Gold
Sad Sweet Dreamer – Sweet Sensation
Down Town – Petula Clark
Easy – Oakridge Boys
Only You Can Do It – Francoiose Hardy
Costafine – Splinter (chorus)
Where Did Our Love Go? – Phil Collins

12 BAR BLUES

12 Bar Blues is a set pattern of chords which repeats every 12 bars.
Here is a 12 Bar Blues in the key of A:

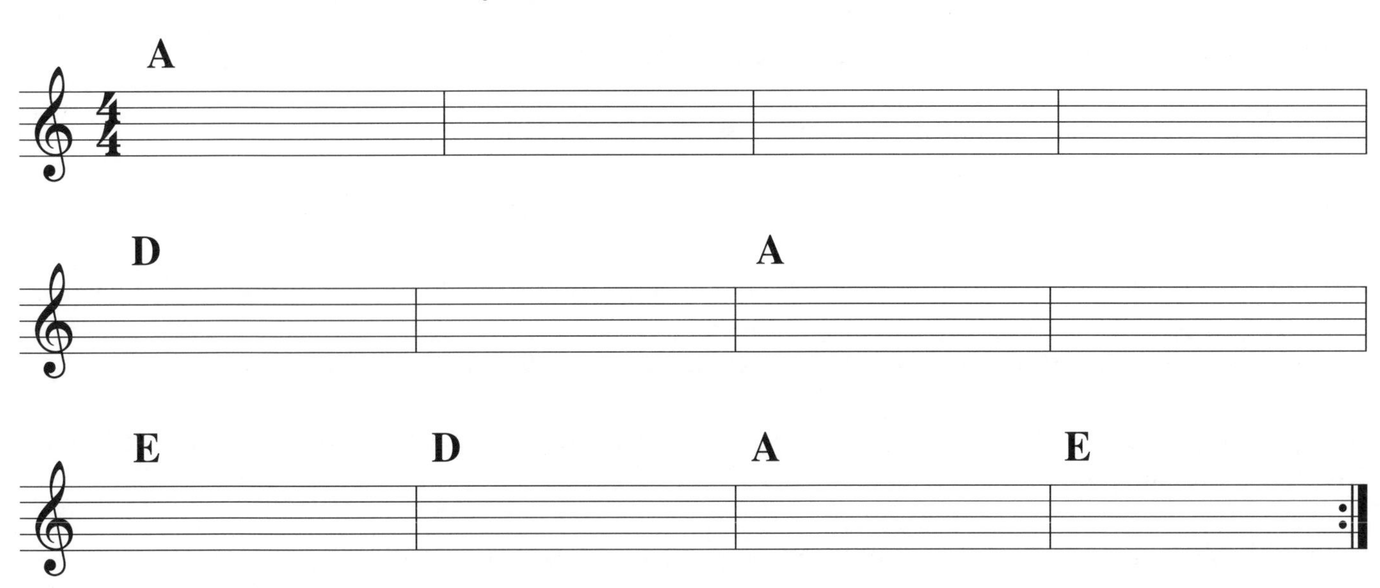

Written below is a list of songs which use 12 Bar Blues.

Be-bop-a-lula – Gene Vincent/John Lennon
Hound Dog – Elvis Presley
Johnny B. Goode – Chuck Berry
Boppin' the Blues – Blackfeather
The Wanderer – Dion
Going up the Country – Canned Heat
Makin' Your Mind Up – Bucks Fizz
Green Door – Shakin' Stevens
In the Summertime – Mungo Jerry
Rock Around the Clock – Bill Haley & The Comets
Barbara Ann – The Beach Boys
Let's Stick Together – Bryan Ferry
Long Tall Glasses (I Know I Can Dance) – Leo Sayer
Blue Suede Shoes – Elvis Presley
School Days (Ring Ring Goes the Bell) – Chuck Berry
Roll Over Beethoven – Chuck Berry
Spirit in the Sky – Norman Greenbaum
Turn Up Your Radio – The Masters Apprentices
Tutti Frutti – Little Richard
Dizzy Miss Lizzy – larry Williams/The Beatles
Peggy Sue – Buddy Holly
Jailhouse Rock – Elvis Presley
Get Down and Get With It – Slade
Good Golly Miss Molly – Little Richard
Lucille – Little Richard
In the Mood – Glen Miller
Surfin' Safari – The Beach Boys
Peppermint Twist – Sweet
Boogie Woogie Bugle Boy – The Andrew Sisters/Bett Midler
I Hear You Knocking – Dave Edmunds
Boy From New York City – Darts/Manhattan Transfer
Mountain of Love – Johnny Rivers
I Love to Boogie – T-Rex
Shake Rattle & Roll – Bill Hayley
Lady Rose – Mungo Jerry
Theme to Batman
Theme to Spiderman
Stuck in the Middle with you – Stealers Wheel
Hot Love – T-Rex
The Huckle Buck – Brendan Bower
Way Down – Elvis Presley
I Can Help – Billy Swan
Rockin' Robin – Michael Jackson
Red House – Jimi Hendrix
Texas Flood – Stevie Ray Vaughan
Killing Floor – Jimi Hendrix
The Jack – ACDC
Ice Cream Man - Van Halen
Oh Pretty Woman – Gary Moore
Give Me One Reason – Tracy Chapman
Why Didn't You Call Me? – Macy Gray

GLOSSARY OF MUSICAL TERMS

"a" — annular finger (ring finger). As used for identifying the right hand fingers in fingerpicking patterns.

Accent — a sign, >, used to indicate a predominant beat.

Accidental — a sign used to show a temporary change in pitch of a note (i.e. sharp ♯, flat ♭, double sharp 𝄪, double flat 𝄫, or natural ♮). The sharps or flats in a key signature are not regarded as accidentals.

Additional notes — a note not belonging to a given scale, but can be used for improvising against most chords in a progression without sounding out of key.

Ad lib — to be played at the performer's own discretion.

Allegretto — moderately fast.

Allegro — fast and lively.

Anacrusis — a note or notes occurring before the first bar of music (also called 'lead-in' notes).

Andante — an easy walking pace.

Arpeggio — the playing of a chord in single note fashion.

Bar — a division of music occurring between two bar lines (also called a 'measure').

Bar chord — a chord played with one finger laying across all six strings.

Bar line — a vertical line drawn across the staff which divides the music into equal sections called bars.

Bass — the lower regions of pitch in general. On guitar, the 4th, 5th and 6th strings.

Bend — a technique which involves pushing a string upwards (or downwards), which raises the pitch of the fretted note being played.

"Blues" Scale — consisting of the I, ♭III, IV, ♭V, V, ♭VII and notes relative to the major scale.

Capo — a device placed across the neck of a guitar to allow a key change without alteration of the chord shapes.

Chord — a combination of three or more different notes played together.

Chord progression — a series of chords played as a musical unit (e.g. as in a song).

Chromatic scale — a scale ascending and descending in semitones.

e.g. **C** chromatic scale:

ascending:	C	C♯	D	D♯	E	F	F♯	G	G♯	A	A♯	B	C
descending:	C	B	B♭	A	A♭	G	G♭	F	E	E♭	D	D♭	C

Clef — a sign placed at the beginning of each staff of music which fixes the location of a particular note on the staff, and hence the location of all other notes, e.g.

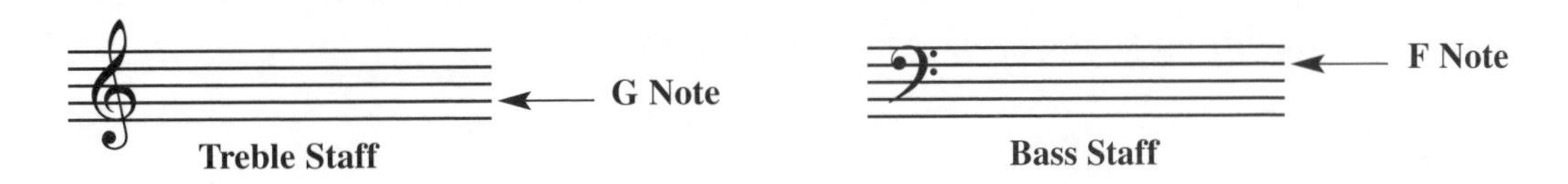

Cliches — small musical phrases that are frequently used.

Coda — an ending section of music, signified by the sign 𝄌 .

Common time — and indication of $\frac{4}{4}$ time — four quarter note beats per bar (also indicated by 𝄴)

Compound time — occurs when the beat falls on a dotted note, which is thus divisible by 3 e.g. $\frac{6}{8}$ $\frac{9}{8}$ $\frac{12}{8}$

D.C al fine — a repeat from the beginning to the word 'fine'.

Dot — a sign placed after a note indicating that its time value is extended by a half. e.g.

𝅗𝅥 = 2 counts 𝅗𝅥. = 3 counts

Double bar line — two vertical lines close together, indicating the end of a piece, or section thereof.

Double flat — a sign (𝄫) which lowers the pitch of a note by one tone.

Double sharp — a sign (𝄪) which raises the pitch of a note by one tone.

D.S. al fine — a repeat from the sign (indicated thus 𝄋) to the word 'fine'.

Duration — the time value of each note.

Dynamics — the varying degrees of softness (indicated by the term 'piano') and loudness (indicated by the term 'forte') in music.

Eighth note — a note with the value of half a beat in $\frac{4}{4}$ time, indicated thus 𝅘𝅥𝅮 (also called a quaver).

The eighth note rest — indicating half a beat of silence, is written: 𝄾

Enharmonic — describes the difference in notation, but not in pitch, of two notes: e.g.

F♯ or G♭ 

Fermata — a sign, 𝄐 , used to indicate that a note or chord is held to the player's own discretion (also called a 'pause sign').

Fill ins — a short lead riff played between one line of a lyric and the next, or between one verse and the next.

First and second endings — signs used where two different endings occur. On the first time through ending one is played (indicated by the bracket ⌈1. ⌉); then the progression is repeated and ending two is played (indicated ⌈2.).

Flat — a sign, (♭)used to lower the pitch of a note by one semitone.

Form — the plan or layout of a song, in relation to the sections it contains; e.g. Binary form containing an "A" section and a "B" section (A B).
Ternary form, containing an "A" section and a "B" section, and then a repeat of the "A" section (A B A).
The verse/chorus relationship in songs is an example of form.

Forte — loud. Indicated by the sign ***f***.

Half note — a note with the value of two beats in $\frac{4}{4}$ time, indicated thus: 𝅗𝅥 (also called a minim). The half note rest, indicating two beats of silence, is written: ▬◄— third staff line.

Harmonics — a chime like sound created by lightly touching a vibrating string at certain points along the fret board.
Harmony — the simultaneous sounding of two or more different notes.

Improvise — to perform spontaneously; i.e. not from memory or from a written copy.

Interval — the distance between any two notes of different pitches.

Key — describes the notes used in a composition in regards to the major or minor scale from which they are taken; e.g. a piece 'in the key of C major' describes the melody, chords, etc., as predominantly consisting of the notes, **C**, **D**, **E**, **F**, **G**, **A**, and **B** — i.e. from the **C** scale.

Key signature — a sign, placed at the beginning of each staff of music, directly after the clef, to indicate the key of a piece. The sign consists of a certain number of sharps or flats, which represent the sharps or flats found in the scale of the piece's key. e.g.

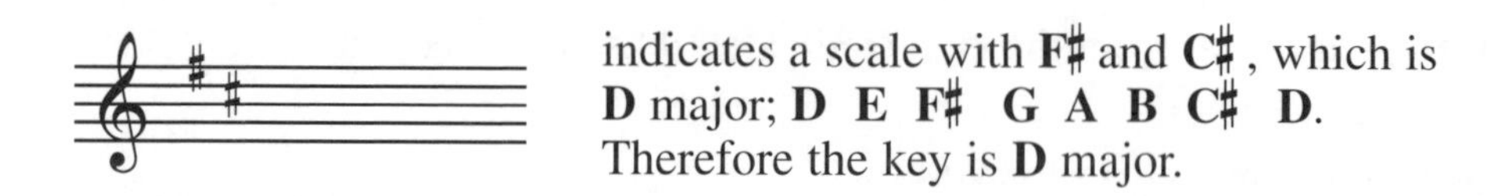

Lead — the playing of single notes, as in a lead solo or melody line.

Lead-In — same as anacrusis (also called a pick-up).

Leger lines — small horizontal lines upon which notes are written when their pitch is either above or below the range of the staff, e.g.

Legato — smoothly, well connected.

Lyric — words that accompany a melody.

"m" — middle finger. As used for identifying the right hand fingers in fingerpicking patterns.

Major Pentatonic Scale — a 5 tone scale based on the interval sequence, T, T, T½, T, T½.

Major scale — a series of eight notes in alphabetical order based on the interval sequence tone - tone - semitone - tone - tone - tone - semitone, giving the familiar sound **do re mi fa so la ti do**.

Melody — a succession of notes of varying pitch and duration, and having a recognizable musical shape.

Metronome — a device which indicates the number of beats per minute, and which can be adjusted in accordance to the desired tempo.

e.g. MM (Maelzel Metronome) ♩ = 60 — indicates 60 quarter note beats per minute.

Minor Pentatonic Scale — a 5 tone scale based on the interval sequence.

Mode — a displaced scale e.g. playing through the C to C scale, but starting and finishing on the D note.

Moderato — at a moderate pace.

Modulation — the changing of key within a song (or chord progression).

Natural — a sign (♮)used to cancel out the effect of a sharp or flat. The word is also used to describe the notes **A**, **B**, **C**, **D**, **E**, **F** and **G**; e.g. 'the natural notes'.

Notation — the written representation of music, by means of symbols (music on a staff), letters (as in chord and note names) and diagrams (as in chord illustrations.)

Note — a single sound with a given pitch and duration.

Octave — the distance between any given note with a set frequency, and another note with exactly double that frequency. Both notes will have the same letter name;

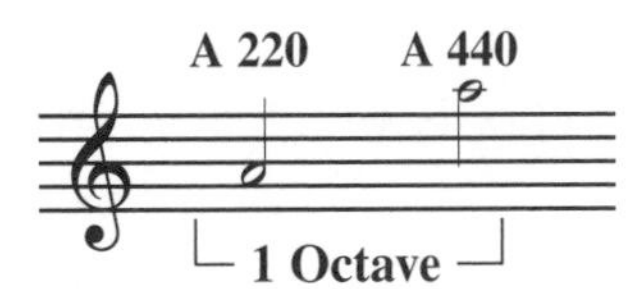

Open chord — a chord that contains at least one open string.

"p" — primary finger (thumb). As used for identifying the right hand fingers in fingerpicking patterns.

Passing note — connects two melody notes which are a third or less apart. A passing note usually occurs on an unaccented beat of the bar.

Phrase — a small group of notes forming a recognizable unit within a melody.

Pitch — the sound produced by a note, determined by the frequency of the string vibrations. The pitch relates to a note being referred to as 'high' or 'low'.

Pivot finger — a finger which remains in position while the other fingers move, when changing chords.

Plectrum — a small object (often of a triangular shape) made of plastic which is used to pick or strum the strings of a guitar.

Position — a term used to describe the location of the left hand on the fret board. The left hand position is determined by the fret location of the first finger, e.g.
The 1st position refers to the 1st to 4th frets. The 3rd position refers to the 3rd to 6th frets and so on.

Quarter note — a note with the value of one beat in $\frac{4}{4}$ time, indicated thus ♩ (also called a crotchet).
The quarter note rest, indicating one beat of silence, is written: 𝄽 .

Reggae — a Jamaican rhythm featuring an accent on the second and fourth beats (in $\frac{4}{4}$ time).

Relative — a term used to describe the relationship between a major and minor key which share the same key signature; e.g. G major and E minor are relative keys both sharing the F♯ key signature.

Repeat signs — in music, used to indicate a repeat of a section of music, by means of two dots placed before a double bar line:

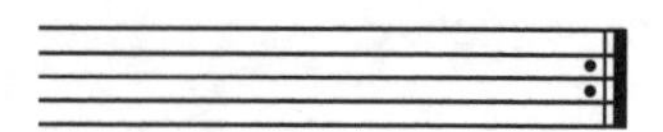

In chord progressions, a repeat sign 𝄎 , indicates an exact repeat of the previous bar.

Rest — the notation of an absence of sound in music.

Rest stroke — where the finger, after picking the string, comes to rest on the next string (for accenting the note).

Rhythm — the aspect of music concerned with tempo, duration and accents of notes (or chord strums). Tempo indicates the speed of a piece (fast or slow) duration indicates the time value of each note or strum (quarter note, eighth note, sixteenth note, etc.); and accents indicate which beat is more predominant (in rock, the first and third beats; in reggae, the second and fourth beats).

Riff — a pattern of notes that is repeated throughout a progression (song).

Root note — the note after which a chord or scale is named (also called 'key note').

Scale Tone Chords — chords which are constructed from notes within a given scale.

Semitone — the smallest interval used in conventional music. On guitar, it is a distance of one fret.

Sharp — a sign (♯) used to raise the pitch of a note by one semitone.

Simple time — occurs when the beat falls on an undotted note, which is thus divisible by two.

Sixteenth note — a note with the value of quarter of a beat in $\frac{4}{4}$ time, indicated thus 𝅘𝅥𝅯 (also called a semiquaver).

The sixteenth note rest, indicating quarter of a beat of silence, is written: 𝄿

Slide — a technique which involves a finger moving along the string to its new note. The finger maintains pressure on the string, so that a continuous sound is produced.

Slur — sounding a note by using only the left hand fingers (an ascending slur is also called 'hammer-on'; a descending slur is also called 'pull-off').

Staccato — to play short and detached. Indicated by a dot placed above the note: 

Staff — five parallel lines together with four spaces, upon which music is written.

Syncopation — the placing of an accent on a normally unaccented beat. e.g.:

Tablature — a system of writing music which represents the position of the player's fingers (not the pitch of the notes, but their position on the guitar). A chord diagram is a type of tablature. Notes can also be written using tablature thus:

Each line represents a string, and each number represents a fret.

Tempo — the speed of a piece.

Tie — a curved line joining two or more notes of the same pitch, where the second note(s) is not played, but its time value is added to that of the first note.

In Example 2, the first note is held for seven counts.

Timbre — a quality which distinguishes a note produced on one instrument from the same note produced on any other instrument (also called 'tone colour'). A given note on the guitar will sound different (and therefore distinguishable) from the same pitched note on piano, violin, flute etc. There is usually also a difference in timbre from one guitar to another.

Time signature — a sign at the beginning of a piece which indicates, by means of figures, the number of beats per bar (top figure), and the type of note receiving one beat (bottom figure).

Tone — a distance of two frets; i.e. the equivalent of two semitones.

Transposition — the process of changing music from one key to another.

Treble — the upper regions of pitch in general.

Treble clef — a sign placed at the beginning of the staff to fix the pitch of the notes placed on it. The treble clef (also called 'G clef') is placed so that the second line indicates as G note:

← **G line**

Tremolo (pick tremolo) — a technique involving rapid pick movement on a given note.

Triplet — a group of three notes played in the same time as two notes of the same kind.

Eighth note triplet ♪♪♪ (3) = ♪♪

Vibrato — a technique which involves pushing a string up and down, like a rapid series of short bends.

Wedge mark — indicates pick direction; e.g: **V** = down pick, **Λ** = up pick

Whole note — a note with the value of four beats in $\frac{4}{4}$ time, indicated thus **o** (also called a semibreve).

The whole note rest, indicating four beats of silence, is written: ▬ ← 4th staff line.

GM 1 TAB VERSION

FOR BEGINNING GUITARISTS

A comprehensive, lesson by lesson introduction to the guitar. Covers notes on all strings, reading music and tablature, picking technique and basic music theory. Incorporates well known traditional, Pop/Rock, Folk and Blues songs.

PROGRESSIVE GUITAR METHOD: LEAD

FOR BEGINNER TO INTERMEDIATE

Covers scales and patterns over the entire fretboard so that you can improvise against major, minor, and Blues progressions in any key. Learn the licks and techniques used by all lead guitarists such as hammer-ons, slides, bending, vibrato, pick tremolo, double notes, slurring and right hand tapping.

PROGRESSIVE GUITAR METHOD: RHYTHM

FOR BEGINNING RHYTHM GUITARISTS

Introduces all the important open chord shapes for major, minor, seventh, sixth, major seventh, minor seventh, suspended, diminished and augmented chords. Learn to play over 50 chord progressions, including 12 Bar Blues and Turnaround progressions.

PROGRESSIVE GUITAR METHOD: CHORDS

FOR BEGINNER TO ADVANCED

Contains the most useful open, Bar and Jazz chord shapes of the most used chord types with chord progressions to practice and play along with. Includes special sections on tuning, how to read sheet music, transposing, the use of a capo, as well as an easy chord table, chord formula and chord symbol chart.

PROGRESSIVE GUITAR METHOD: THEORY

FOR BEGINNER TO ADVANCED

A comprehensive, introduction to music theory as it applies to the guitar. Covers reading traditional music, rhythm notation and tablature, along with learning the notes on the fretboard, how to construct chords and scales, transposition, musical terms and playing in all keys. A useful tool for songwriting and composition, and essential for any guitarist who wants to become a better musician.

PROGRESSIVE BLUES GUITAR

FOR BEGINNING BLUES GUITARISTS

A great introduction to the world of Blues Guitar. Covers all the essential rhythms used in Blues and R&B along with turnarounds, intros and endings, and gaining control of 12 and 8 bar Blues forms. Also explains and demonstrates the Blues scale, major and minor pentatonic scales and 7th arpeggios in a logical system for playing over the entire fretboard. Contains all the classic Blues sounds such as note bending, slides, and vibrato demonstrated in over 100 licks and solos in a variety of Blues styles.

PROGRESSIVE BLUES LEAD GUITAR TECHNIQUE

INTERMEDIATE TO ADVANCED

The central approach of this book is the development of musical technique, dealing with rhythm as it applies to lead guitar playing and concentrating on the development of phrasing and timing and how to really get the most out of the notes you play. Along the way, the book introduces the Blues scale and other important scales and arpeggios commonly used by Blues players. Also contains lots of great solos.

PROGRESSIVE COUNTRY GUITAR METHOD

FOR BEGINNER TO ADVANCED

Teaches the all important basic chords and rhythms used in Country Guitar by means of the two main classifications of Country guitar, rhythm and lead playing. Includes Country chord progressions, bass note picking and basic Country licks. There is also a special section dealing with tuning, the basics of music for Country guitar and an easy to read chord chart.

PROGRESSIVE ROCK GUITAR TECHNIQUE

FOR INTERMEDIATE ROCK GUITARISTS

This book continues on from *Progressive Rock Guitar Method,* dealing with all the Rhythm and Lead guitar styles of Rock. Rhythm guitar will be developed further by learning Bar chords, Rock progressions and advanced rhythm techniques. Lead guitarists will learn scale patterns, licks and solos using techniques such as Hammer-ons, Pull-offs, Slides, Bends, Vibrato and Double Note Licks. All licks and solos are clearly notated using standard music notation and 'Easy Read' guitar tab.

PROGRESSIVE CLASSICAL GUITAR METHOD

FOR BEGINNER TO ADVANCED

A comprehensive, lesson by lesson method covering all aspects of basic classical guitar technique such as proper hand techniques, progressing through the most common keys and incorporating some of the world's most popular classical guitar pieces in solo or duet form. Music theory including the introduction of several different time signatures, open and bar chords and scales are also part of this easy to follow classical guitar method.

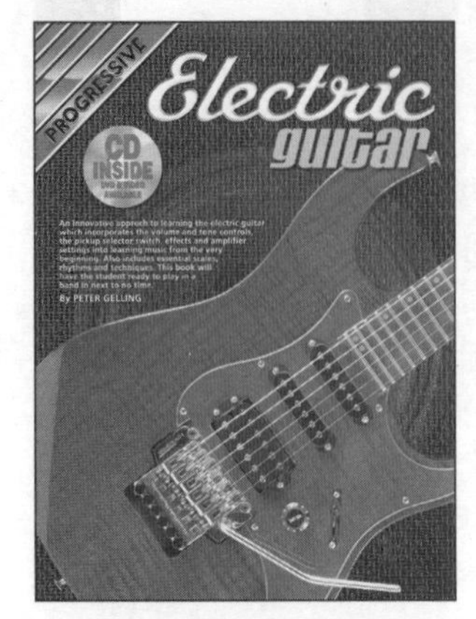

PROGRESSIVE ELECTRIC GUITAR

FOR BEGINNER TO INTERMEDIATE GUITARISTS

An innovative approach to learning the electric guitar which incorporates the volume and tone controls, the pickup selector switch, the tremolo arm, effects and amplifier settings into learning music from the very beginning. Explains and demonstrates all the essential chords, scales, rhythms and expressive techniques such as slides, bends, trills and vibrato. Also contains lessons on understanding the bass and drums and how to create parts which work with them. This book will have the student ready to play in a band in next to no time

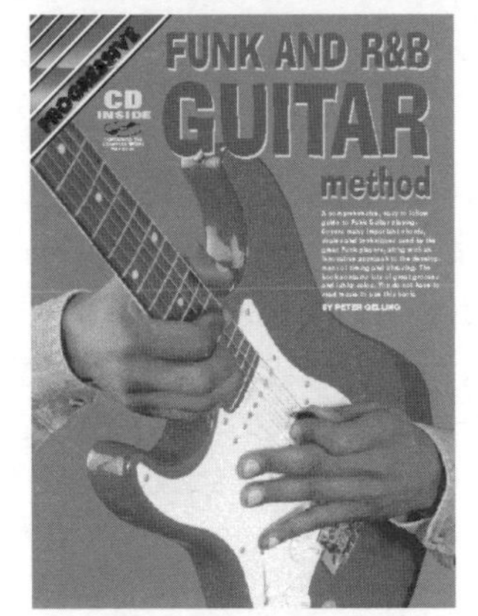

PROGRESSIVE FUNK AND R&B GUITAR METHOD

FOR BEGINNER TO ADVANCED

This book demonstrates many of the classic Funk sounds, using both rhythm and lead playing, since a good Funk player needs to be equally comfortable with both. A variety of chord forms are introduced within a framework that quickly allows the student to play confidently over the entire fretboard. Features an innovative approach to learning rhythms and applying them to riffs and grooves.

PROGRESSIVE JAZZ LEAD GUITAR METHOD

INTERMEDIATE TO ADVANCED

A great introduction to the world of Jazz lead guitar playing. Starting with a simple approach to improvisation using the major scale, the book demonstrates all the essential rhythms, scales, modes and arpeggios needed to become a confident Jazz player. Also deals with playing over chord changes and various approaches to Blues playing. A variety of techniques are used and all new sounds and techniques are demonstrated with authentic Jazz riffs, lines and solos.

PROGRESSIVE SCALES AND MODES FOR GUITAR

FOR BEGINNER TO ADVANCED

Progressive Scales and Modes gives the student a complete system for learning any scale, mode or chord and makes it easy to memorize any new new sound as well as building a solid visual and aural foundation of both the theory and the guitar fretboard. The book also shows you how to use each scale as well as how and why it fits with a particular chord or progression. The final section contains jam along progressions for every scale and mode presented in the book.

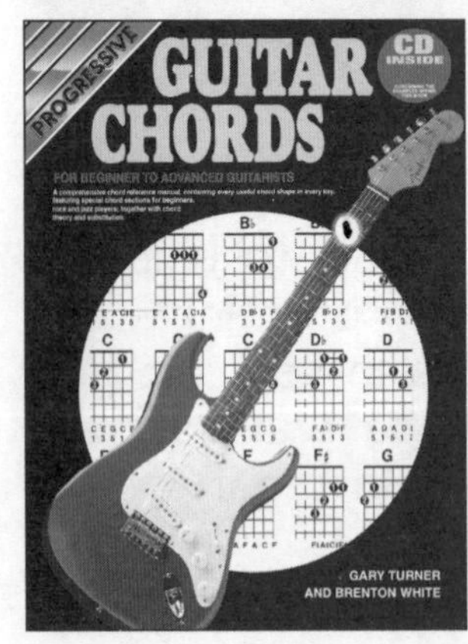

PROGRESSIVE GUITAR CHORDS

FOR BEGINNER TO ADVANCED GUITARISTS

Shows you every useful chord shape in every key. An open chord section for beginners contains the simplest and most widely used chord shapes in all keys. A bar chord section for the semi-advanced player who will need a thorough knowledge of bar chord shapes in all positions. A section for the advanced player listing the moveable shapes for chords widely used by Jazz guitarists. Other sections contain important music theory for the guitarist including scales, keys and chord construction.